Praise for *Designing Autonomous AI*

An easy and comprehensive introduction to machine teaching, a powerful new paradigm of useful AI for industrial applications that empowers engineers, expert operators, innovation leaders, and business owners to optimize industrial processes by teaching the AI the expertise that took them decades to learn.

—*Teresa Escrig, Principal Project Manager, Microsoft*

By steering clear of the morass of AI's mathematical and programming details, Kence Anderson has produced an engaging book that will appeal to a wide swath of readers with an interest in this transformational technology. His thoughtful examples illustrate the key ideas behind AI in ways that will resonate with readers.

—*Jonathan Schaeffer, Distinguished Professor of Computer Science, University of Alberta*

The insight that learning systems, by design, must be taught spawned the machine teaching paradigm. This book captures hard-won patterns and practices to make applying it to real-world applications successful. If you're building an autonomous system, you couldn't ask for a better guide than Kence Anderson.

—*Mark Hammond, VP, Autonomous Systems, Microsoft; Cofounder and CEO, Bonsai AI Inc.*

Machine teaching is a key skill in the next wave of useful, applied AI. This book is a practical, real-world guide, developed from a wealth of experience empowering subject matters in applying AI to business-valuable projects.

—*Phil Harvey, Autonomous Systems Architect, Bonsai, Microsoft Research*

Designing Autonomous AI
A Guide for Machine Teaching

Kence Anderson

Beijing · Boston · Farnham · Sebastopol · Tokyo

Designing Autonomous AI

by Kence Anderson

Published by O'Reilly Media, Inc., 1005 Gravenstein Highway North, Sebastopol, CA 95472.

O'Reilly books may be purchased for educational, business, or sales promotional use. Online editions are also available for most titles (*http://oreilly.com*). For more information, contact our corporate/institutional sales department: 800-998-9938 or *corporate@oreilly.com*.

Acquisitions Editor: Nicole Butterfield	**Indexer:** Ellen Troutman-Zaig
Development Editor: Sarah Grey	**Interior Designer:** David Futato
Production Editor: Jonathon Owen	**Cover Designer:** Karen Montgomery
Copyeditor: Justin Billing	**Illustrator:** Kate Dullea
Proofreader: Piper Editorial Consulting, LLC	

June 2022:   First Edition

Revision History for the First Edition

2022-06-10:   First Release

See *http://oreilly.com/catalog/errata.csp?isbn=9781098110758* for release details.

The O'Reilly logo is a registered trademark of O'Reilly Media, Inc. *Designing Autonomous AI*, the cover image, and related trade dress are trademarks of O'Reilly Media, Inc.

978-1-098-11075-8

[LSI]

This book is dedicated to my father, Lawrence Anderson (1916–2002), the maestro and master teacher.

Table of Contents

Part II.   What Is Machine Teaching?

Part III.   How Do You Teach a Machine?

Part IV.   Tools for the Machine Teacher

Foreword

It gives me great pleasure to enthusiastically recommend *Designing Autonomous AI*, written by a leading real-world practitioner in emergent autonomous AI: Kence Anderson.

As the Corporate Vice President currently responsible for new product incubations at Microsoft, and as someone who has been closely involved with creation of new product categories like VPNs, real-time communications and now autonomous systems at Microsoft, I have learned that creating new categories is not a straightforward path.

Established product categories and their underlying technologies and business models are well honed for the real world with well understood problems and solutions. These are things we use in our daily lives.

Fundamental research is important to new category creation but lives in the ether of science, generally abstracted from real world considerations. Researchers create novel methods and demonstrate their promise through results in carefully crafted experiments—the amazing state of the art in AI is a recent example of this.

Importantly, not every method created by researchers is sufficient or workable in the real world. New categories can be created when one or more of these new methods are developed further, grounded in and applied to the real-world environment.

New category creation is a chaotic, primordial process entailing a loop of exploration, learning, and adaptation. This process is very high dimensional and domain dependent; there is no single formula here. However, at the core of new category creation, inevitably there is always a breakthrough clinching idea that solves the most difficult aspects of the real-world problem.

The new category of autonomous AI, which is so significant that it is being called the Fourth Industrial Revolution, is particularly challenging in this regard because the underlying real-world considerations are extremely onerous. Building adequate systems that are safe and performant in the real world is nontrivial. This is a key reason for why we haven't seen flying cars outside our window yet.

For autonomous AI, one of those breakthrough clinching ideas is machine teaching. In the same way languages and compilers made the once complex and kludgy task of computing easy, efficient, and accessible to millions of programmers, machine teaching is enabling experts from any discipline (mechanical, electrical, or aeronautical engineering, etc.) to build powerful and usable autonomous systems easily, without requiring a PhD in AI or data science.

Machine teaching, without apologies, borrows from well-established techniques from all schools of thoughts of AI: connectionist, symbolist, and experiential, and from proven methods in pedagogy. Machine teaching provides an easy way to codify human expertise in any domain and to apply the power of learning methods automatically, abstracting away the tyranny of abstruse AI algorithms.

Kence Anderson writes about machine teaching with the lucidity and authority of someone who had a hand in its creation (which he did).

— Gurdeep Pall (Seattle, WA, 2022)

Preface

There's a saying that "those who can't do, teach; and those who can't teach, write." Well, that's not how this book came to be. I spent four years traveling around the world to steel mills, mines, factories, testing facilities, design studios, machine shops, chemical plants, oil fields, refineries, warehouses, and logistics centers, learning from subject matter experts about the challenges and opportunities of industrial decision-making, then working with them to design useful Artificial Intelligence (AI) that can help them make better decisions.

What Is Autonomous AI?

Autonomous AI is AI-powered automation that optimizes equipment and processes by sensing and responding in real time.

The great feat of modern AI is programming algorithms that can adapt and change their behavior based on feedback. The goal of *Designing Autonomous AI* is to show you how to put these learning algorithms to work by teaching AI to make successful decisions in real, production environments.

I'm not claiming that AI brains can achieve parity with humans or match human capability in any area (I will often refer to a specific instance of autonomous AI as a brain). I'm saying that when an autonomous AI is designed properly and makes full use of existing AI and automation components, it can radically outperform systems that calculate actions from known mathematical relationships, search and select actions using objective criteria, or look up actions from recorded human expertise. Let's look at each of the attributes a little more deeply.

There's a large gap to bridge between AI research and useful human-like decision-making in industrial situations. So, when AI research demonstrated that AI can *learn* to perform complex tasks, I took on the task to figure out what kinds of decisions AI can learn to make in the real world. You see, at that time (four years ago), when I started on this journey to probe the capabilities of AI decision-making, the only decisions that learning AI was shown to effectively make were in video games and drastically oversimplified "toy" control problems like you'd find in a first-year university physics or engineering textbook: simplified to the point that a student can calculate what to do next as a word problem.

Fast forward to today and I've designed over 150 autonomous AI for real applications at large companies. Many of them were built and some of them make valuable, effective decisions that previously only human beings could make. Each one performs a single useful, specific, material task in an enterprise process.

After all of those AI projects about everything from controlling bulldozers to warehouse scheduling to food manufacturing, here's my conclusion: *real, industrial processes are complex and the decisions to control and optimize them are fuzzy and full of tradeoffs.* The human expertise that drives these processes is vast and deep and can't be replaced by algorithms that search options for solutions or even advanced calculating control systems. Autonomous AI can make a material improvement in control and optimization of these systems and processes, but you have to be willing to wade into how these processes work and learn from subject matter experts to design AI that will produce these kinds of breakthrough results.

 If you're looking for diatribes about whether AI is overhyped or whether AI will ever achieve the full capabilities of the human mind, then this isn't the book for you.

Every day I read rants about how AI is either complete marketing hype that has little differentiated value (as if AI is really an element of fiction) or that AI is tracking toward superintelligence and is a serious competitor with the human mind in general cognitive ability (this perspective is more like science fiction). Both of these perspectives cannot be true. My opinion is and my experience shows that AI does have unique decision-making capabilities that differentiate it from other technology, but that it is best used to make specific high-value decisions that complement—not replicate—the human mind. So, if you're looking for a discourse about how stupid or about how scary intelligent AI is, you're not likely to find what you're looking for here in this book. If you're looking for a path, a plan, and the tools to design AI that can solve even currently unsolvable problems, right now, then you're in the right place.

One of the reasons that some make wild claims about AI capability, while others simultaneously constantly cry "Hype!" about AI feats and techniques is because the discourse is missing requisite nuanced discussion about the capabilities of AI *compared to current methods for a particular task.* Take natural language processing as the first example. I'm writing this introduction from Spain. I don't need an AI that can understand and comprehend human language to find out how to say my hotel room number in Spanish. The machine translation of 143 (ciento cuarenta y tres) was particularly useful for me on this trip. I used it every day to get into the hotel breakfast area. However, the AI that translated my room number for me is not suitable at all for summarizing paragraphs (another language related task) or writing novels (an even more difficult language related task).

The exact same is true for most every autonomous AI I've ever designed. If you take it outside of the context of the task that I designed it for, it very well might be "hype." But if you use it for the task that I designed it for, the task that it practiced mastering over time, that's no hype. It will outperform existing automation and sometimes attain human expert status. This book is full of examples of such performance achievements, which you will be able to produce in your own AI by the time you've finished reading. The first step to successful brain design puts the right brain in the right place. Find situations where machines are making bad decisions that autonomous AI can make more effectively.

Who Should Read This Book?

Process Experts

This book is for the 100 million subject matter experts out there who manage and seek to automate complex equipment and processes.

Gartner reported in 2018 that there were approximately 10,000 data scientists in the world. Let's approximate that this means there are on the order of 10,000 AI experts who can design and build autonomous AI from scratch using code. Most of these experts hold PhD degrees in areas related to AI. In contrast, there are on the order of ten million software engineers in the world. Most of these developers specialize in writing software applications but are not specialists in AI. Their area of subject matter expertise is writing software and they can do this across many diverse applications. Then there's the 100 million or so subject matter experts in the world. These mechanical engineers, chemical engineers, process engineers, controls engineers, supply chain analysts, logistics analysts, and many others design and manage complex equipment and processes and they know this equipment and these processes inside and out. These populations are visualized in Figure P-1.

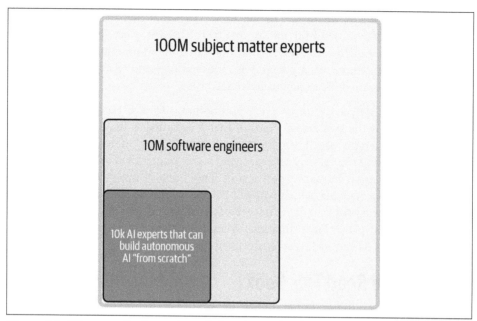

Figure P-1. Diagram of primary intended audience for this book.

While AI experts, data scientists, and software engineers can certainly use this book to design autonomous AI, I wrote this book for 100 million subject matter experts who want to make their systems and processes more autonomous. I didn't need a PhD in AI to devise this framework for designing autonomous AI, and you don't need one to use it.

Data Scientists and Software Engineers

The field of data science is booming. Unfortunately, I've seen innovation organizations pair up process experts and software engineers to great success, but I've seen many more organizations expect data scientists to solve process problems as if they're wizards wielding magic, with limited influence from and access to process experts. This book can help data scientists learn how to take a bird's-eye view of systems and processes to effectively integrate process expertise. The result will be better, more deployable autonomous AI.

Tip for AI Experts, Software Engineers, and Data Scientists

I'm glad that you are reading this book. This book is for you and there are very special parts of the autonomous AI development process that only you can perform. For example, analyzing process data is critical to designing and building autonomous AI and few can perform this function better than data scientists. The same is true for building and integrating machine learning models. Integrating software application components for building autonomous AI requires software engineering expertise. My only word of caution is that the process of designing autonomous AI requires an extreme amount of curiosity about systems and processes that are outside your area of expertise. While you might be able to write software and build machine learning models with minimal knowledge of the people and processes (e.g., in a factory or a logistics operation), you will need to acquire deep expertise from subject matter experts in order to effectively design autonomous AI.

Innovation Leaders

I've had many innovation leaders who manage R&D organizations and consulting practices take my in-person classes, which are a big commitment for them. They take my class because it frames the context and value of autonomous AI as a driver for their business. These leaders absorb the technical information because they want to separate the fact from fiction as they evaluate autonomous AI and its capabilities. Innovation leaders, I invite you to read this book to help you select use cases for autonomous AI and build an autonomous AI practice.

Teachers

This book is also for teachers. The practice of teaching is crucial to designing autonomous AI systems well. The practice of teaching machines exposes, and forces us to articulate, aspects of teaching that we can translate back to help us do a better job teaching humans.

Teachers reading this book should look for ways that machine teaching can sharpen their teaching mindset and practice.

Problem Solvers

Finally, this book is for people who want to solve important problems in our world using autonomous AI.

We reclaim this nascent but powerful technology from science fiction, which pigeon-holes autonomous AI as "killer robots," because this technology, in the right creative hands, can do much good for people. If you come to this book hoping to solve key problems in society and to make a positive difference in the world, I encourage you to wade through the technical details and examples and grab hold of the framework for teaching AI to do something truly useful. I've designed AI to help wind farms generate more sustainable energy, factories reduce emissions, and buildings reduce energy usage. My students have designed AI for sustainable fishing, vertical agriculture, and many other important purposes. You can, too.

What Can You Expect to Learn from This Book?

By the end of this book, you'll know how to design advanced AI without needing to manipulate neural networks or machine learning algorithms. I'll present a little bit of theory, lots of concrete examples, and a proven architectural framework for designing autonomous AI systems to show you how to teach AI explicit skills and strategies. You'll learn a variety of AI design patterns, when to use each pattern, and how to combine patterns. If you follow this book and practice on real problems, you'll learn:

- The difference between automated and autonomous decision-making systems
- The unique advantages of autonomous AI for real-time decision-making
- How to design autonomous AI from modular components
- How to apply design patterns to create explainable AI designs from human expertise
- How to teach autonomous AI known skills and strategies explicitly

Automated systems can be brittle and require constant supervision and intervention from humans. Autonomous systems provide more human-like decision-making capabilities in an explainable way. They can also assist humans in acquiring important industrial skills. I want to teach you the framework that I have used to select use cases and design over one hundred autonomous AI brains for companies like PepsiCo, Bell Flight, Shell, and many others. Designing Autonomous AI has many material benefits to businesses, but I hope and expect that many readers will use their new knowledge of autonomous AI to do good solving pressing problems. I wrote this book because I want to empower you to design autonomous AI that will beat benchmarks, revolutionize industries, and make a material positive impact on the world.

At the end of the day, I hope to influence how you think about building skills, making decisions, and solving problems.

Conventions Used in This Book

The following typographical conventions are used in this book:

Italic
> Indicates new terms, URLs, email addresses, filenames, and file extensions.

`Constant width`
> Used for program listings, as well as within paragraphs to refer to program elements such as variable or function names, databases, data types, environment variables, statements, and keywords.

`Constant width bold`
> Shows commands or other text that should be typed literally by the user.

`Constant width italic`
> Shows text that should be replaced with user-supplied values or by values determined by context.

 This element signifies a tip or suggestion.

 This element signifies a general note.

 This element indicates a warning or caution.

O'Reilly Online Learning

 For more than 40 years, *O'Reilly Media* has provided technology and business training, knowledge, and insight to help companies succeed.

Our unique network of experts and innovators share their knowledge and expertise through books, articles, and our online learning platform. O'Reilly's online learning platform gives you on-demand access to live training courses, in-depth learning paths, interactive coding environments, and a vast collection of text and video from O'Reilly and 200+ other publishers. For more information, visit *http://oreilly.com*.

How to Contact Us

Please address comments and questions concerning this book to the publisher:

O'Reilly Media, Inc.
1005 Gravenstein Highway North
Sebastopol, CA 95472
800-998-9938 (in the United States or Canada)
707-829-0515 (international or local)
707-829-0104 (fax)

We have a web page for this book, where we list errata, examples, and any additional information. You can access this page at *https://oreil.ly/designing-ai*.

Email *bookquestions@oreilly.com* to comment or ask technical questions about this book.

For news and information about our books and courses, visit *http://oreilly.com*.

Find us on Facebook: *http://facebook.com/oreilly*

Follow us on Twitter: *http://twitter.com/oreillymedia*

Watch us on YouTube: *http://youtube.com/oreillymedia*

Acknowledgments

First, my family! My son Christien knows about all the "robot brains" I work on and my wife Poppy is the driving force behind everything I do. Mom and Kate, thanks for supporting my ideas all these years.

Thanks to the Microsoft Autonomous Systems solution architects who practiced machine teaching with me day in and day out for years on real customer projects including Jeff Bennett, who first inspired me to write this book back in 2018, Marjorie Adriaenssens, Phil Harvey, Heather MacKinnon-Miller, Andy Wylie, and Amanda Skrabut.

The machine teaching community that consistently teaches me how things work in the real world. I love our discussions: Dale Erickson, Winston Jenks, Grant Bristow,

Sean Eichenlaub, Prabu Parthasarathy, Bridget Fitzpatrick (we miss you), Ed Van Valkenburg, Derek Bevan, and Bryan DeBois.

Thanks to Max Petrie, Ashe Menon, David Pugh, Pitak Jongsuwat, Yanon Lorpatarapong, Atik Suvittham, Francisco Green, and Asim Ghanchi for sharing so much knowledge of real systems and processes with me, and for your quotes!

Thanks to my teammates at Microsoft Project Bonsai, starting with the founders Mark Hammond and Keen Browne, who originally inspired me about machine teaching; Marcos Campos, who developed some of the early foundations of machine teaching; Victor Shnayder and Brice Chung, who always challenged me to think rigorously about machine teaching; Gurdeep Pall for writing the foreword; Dave Cahill and Kevin McCall, who I traveled the world with talking to experts about autonomous AI; Julian Ostrow, Sandeep Kulkarni, Enes Bilgin, Hossein Khadivi Heris, Aydan Aksoylar, Khadija Mustafa, Ade Famoti, Mike Estee, Eric Traut, David Coe, Cyrill Glockner, Varsha Raju, Karen Veldeman, and Brad Kerr.

Special thanks to Teresa Escrig, your edits and talks about book structure were invaluable; Kingsuk Maitra, your ideas are constantly inspiring me; Scott Stansfield, I absolutely love your technical storytelling; Brian Evergreen, Denise Feirstein, and John Alexander; and Kalyan Bansu and Kartavya Neema for developing the task algebra that we present in this book. Andrii Antilikatorov for your rubber factory brain design. Thank you Dr. Jonathan Schaeffer for speaking with me about the checkers optimization project and about your AI research.

Special thanks to John Bilorusky, president of the Western Institute for Social Research (WISR). Your mentorship, discussion about the topics in this book, and expertise on teaching have been invaluable. Most of the research for this book was performed at WISR. The rest was performed at Microsoft.

Thanks to the IBM content development team, for giving a Mechanical Engineer with no writing experience a chance, then teaching me how to write: Hai-Nhu Tran, Frank Eldredge, Shannon Rouiller, Ellen Patterson, Michelle Carey, Kristin Vincent, Dell Burner, Robert Heath, and Andrea Ames. Finally, thanks to my amazing editors: Rebecca Novak for giving me the opportunity to write this book and Sarah Grey and Jonathon Owen for the fantastic editing. It's been a joy writing this book together.

Introduction: The Right Brain in the Right Place (Why We Need Autonomous AI)

Though the problems industry has asked me to solve with autonomous AI are many and varied, they can nonetheless be divided into three clear categories, which I will now explain in detail.

I consulted for a company that uses computer numerical control (CNC) machines to make cell phone cases. Spinning tools cut metal stock into the shape of the phone. After each case is cut, the CNC machine door opens. A robotic arm loads the finished part onto a conveyor, then grasps the next part from a fixture, and loads it into the CNC machine to be cut. If the part does not orient in the fixture at precisely the right angle, the robot arm will fail to grasp the part or will drop the part before it reaches the CNC machine. And if the arriving case is wider or thinner than expected, even just a little, the robot arm will again fail to grasp the part or drop it before it reaches the CNC machine.

The automated system is inflexible. An automated system is one that makes decisions by calculating, searching, or lookup. The robot arm controller was programmed by hand to travel from one fixed point to another and perform the task in a very specific way. It succeeds only if the phone case is the perfect width and sits in the fixture at the perfect angle, as depicted in Figure I-1.

This organization needs more flexible and adaptable automation that can control the robot arm to successfully grasp cases of a wide variety of widths from a range of fixture orientations. This is a great application for autonomous AI. Autonomous AI is flexible and adapts to what it perceives. For example, it can practice grasping cases of various widths that sit in the fixture at various angles and learns to succeed in a wider variety of scenarios, as shown in Figure I-2.

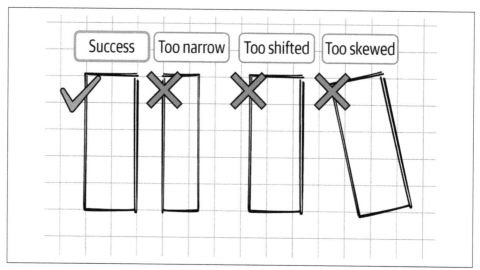

Figure I-1. Width and fixture angle variations that might challenge an automated system during a cell phone manufacturing process.

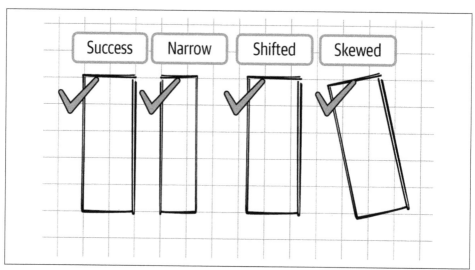

Figure I-2. Width and fixture angle variations that an autonomous AI might learn to adapt to for a cell phone case manufacturing process.

The Changing World Requires Adapting Skills

An executive from a global steel company asked me to travel to Indiana to examine part of their steel making operation, determine where an AI brain could help, and to design that brain. We arrived at the steel mill early in the morning and met with the site CTO, who directed us to the building that housed the process he wanted us to focus on and give us a bit of direction, then we put on protective shoes, hard hats, and metal sleeves and went in for a tour. The foreman came out to meet us and took us on a tour of a "building" that could fit many tall buildings inside of it and was many city blocks wide and long (see Figure I-3). This was the last phase of the steel-making process, where a strip of steel is rolled between what look like two paper towel rolls, then sent through a furnace to temper it and finally through a bath of molten zinc to protect it from rust (this is called "galvanizing").

We talked to the operator at each control room (at steel mills these are called "pulpits"). I interviewed them about how they make decisions to run the machines (what information they use to make the decision and how they operate the machines differently under different scenarios). Then, my hosts whisked me away to a research center, where I reported my recommendations to the chief digital officer (CDO) and a group of researchers about which of the mill's decisions could be improved using AI. I recommended involving AI in galvanization, the last step of the process.

Figure I-3. Photograph of steel mill.

The operators control the coating equipment in real time to make sure that the zinc coating is even and the correct thickness. This job used to be a lot easier when the plant made most of its steel with the same thickness, the same width, and the same coating thickness for the big three US auto manufacturers. Now there are many more customers who ask for many different thicknesses and widths of steel for heating ducts, construction, and all kinds of other things. The operators were having a hard time keeping the coating uniform and the thickness correct across all these variations. Some customers required wide, thin steel with a thin coating; others ordered narrow, thick steel with a thick coating. The world of steel manufacturing had changed and this company was looking to autonomous AI for solutions.

This company is facing a difficult situation. Their business environments (customers, markets, processes, equipment and workers) are changing and they are struggling to adapt their decision-making. Often, their automated systems, which were built to automate repeatable, predictable processes, cannot change their programmed behavior in response to these changing environments. As conditions change, they make worse decisions and sometimes are taken out of service altogether because their decisions are no longer relevant or of sufficiently high quality.

Problems Need Solutions, Not AI

Humans and automated systems are reaching the limits of improvements they can make to industrial processes. Now, enterprises are turning to AI for answers. Unfortunately, much of the discussion about AI focuses on AI as fiction (overhyped and overpromised capability) or science fiction (whether AI will ever reach superintelligence and if it does, what are the philosophical and ethical implications). Neither of these discussions help organizations improve their operations. What enterprises need instead is a playbook for how to design useful AI into autonomous systems where it can make decisions more effectively than humans or automated systems.

When I first started designing autonomous AI, I pitched "a new form of AI" that was different from other kinds of AI and machine learning. I quickly realized that the companies I consulted didn't care about AI. They sought technology that had unique capabilities to control and optimize their high-stakes business processes well compared to their existing solutions. They cared that their operators and automated control systems were effective but struggled to deliver additional process improvement. They understood that control and optimization technology is always evolving and that autonomous AI is simply an evolution of control and optimization technology with unique differentiating characteristics.

What Can AI Do for Me in Real Life?

The AI Index Report (*https://aiindex.stanford.edu/report/*) cites that over 120,000 AI related peer-reviewed academic papers were published in 2019. More than a few of these papers were highly publicized in the press. Some call this the "research to PR pipeline" because of how companies shuttle research breakthroughs straight from the laboratory into press announcements. While it's great to have access to cutting edge research, this research to PR pipeline can make it seem that every new algorithm is ready to solve real-life problems. The challenge is that people and process concerns, combined with the uncertainties of real-life production processes, render many algorithms which seem very promising in controlled laboratory experiments practically useless. Let me give you an example.

A major US rental car company came to us asking whether AI could help them schedule the daily delivery of cars between their locations. Every day, in most major cities, about a dozen drivers shuttle cars from the rental outlet where they were dropped off, to rental locations where they are needed for pickup. A human scheduler plans the routes for each driver, to deliver the right vehicles to the right place. Those familiar with the field of operations research, which is very active in solving logistics and delivery problems, might call this the "Vehicle Routing Problem." Then, they might tell you that there are various optimization algorithms that can search and find the "optimal" solution of routes for each driver so that together, the drivers travel the shortest distance. So, what's the problem? Why would this company be using human schedulers? Don't they know about Dijkstra's algorithm for finding routes that travel the shortest total distance? Wait a minute. It's not that simple.

Dijkstra's shortest path algorithm searches possible routes and schedules routes for each driver that place each stop as close together as possible. So, if you are in a city where the best policy is to always schedule each next stop as closely as possible, Dijkstra's algorithm will give you the best possible answer every time. Here's the problem. For most metropolitan cities, the determining factor for the time each trip leg takes is *traffic*, not distance. But operations research defines the vehicle routing problem without considering traffic. There are plenty of situations where the next best stop is not the closest because of bad traffic conditions. This is especially true during rush hour traffic. Each city has unique traffic patterns, but traffic varies based on a number of factors. Dijkstra's algorithm doesn't consider traffic at all and it doesn't change its scheduling behavior based on any of the factors that dictate traffic patterns. So, even if every rental car company knows how to program and utilize Dijkstra's algorithm, it won't effectively replace human route schedulers. Dijkstra's algorithm also has limited ability to train inexperienced schedulers or augment the expertise of experienced schedulers.

Instead, here's a brain that might adapt to traffic patterns better than Dijkstra's algorithm. This brain can also be used to coach inexperienced schedulers or advise experienced schedulers. Figure I-4 is a hypothetical AI brain example, not one that was designed for a real company, but using the techniques in this book, you can easily design similar brains and modify this brain design for similar applications.

The example brain in Figure I-4 works like a taxi dispatch. Each time a driver arrives delivering a car, it decides to which location the driver should deliver their next car. The goal is to deliver all cars to the locations where they are needed in the least amount of time.

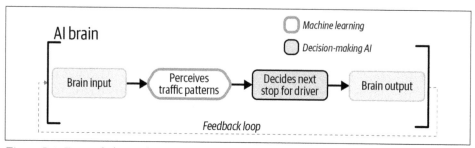

Figure I-4. Example brain for real-time scheduling of rental car deliveries in a major city.

Here's how to read the brain design diagram. The ovals represent the input and the output of the brain. The brain receives information about traffic, vehicles that need to be delivered, and delivery locations. For example, the brain might receive information that it is Wednesday during morning rush hour commute time, that 5 cars have been delivered so far, and that 98 cars await delivery so far for the day through its input node. The modules represent skills that the brain learns to make scheduling decisions. We design a machine learning module into the brain (represented by a hexagon) to predict the trip length to each possible destination based on traffic patterns for the city. This module works a lot like the algorithms in Google and Apple Maps that predict how long each trip will take. The rectangle represents an AI decision-making module that determines which destination to route the driver to. See "Visual Language of Brain Design" on page 113 for more details on how we visually represent brain designs. The brain learns to make scheduling decisions that better adapt to traffic patterns and create schedules that deliver the daily stable of cars more quickly than Dijkstra's algorithm.

This example doesn't suggest that software algorithms are not useful to solve real-life problems. It's a warning against picking a software algorithm or a technique that's been demonstrated in research from a list and applying it to solve a real-world problem without considering all the requirements for a solution to that problem. Earlier, I posed the question, "Why hasn't software solved more problems in manufacturing?" My response is that if you pick from a "list of software algorithms" without deeply understanding the operations and the processes that you are trying to improve, you will be unable to effectively solve real-life problems well.

Instead of simplifying decision-making processes until a particular algorithm can make a decision well, add nuance to your decision-making capabilities until it can solve the realistic problem well.

AI Decision-Making Is Becoming More Autonomous

In his 1970 book *The Structure of Scientific Revolutions* (University of Chicago Press), Thomas Kuhn describes research breakthroughs as the punctuation between long periods of incremental improvement and experimentation. For example, in 1687 Sir Isaac Newton made an important discovery about gravity. In 1915, Albert Einstein made breakthroughs that provided a more nuanced and accurate picture of gravity (*https://oreil.ly/MMK5g*). Einstein's breakthrough doesn't contradict Newton's Law, but it provides a more comprehensive and nuanced view of how gravity works. In the same way, quantum leaps in autonomous decision-making capability punctuate long periods of incremental improvement and experimentation within established paradigms. Stephen Jay Gould observes the same phenomena in his discussion of punctuated equilibrium.[1] Figure I-5 illustrates how scientific revolutions and mainstream democratization advance science over time.

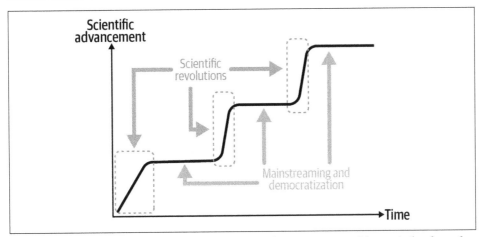

Figure I-5. Scientific advancement over time: revolutions separated by periods of puzzle solving where mainstreaming and democratization occurs.

Throughout the history of AI and other research technologies, these periods of puzzle solving and incremental change between research breakthroughs have added more nuanced decision-making capabilities that spin off from research and become useful for solving real problems in industry. The jet fighter engine was developed in German research laboratories during WWII and used for the first time in a production fighter, the Messerschmitt Me 262. War drove the innovation of jet aircraft, which was then mainstreamed into commercial aircraft over years after WWII.

---

1 Stephen Jay Gould, *The Structure of Evolutionary Theory* (Belknap Press, 2002).

The same is true for AI and automation-related technologies. Let's take the expert system, for example: a method for making automated decisions based on human experience. Expert systems were developed during the second major wave of AI research (1975–1982). Expert systems are great at capturing existing knowledge about how to perform tasks but proved to be inflexible and difficult to maintain. At one point, expert systems (which some thought would reach full human comparable intelligence) comprised much of what was then considered AI research, but by the 1990s they had all but disappeared from AI research efforts. While it's true that most of the fundamental research questions about expert systems had been answered by this time, expert systems hadn't delivered the anticipated autonomy. Simultaneously, the period of puzzle solving began to mainstream and democratize expert systems into useful decision-making automation for real systems, while work began that led to new revolutions which addressed the weaknesses of expert systems for autonomous decision-making.

Expert systems are widely used today in finance and engineering. NASA developed a software language for writing them in 1980. In this book, I'll show you how to combine expert systems with other AI techniques as we design autonomous AI. The first takeaway here is that research breakthroughs often aren't ready to add value to production systems and processes until they mature to meet the people and process concerns of those who run these processes. The second takeaway here is that new revolutions will continue to improve autonomous decision-making.

One of these revolutions is machine learning (*https://oreil.ly/iKAcx*), defined in the linked Wikipedia article at the time of writing this book as the study of computer algorithms that can improve automatically through experience and by the use of data. Machine learning is a powerful paradigm for prediction and prescriptive decision-making, and a fundamental building block for modern autonomous AI that I'll discuss extensively in this book. It is not, however, a replacement for all preceding decision-making paradigms. Machine learning is to previous decision-making paradigms as Einstein's theory of relativity is to Newtonian physics: Newtonian physics applies when looking at objects of a certain size traveling at certain speeds. Relativity is a more nuanced paradigm that applies to situations where Newtonian Physics doesn't describe reality well. Discarding previous decision-making paradigms in favor of machine learning leads to a phenomenon that I call *data science colonialism*.

Beware of Data Science Colonialism

In the same way that software hasn't solved more problems in manufacturing, it appears that the burgeoning field of data science hasn't produced the anticipated sweeping positive effect on industry either. Data science (*https://oreil.ly/3G1u6*), again using a definition from the linked Wikipedia article, is an interdisciplinary field that uses scientific methods, processes, algorithms, and systems to extract knowledge and insights from noisy, structured, and unstructured data, and to apply knowledge and actionable insights from data across a broad range of application domains. The field is on fire, and companies look to data scientists to solve a wide range of problems. Unfortunately, though, as VentureBeat reports (*https://oreil.ly/IEd0d*), 87% of machine learning models that data scientists create never make it into production. Data science colonialism is a practice of using only data to dictate how to control a system or optimize a process, without sufficient understanding of the process. It ignores previous experience controlling a process and engineering experience gained from designing it. Sometimes it even ignores the physical and chemical laws that govern the process. Data science colonialism ignores important details and condescends to experts who should be involved in designing and building autonomous AI.

There's a flavor of data science that functions a lot like colonialism. Colonialism is a practice in which countries explore or even invade other territories claiming intentions to improve the societies they encounter, usually without consideration for the existing culture and values. A colonialistic mindset might ask, "Why would I need to consult a more primitive society about what help they need from me? I should just be telling them what to do!" That's one of the most egregious perspectives of colonialism: the arrogance that you don't need to learn or consider anything about the people whose culture and way of life you are destroying. Unfortunately, I see a similar perspective among some misguided data science practitioners who don't see the need to slow down, listen, and learn about the process from people before attempting to design a "superior" solution.

I was in Canada at a large nickel mine consulting with process experts about using AI to control a SAG mill (think about an eight-story-tall cement mixer). I stepped outside to take a phone call, and when I walked back down the hallway, I found one of the data scientists arguing with one of the experts. It wasn't anything that professionals can't work through together, but the disagreement was about whether we should trust and respect the operators' existing expertise about how to run the mill.

Another time, I spoke with an executive who had an advanced degree in AI and oversaw optimization of processes at a manufacturing company. I explained to him that my approach to designing AI for industrial processes relies heavily on existing subject matter expertise about how to control or optimize the system. He thanked me for not being one of the many companies that have come in, told him that all they needed was some of his data, and that with that data they would build him an AI based control system. He didn't believe that it was possible to ignore decades of human expertise and come up with a control system that would both function well and address all the people and process concerns related to running expensive safety-critical equipment. Neither do I.

Multiple companies have recently tried to solve problems in healthcare using machine learning algorithms. Activities like reading radiology scans to check for cancer can be life-saving. However, some firms have exaggerated the capabilities of algorithms and underemphasized the expertise of medical practitioners with disappointing results. Perhaps more respect for the experts would lead to better technology and stronger results.

Here's another example of data science colonialism. Remember the bulldozer AI that I told you about in the introduction? One of the subject matter experts, a PhD controls engineer named Francisco, thanked me during the AI design process. He felt condescended to by others who had consulted him about AI in the past. What?! Francisco was brilliant in mathematics and control theory—why would anyone condescend to him about AI? The best brain designers are curious, humble, and resist the temptation to view data science, machine learning, or AI, as superseding the value of subject matter expertise.

This is not to say that all data scientists believe their trade is a cure-all; there are data scientists who are curious and practice great empathy. The humility and curiosity to inquire and learn what people already know about making decisions will go a long way when designing autonomous AI.

 Any AI brain that you design to make real decisions for real processes should address the changing world, the changing workforce, and pressing problems.

The Changing Workforce Demands Transferred Skills

When automation systems don't perform well or make good decisions, factories and processes revert back to human control. Humans step in to make high-value decisions for some processes only when the automated systems are making bad decisions, but humans retain complete control of other processes that they haven't figured out how to automate well. However, experts are retiring at an alarming rate and taking decades of hard earned knowledge about how to make industrial decisions out of the workforce with them. After talking to expert after expert and business after business, I realized that people look to AI for answers to their changing workforce because expertise is hard to acquire and equally hard to maintain. To make matters worse, expertise is relatively easy to teach, but takes a lot of practice.

Expertise Is Hard to Acquire

I visited a chemical company that makes plastic film for computer displays and other products on an extruder. An extruder takes raw material (soap, cornmeal for food, or in this case plastic pellets) and heats them up in a metal tube with a turning screw inside. The screw forces the material out a slit to make the plastic. Then the plastic film (it looks just like Saran Wrap) gets stretched in both directions, cooled and sometimes coated. The control room was filled with computer screens and keyboards to check measurements and make real-time adjustments. Can you guess how long an operator trains before they can "call the shots" in the control room as a senior operator? Seven years! Many operators put themselves through university chemical engineering programs during this time. It takes a whole lot of practice turning the knobs on a process until you can control it well for different products, across varying customer demand, types of plastic, types of coating and machine wear. And after your experts get really, really good at controlling your process, it's time for them to retire and you need a way to pass on this expertise to others who are less experienced.

Expertise Is Hard to Maintain

Navasota, Texas, is a small town about two hours' drive from Houston. I went there to help a company called NOV Inc. with their machine shop operations. We arrived in a pickup truck, to a parking lot full of pickup trucks and I felt out of place because I was only one of two people I saw that day who weren't wearing cowboy boots. Our executive sponsor was a forward thinking executive named Ashe Menon who wanted to use AI as a training tool. Many are afraid that AI will take away people's jobs, but he told me the opposite: "I want to be able to hire a 16 year-old high school dropout, sit a brain next to him and have him succeed as a machine operator." He wants to augment human machinists with autonomous AI, not replace them.

We sat down in a no-frills, industrial conference room over strong coffee and he introduced me to a machinist named David. I prefer discussing AI in plain language instead of using research jargon, so I explained to this 35-year expert machinist that a new form of AI can learn by practicing and getting feedback just like he has over all these years, and that we can even use his valuable expertise to teach the AI some of the things he already knows so that it gets better faster as it practices.

You see, when David and other expert machinists control the cutting machines (give them instructions about where to move and how fast to spin the cutter), the cutting jobs get done much quicker and at higher quality than when the engineers use automated software to generate the instructions. David has practiced cutting many different kinds of parts using over 40 different machine makes and models. Some of the machines are new and some of the machines in the shop are over 20 years old. These machines all behave quite differently while cutting metal and David learned how to get the best out of each machine by operating it differently.

NOV and many other companies want to capture and codify the best expertise from their seasoned operators, upload this experience into an AI brain, and sit that brain next to less experienced operators to help them get up to speed more quickly and perform more proficiently. This requires interviewing experts to identify the skills and strategies that they practiced in order to succeed at a task. Then you will be able to design an AI that will practice these same skills, get feedback, and also learn to succeed at the task.

An executive in the resources industry told me that their 20- and 30-year experts are retiring in large groups and that it feels like their hard fought, valuable experience about how to best manage their business is walking out the door, never to return. Humans can learn how to control complex equipment that changes in really odd ways, but it takes a lot of practice time to build the nuances into our intuition. Most expert operators tell me that it took years or decades to learn to do their job well.

 Designing autonomous AI allows you to package expertise into AI as neat units of skill that can be passed onto other humans, saved for later, combined in new and interesting ways, or used to control processes autonomously.

Expertise Is Simple to Teach, but Requires Practice

Whether playing chess, learning a sport, or controlling a process in a factory, gaining skill requires a lot of practice to understand the nuances of what to do in many complex situations. Expertise is complex and situationally nuanced. Teachers guide this practice in a way that leads to more efficient skill acquisition. Coaches and teachers do this all the time when they introduce (describe) a skill, then ask students to practice it. When teachers do this, they often have an opinionated sequence that they want skills to be introduced and practiced. If the lesson plan is good, it accelerates learning, but even the best teaching plan does not take away from the situational improvisation and nuance that the learner displays while practicing (acquiring) the skills.

SCG Chemicals is part of a 100-year-old company that manufactures plastic. For one type of plastic, they invented the process, learned to run the reactors efficiently, and even researched advanced chemistry to simulate the process. The operators practiced controlling the reactors well for all the different plastic products they make and for the catalysts they use to make them. One of the first questions that I asked the experts was "How do you teach new operators this complex skill of controlling reactors?" The answer was concise and easy to understand: there are two primary strategies that we teach every boardman (operators of all genders at SCG are called boardmen).

1. Add ingredients until the density reaches the target range. Ignore the melting point measurements for the process while you are using this first strategy.

2. Then, when the density of the plastic is in target range, switch over to the second strategy. While using this strategy, ignore the density and add ingredients until the melting point for the plastic reaches product specification.

Because of the way the chemistry works, if you work the strategies in the prescribed order, both the density and the melting point will turn out right. They invented this process, but even they don't have all the chemistry that explains why it works this way. It works every time though, so SCG Chemicals teaches this sequence for the strategies to their operators.

Do you see how teaching the skills is relatively straightforward for a competent teacher, but how each skill still requires a lot of practice? In the hands of a good teacher, these skills are easy to outline but require a whole lot of practice to build into your intuition. Each minute, the boardman needs to decide how much of each ingredient (called reagents in chemistry) to add. They will need to add less reagent when the density is close to the target and more reagent when the temperature is higher. How much more will depend on which variant of plastic they're making and which catalyst they're using to drive the reaction.

The supervising engineer, Pitak, writes customized recipes that boardmen can follow to successfully execute each of the strategies even if they haven't had enough practice to master the skills yet. The boardman leans on these rigid recipes to help them succeed until they have practiced enough to internalize the nuances and variations.

Even though every boardman knows the two strategies and has a procedure for how to use them, it takes a lot of practice to modify the strategies to match the changing process conditions. For example, a boardman might add reagents to the reactor in different amounts while making one kind of plastic using one type of catalyst, but might add ingredients to the reactor in slightly different amounts while making a different kind of plastic using a second type of catalyst. So, Pitak updates the recipes as conditions change.

This is very similar to what happens while baking (baking is a complex chemical reaction after all). Your father might have taught you to mix the dough while adding the first set of ingredients until it feels sticky and smells like almonds. This is the first strategy. He might have also taught you that, next, you add a different set of ingredients and knead the dough until it's firm. This is the second strategy. Your father taught you two strategies and how to sequence them, as illustrated in Figure I-6.

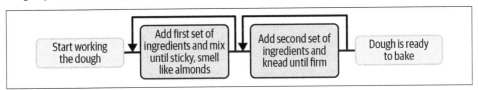

Figure I-6. Baking preparation process with two skills used in sequence.

The strategies are pretty easy to teach and understand, but take practice to master. That's what recipes are for. They tell you exactly how much of each ingredient to add during each step of the process and recommend how long to mix and how long to knead. The problem with recipes (for baking, manufacturing plastic, and many other tasks) is that the recipe is rigid. An expert baker knows that if it's hot and humid outside you will mix for a shorter period of time before you start kneading, the same way that Pitak knows that if it's more hot and humid outside, the boardman will need to add more reagents or more catalyst to the reactor. That's why Pitak updates the recipes for the boardman to follow as the temperature and humidity change over time. With a lot more practice, bakers and boardmen no longer need the recipes. They create their own recipes on the fly (bakers based on the feel and smell of the dough, boardmen based on the temperature and pressure in the reactor). This is why my mom never uses recipes when she cooks. She started decades ago with a recipe for each dish, but now when she cooks each dish, she adjusts the ingredients to taste as she goes. When she first taught me how to make our family's chili recipe, I followed the instructions "to a T," but now I improvise while making chili just like she does!

Pressing Problems Demand Completely New Skills

Climate change is a pressing societal problem. Many companies have made pledges to take action to slow the effect of climate change (*https://oreil.ly/kbzSr*). Is there a way that AI can help?

Well, less energy consumption means less need for energy from fossil fuels. Did you know that 50% of energy usage in buildings comes from heating, cooling, air conditioning and ventilation (HVAC) systems? It turns out that this is an opportunity for AI to make a material difference on climate change. Many commercial HVAC systems, like those that cool and heat office buildings, rely on human engineers and operators to tune and control them.

Driving various rooms toward the right temperature while carefully managing energy usage is not as easy or intuitive as it appears. Managing energy consumption for a building or campus adds several layers of variability like the controls for cooling towers, water pumps, and chillers. This is further complicated by occupants entering and leaving the building constantly throughout the day. There's a pattern to it (imagine commute times and traffic conditions) but they are complex to perceive. The price of energy changes throughout the day. There are peak times where energy is most expensive and off-peak times where energy is cheaper. You can recycle air to save money from heating outside air, but legal standards dictate how much carbon dioxide is allowed in the building, which limits your ability to recycle. Each layer of complexity makes it harder for a human to understand how each variable will impact the outcome of a control setting.

Microsoft built an autonomous AI to control the HVAC systems on its Redmond West Campus (*https://oreil.ly/k4XxA*). The campus had automated systems, but those systems cannot make supervisory decisions based on occupancy and outdoor temperature in real time. My team worked with mechanical engineers to design a brain to make those decisions, and the new system is currently using about 15% less energy. Two years earlier, Google successfully tested an AI that reduced energy consumption in data centers by 40% (*https://oreil.ly/rK7Ki*). If you're wondering why the earlier AI generated more improvement, it's because data centers are easier to control. They have less influence from outside factors. Commercial buildings have to deal with things like solar irradiation (most of the heat in commercial buildings comes from sun shining in the windows from different angles at different times) and large numbers of people constantly exiting and entering the building.

AI Is a Tool; Use It for Good

Every day I see people debating the ethics and perils of AI on social media. While I agree that ethics are important and that we should be very careful as a society about how we approach AI, the only way to ensure that AI gets used for good is to design and build AI that explicitly does useful, helpful, things.

I just finished teaching my first Designing Autonomous AI cohort to underrepresented minority students in New York City with the Urban Arts Partnership (*https://www.urbanarts.org*). What an amazing experience working with such energetic and talented college students!

As a Black man who works in AI research, I feel the weight of unequal access to advanced technologies like AI every day. If the Fourth Industrial Revolution can endow superpowers, tremendous wealth, and expansive opportunity for those who lead it, then unequal access to AI presents something of a calcifying caste system: 4% of the workforce at Microsoft and at Facebook are Black; 2.5% of the workforce at Google is Black. Less than 20% of all AI professors are women, 18% of major research papers at AI conferences are written by women, and only 15% of Google AI research staff are women.[2]

Robert J. Shiller, 2013 Nobel laureate in economics, says it well:

> You cannot wait until a house burns down to buy fire insurance on it. We cannot wait until there are massive dislocations in our society to prepare for the Fourth Industrial Revolution.

Almost everyone has limited access to advanced technology to some extent, but those who are marginalized in additional ways, such as due to their income, race, and ability, are multiplicatively less likely to experience the benefits of working with autonomous AI.

---

2 A version of this paragraph was originally published in *Cases and Stories of Transformative Action Research: Five Decades of Collaborative Action and Learning* by John Bilorusky (Routledge).

Starting with the principles and techniques in this book, I intend to further democratize access to decision-making autonomous AI and put it into the hands of the underrepresented and the underprivileged as a means for solving societal problems and economic advancement.

First, imagine an operator at the chemical company that I talked about above (the one with the plastic extruder) not just learning to control the extruder well, but designing and building AI that they will take with them into the control room to help them make decisions. Next, imagine a squad of chess players from inner city East Oakland, California, all minorities, who learned how to play chess by playing with and against autonomous AI that they designed and taught. We have much work to do to fulfill this vision, but the progress is real and I invite you to use your skills designing autonomous AI to do good in areas that you are passionate about.

PART I

When Automation Doesn't Work

I recently participated in a workgroup organized by the National Science Foundation to investigate the use of AI in manufacturing (*https://oreil.ly/liAFY*). About 20 of us in Workshop 2 Roundtable 4 started by pondering why "software hasn't had more impact on the manufacturing industry." Some industries like finance have embraced software and data science in a more significant way than what we see in manufacturing. We came to two conclusions. First, the long list of software algorithms that are available to solve problems are not accessible without training in programming and using algorithms. Many times I've spoken to software engineers about industry problems, who asked: doesn't this industry know about this algorithm? No, they don't. And even if they did, they would not be able to manipulate it the way a software engineer can and even then there's no guarantee that the algorithm will solve the real-life problem in all of its complexity without getting to know the process.

My second and more important takeaway from the workgroup was that *the manufacturing industry runs on the exchange of skills, not algorithms*. In manufacturing, operators, supervisors, and engineers practice building, refining and teaching high-value skills for controlling equipment and processes. Just a few weeks ago a manufacturing executive told me that the most important asset of this multi-billion dollar company was the expertise (skills) of its operators and process controllers. This suggests to me that any mechanism for process improvement in manufacturing must be compatible with the exchange of skills. In the workgroup, we discussed many possible assets that can be accumulated and stored to accelerate improvement in manufacturing. Assets like part blueprints and manufacturing recipes are very specific and proprietary. Skills, on the other hand, can be common to similar processes, and can be stored and customized to the processes of specific companies, manufacturing lines, and product types.

So, how is it possible to accumulate and store skills using software? That's what an instance of autonomous AI is, an agent that can acquire and perform specific skills. And machine teaching provides the organizing structure for these skills. These skills can be stored, perhaps along with specialized virtual environments for practicing skills in certain scenarios. Imagine training the best experts in your organization in machine teaching, which enables them to codify their most valuable skills, and designing AI that will practice and master these skills. This is especially important to the many organizations that are at risk of losing large amounts of expertise as their experts retire.

In this first part of the book, I make the case for considering skills as the right level of abstraction for advanced problem solving instead of algorithms, rules, or recipes. In Chapter 1 I discuss the limitations of automation, and in Chapter 2 I discuss the promising contributions of autonomous AI to the quest for more humanlike decision-making.

- Chapter 1, "Sometimes Machines Make Bad Decisions"
- Chapter 2, "The Quest for More Human-Like Decision-Making"

Sometimes Machines Make Bad Decisions

Why do humans so frequently manage, supervise, step in to assist, or override automated systems? What are the qualities of human decision-making that automated systems cannot replicate? Comparing these strengths and weaknesses helps us design useful AI and avoid thinking that AI is a magical cure-all or complete hype.

I took a trip to Australia and while I was there, a resources company asked for help with their aluminum production process. The company uses an expert system to make automated decisions during the process.

Aluminum is made in large tubs called cells (see Figure 1-1). Aluminum is smelted using a process called electrolysis. In aluminum electrolysis, alumina powder is injected into a cell full of cryolite. Electricity passes through the cryolite, and the resulting reaction produces aluminum. Here's the problem: it's almost impossible to tell exactly what's going on in the cell because the temperature is high enough and the cryolite is corrosive enough to destroy sensors. So experts and automated systems rely on changes in the electrical properties of the cell for feedback. Voltage is how hard the electricity is pushing through the system. Current (measured in amps) is the amount of electricity that flows through the system, and resistance is the amount of opposition the system provides to the flow of electricity.

So standard practice for controlling alumina cells (across the industry, not just at this particular company) is to employ the following two strategies:

- Overfeed the cell (inject more alumina than is likely needed to feed the reaction) until the cell resistance drops. This is a sign that it is time to change strategy.
- Underfeed the cell (inject less alumina than is likely needed to feed the reaction) until the cell resistance rises.

Good aluminum production swings back and forth between these two strategies. The trick is to know when to switch to the opposing strategy. This decision about how to navigate between strategies is nuanced and requires paying attention to how cell resistance changes as well as other variables. This company uses an automated expert system to make this decision for each cell. Expert systems store expert rules (and sometimes equations that describe relationships between variables) to make decisions. I discuss the pros and cons of expert systems in detail in "Expert Systems Recall Stored Expertise" on page 21.

In most situations, the expert system makes great decisions about when to transition between strategies, but the boundary between the strategies is fuzzy. In some scenarios, the expert system transitions too early or too late. Both early and late transitions result in effects that degrade aluminum production. When these effects occur, human experts are called in to override the expert system and make the nuanced decisions about when and how to execute the strategies.

Figure 1-1. Alumina cells for manufacturing aluminum. The example of expert systems in aluminum manufacturing illustrates how automated processes require humans to step in and make decisions when automated systems make bad decisions.

Curiosity Required Ahead

There are a lot of examples in this book! Why are there so many use case examples in this book? Or, put differently, "Why do you keep bringing up so many different engineering processes that I've never heard of? It's a lot to take in!" Here's my answer: the practice of machine teaching requires curiosity and interest in learning new things above all. I've been asked to formulate autonomous AI designs for all kinds of machines, systems, and processes, most of which I had never heard of in my life (including aluminum smelting). Sometimes, I was asked to come up with these designs very quickly, in hours, or even minutes. This was made possible by my intense curiosity about engineering processes and by the framework that I teach in this book. As you read through the examples in this book, hopefully you will appreciate that in order to design effective autonomous AI, you need to have an appetite for learning.

Math, Menus, and Manuals: How Machines Make Automated Decisions

If you want to design brains well, you first need to understand how automated systems make decisions. You will use this knowledge to compare techniques and decide when autonomous AI will outperform existing methods. You will also combine automated decision-making with AI to design more explainable, reliable, deployable brains. Though there are many subcategories and nuances, automated systems rely on three primary methods to make decisions: math, menus, and manuals.

Control Theory Uses Math to Calculate Decisions

Control theory uses mathematical equations to calculate the next control action, usually based on feedback, using well-understood mathematical relationships. When you do this, you must trust that the math describes the system dynamics well enough to use it to calculate what to do next. Let me give you an example. There's an equation that describes how much space a gas will take up based on its temperature and pressure. It's called the ideal gas law (*https://oreil.ly/XF560*). So if we wanted to design a brain that controls a valve that inflates party balloons, we could use this equation to calculate how much to adjust the valve open and closed to inflate balloons to a particular size.

In the example above, we rely on math to describe what will happen so completely and accurately that we don't even need feedback. Controlling based on equations like this is called open loop control because there is no closed feedback loop telling us whether our actions achieved the desired results. We trust the equation so much that we don't even need feedback. But what if the equation doesn't completely describe all of the factors that affect whether we succeed or not? For example, the ideal gas law doesn't model high-pressure, low-temperature gases, dense gases, or heavy gases well (*https://oreil.ly/svtIq*). Even when we control responding to feedback, limitations of the mathematical model might lead to bad decisions.

I see the history of control theory as an evolution of capability where each control technology can do things that previous control technologies could not. The U.S. Navy invented the Proportional Integral Derivative (PID) controller (*https://oreil.ly/qzfYf*) to automatically steer ship rudders and control ship headings (the direction the ship is pointing). Imagine that a ship is pointing in one direction and the captain wants to change headings to point the ship in a different direction, as shown in Figure 1-2.

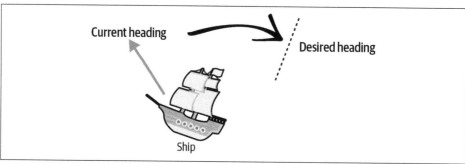

Figure 1-2. Ship changing heading.

The controller uses math to calculate how much to move the rudder based on feedback it gets from its last action. There are three numbers that determine how the controller will behave: the P, the I, and the D constant. The P constant moves you toward the target, so for the ship, the P constant makes sure that the rudder action causes the ship to move towards its new heading. But what if the controller keeps turning the rudder and the ship sweeps right past the target heading? This is what the I constant is for. The I constant tracks how much total error you have in the system and keeps you from overshooting or undershooting the target. The D constant ensures that you arrive at the target destination smoothly instead of abruptly. So a D in the ship controller would make it more likely that the ship will decelerate and arrive more precisely to its destination heading.

A ship with a P controller (no I and no D) might overshoot the target, sweeping the boat past the new heading. After the ship sweeps past the target, you'll need to turn it back. The leftmost diagram in Figure 1-3 shows what this might look like. The horizontal line represents the destination heading. A PI controller will more quickly converge on the target because the I term makes sure that you overshoot the target as little as possible. The PD controller approaches the target more smoothly, but takes longer to reach it.

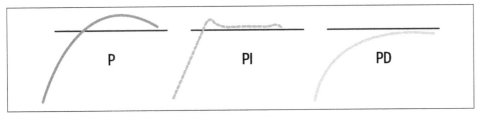

Figure 1-3. Example behaviors of various controllers.

The PID controller can be very effective and you can find it in almost every modern factory and machine, but it can confuse disturbances and noise for events that it needs to respond to. For example, if a PID controller controlled the gas pedal on your car, it might confuse a speed bump (which is a minor and temporary disturbance) for a hill which requires significant acceleration. In this case, the controller might overaccelerate and exceed the commanded speed, then need to slow down.

The feedforward controller separately measures and responds to disturbances, not just the variable you are controlling. In contrast to PID feedback control, Jacques Smuts writes:

> feedforward control acts the moment a disturbance occurs, without having to wait for a deviation in process variable. This enables a feedforward controller to quickly and directly cancel out the effect of a disturbance. To do this, a feedforward controller produces its control action based on a measurement of the disturbance.
>
> When used, feedforward control is almost always implemented as an add-on to feedback control. The feedforward controller takes care of the major disturbance, and the feedback controller takes care of everything else that might cause the process variable to deviate from its set point.[1]

In our cruise control example, this means that the controller can better tell the difference between a speed bump and a hill by measuring and responding to the disturbance (the change in road elevation) instead of measuring and responding only to the change in the vehicle's speed. See Figure 1-4 for an example showing how much better feedback with feedforward control responds to a disturbance than feedback control alone.

The more sophisticated feedforward controller has limitations too. Both PID and feedforward controllers can only control for one variable at a time for one goal per feedback loop. So you'd need two feedback/feedforward loops, for example, if you needed to control both the gas pedal and the steering wheel of the car. And neither of those loops can both maximize gas mileage and maintain constant speed at the same time.

1 Jacques Smuts, "A Tutorial on Feedback Control," *Control Notes: Reflections of a Process Control Practitioner,* January 17, 2011, *https://blog.opticontrols.com/archives/297.*

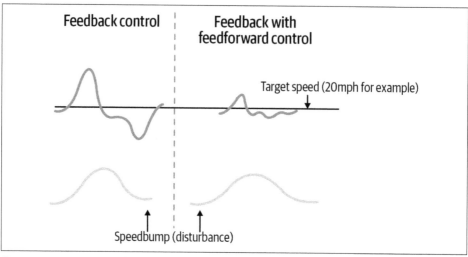

Figure 1-4. Comparing how a car controlled by PID feedback control responds to a speed bump versus one controlled by feedforward; the fluctuation in speed is much smaller with feedforward control.

So what happens if you need to control for more than one variable or pursue more than one goal? There are ways to solve this, but in real life we often see people create separate feedback loops that can't talk to each other or coordinate actions. So in the same way that humans duplicate work and miscalculate what to do when we don't coordinate with each other, separate control loops don't manage multiple goals well and often waste energy.

Enter the latest in the evolution of widely adopted control systems: model predictive control (MPC). MPC extends the capability of PID and feedforward to control for multiple inputs and outputs. Now, the same controller can be used to control multiple variables and pursue multiple goals. The MPC controller uses a highly accurate system model to try various control actions in advance and then choose the best action. This control technique actually borrows from the second type of automated decision-making (menus). It has many attractive characteristics, but lives or dies by the accuracy of the system model, or the equations that predict how the system will respond to your actions. But real systems change: machines wear, or equipment is replaced, the climate changes, and this can make the system model inaccurate over time. Many of us have experienced this in our vehicles. As the brakes wear, we need to apply the brakes earlier to stop. As the tires wear, we can't drive as fast or turn as sharply without losing control. Since the MPC uses the system model to look ahead and try potential actions, an inaccurate model will mislead it to decide on actions that won't work well on the real system. Because of this, many MPC systems that were installed, particularly in chemical plants in the 1990s, were later decommissioned when the plants drifted from the system models. The MPC controllers that relied heavily on these system models in order to be accurate no longer controlled well.

In 2020, McKinsey QuantumBlack built an autonomous AI to help steer the Emirates Team New Zealand sailing team to victory by controlling the rudder of their boat. This AI brain can input many, many variables including ones that math-based controllers can't, like video feeds from cameras and categories (like forward, backward, left, right). It learns by practicing in simulation and acquires creative strategies to pursue multiple goals simultaneously. For example, in its experimentation and self-discovery, it tried to sail the boat upside down because for a while, during practice in simulation, it seemed like a promising approach to accomplish sailing goals.

Control theory uses math to calculate what to do next, the techniques to do this continuously evolve, and autonomous AI is simply an extension of these techniques that offers some really attractive control characteristics such as the ability to control for multiple variables and track toward multiple goals.

When Should You Use Control Theory to Make Decisions?

- Use control theory when you need reliable, predictable control of processes that you can measure well.
- Use control theory when you understand the system dynamics well and can express them in mathematical terms.

Limitations of Control Theory

- Controllers that use math to make decisions rely heavily on the mathematical model. If you can't model the system well with math, you can't control it well with control theory.
- The settings on controllers make them work well for linear systems, but not as well when there are nonlinear relationships between the variables.
- The controller will not change its behavior unless human experts retune the constants.

Optimization Algorithms Use Menus of Options to Evaluate Decisions

Optimization algorithms search a list of options and select a control action using objective criteria. Think about the way optimization works, like selecting options from a menu. For example, an optimization system might list all possible routes to deliver a package from manufacturing point A to delivery point B, then select sequential routing decisions by sorting the shortest route to the top of the list of options. You might come up with different control actions if you sort for the shortest trip duration. In this example, the route distance and the trip durations are the objective criteria (the goals of the optimization). Imagine playing tic-tac-toe this way. Tic-tac-toe is a simple two player game played on a grid where you place your symbol, an X or an O, in squares on the grid and you win when you are the first player to occupy three squares in a row with your symbol. If you want to play the game like an optimization algorithm, you could use the following procedure:

1. Make a list of all squares (there are 9, see Figure 1-5 for an example).
2. Cross out (from the list) the squares that already have an X or an O in them.
3. Choose an objective to optimize for. For example, you might decide to make moves based on how many blank squares there are adjacent to each square. This objective gives you the most flexibility for future moves. This is why many players choose the center square for their first move (there are 8 squares adjacent to the middle square).
4. Sort your options based on the objective criteria.
5. The top option is your next move. If there are multiple moves with the exact same objective criteria score, choose one randomly.

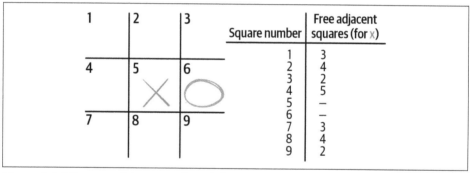

Figure 1-5. Diagram of tic-tac-toe board showing X making the first move, O making the second move, the number of adjacent squares that are open or under X's control for each option available for X's next move, and a list that tracks the attributes of each square.

This exercise shows the first limitation of optimization algorithms. They don't know anything about the task. This is why you need to choose a square randomly if there are multiple squares with the same objective score at the top of your search. Claude Shannon, one of the early pioneers of AI, talked about this in his famous 1950 paper about chess-playing AI.[2] He observed that there were two ways to program a chess AI. He labeled them System A and System B. System A, which is actually the third method of automated decision-making (manuals), programs chess strategies. These

---

2 Claude E. Shannon, "Programming a computer for playing chess," *Philosophical Magazine*, 7th series, 41, no. 314 (March 1950): 256-75.

rules and exceptions are difficult to manage and update, but they express understanding of the game. System B, which is optimization, searches possible legal chess moves with a single easy-to-maintain algorithm, but has no actual understanding of the concepts or strategies of chess.

Strategy Versus Search

I believe that strategy is one of the missing key ingredients of AI research. I think that Claude Shannon (an early pioneer of AI) would agree with me. Strategy is a key way that we make sense of the world, and Shannon predicted a long time ago that there would be friction about whether to use strategy or search options, as shown in Figure 1-6.

Figure 1-6. Two approaches for making complex sequential decisions.

Solutions Are like Points on a Map

Optimization algorithms are like explorers searching the surface of the earth for the highest mountain or the lowest point. The solutions to problems are points on the map where, if you arrive, you achieve some good outcome. If your goal is altitude, you are looking for the peak of Mt. Everest, at 8,848 meters above sea level (see Figure 1-7 for a map of Earth relief by altitude in relation to sea level). If your goal is finding the location that is most packed with people (population density), you are looking for the Chinese island of Macau, which has a population density of 21,081 people/km² (see Figure 1-8 for a map of Earth relief by population density). If you're looking for the coldest place on earth on average, then you're looking for Vostok Station, Antarctica.

Now, imagine that you are an optimization algorithm searching the earth for the highest peak. One way to ensure that you find the highest peak is to set foot on every square meter of earth, take measurements at each point and then, when you are done, sort your measurements by altitude. The highest point on earth will now be at the top of your list.

Since there are 510 million square kilometers of land mass on earth, it would take many, many lifetimes to get your answer.[3] This method is called brute force search

---

3 George Heineman's *Learning Algorithms* (O'Reilly) provides details on how to benchmark these algorithms.

and is only feasible when the geographical search area of possible decisions is very small (like in the game tic-tac-toe). For more complex problem geographies, we need another method.

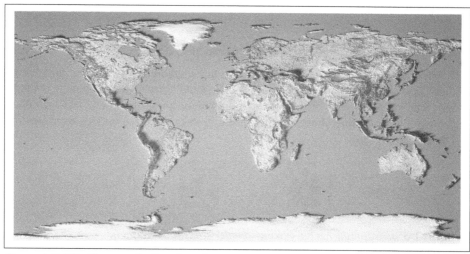

Figure 1-7. World map relief by altitude.

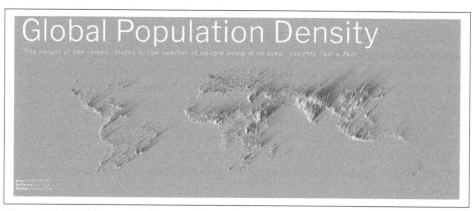

Figure 1-8. World map relief by population density.

A more efficient way to search the earth for the highest peak is to walk the earth and only take steps in the direction that slopes upward the most. Using this method, you can avoid exploring much of the geography by only traveling uphill. In optimization, this class of methods is called gradient-based methods because the slope of a hill is called a grade or a gradient. There are two challenges with this method. The first is that, depending on where you start your search exploration, you could end up on a tall mountain that is not the highest point on earth. If you start your search in Africa, you could end up on Mt. Kilimanjaro (not the world's tallest peak). If you start in North America, you could end up on top of one of the mountains in the Rocky Mountain range. You could even end up on a much lesser peak because once you ascend any peak using this search method, you cannot descend back down any hill. Figure 1-9 demonstrates how this works.

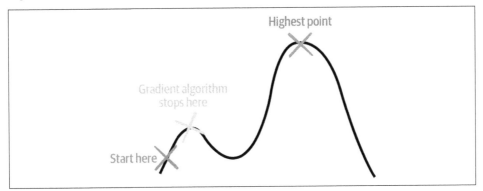

Figure 1-9. A gradient-based algorithm will stop searching in relation to the highest point on a curve.

The second limitation of this method is that it can only be used in situations where you can calculate the slope of the ground where you walk. If there are gaps in the terrain (think vertical drops or bottomless pits), it is not possible to calculate the slope (technically it's infinite) at the vertical drops, so you can't use gradient-based optimization methods to search for solutions in that space. See Figure 1-10 for examples of solution terrain that gradient algorithms cannot search.

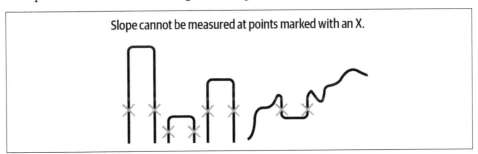

Figure 1-10. These examples of function curves cannot be searched using gradient-based methods.

Now, imagine if you employed multiple explorers to start at different places in the landscape and search for the highest point. After each step, the explorers compare notes on their current altitude and elevation and use their combined knowledge to better map the earth. That might lead to a quicker search and avoid all explorers getting stuck in a high spot that is not the peak of Mt. Everest. These and other innovations allow optimization algorithms to more efficiently and effectively explore more kinds of landscapes, even the ones shown in Figure 1-10. Many of these algorithms are inspired by processes in nature. Nature has many effective ways of exploring thoroughly, much like water flowing over a patch of land. Here are a few examples:

Evolutionary algorithms
> Inspired by Darwin's theory of natural selection (*https://oreil.ly/Vk1mR*), evolutionary algorithms (*https://oreil.ly/XTEhN*) spawn a population of potential solutions decisions, test how well each of the solutions in the population achieve the process goals, kill off the ineffective solutions, then mutate the population to continue exploring.

Swarm methods
> Inspired by how ants (*https://oreil.ly/Iv1MN*), bees (*https://oreil.ly/3YtEp*), and particles (*https://oreil.ly/zKbdt*) swarm, move, and interact, these optimization methods explore the solution space with many explorers that move along the landscape and communicate with each other about what they find. Figure 1-11 illustrates how these explorers work.

Tree methods
> These methods treat potential solutions as branches on trees. Imagine a choose-your-own-adventure novel (and other interactive fiction) that asks you to decide which direction to take at a certain point in the story. The decisions proliferate with the number of options at each decision point. Tree-based methods use various techniques to search the tree efficiently (not having to visit each branch) for solutions. Some of the more well known tree methods are branch and bound (*https://oreil.ly/Sxq77*) and Monte Carlo tree search (MCTS) (*https://oreil.ly/uUyJd*).

Simulated annealing
> Inspired by the way that metal cools, simulated annealing searches the space using different search behavior over time. All metals have a crystalline structure that cools in a common way. That structure changes more when the metal is hotter and less when cooler. Annealing is a process by which a material like metal is heated above its recrystalization temperature and then slowly cooled in order to render it more malleable for the next steps in various industrial processes. This algorithm imitates that process. Simulated annealing casts a wide search net at first (exploring more), then becomes more sure that it's zeroing in on the right area (exploring less) over time.

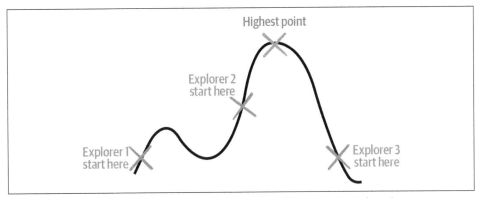

Figure 1-11. Some optimization algorithms use multiple coordinated explorers.

Solving the Game of Checkers

There is a scene in the movie *The Matrix* where the main character Neo finds a child, dressed as a Shaolin monk, bending a spoon with his mind. Seeing that Neo is perplexed, the child explains that there is no spoon. Neo and the child are in a manipulative virtual digital world that a rogue machine AI conjured to entrap humans in their minds. The child is manipulating the imaginary code-based world that their human minds occupy.

I feel similarly about making the perfect sequential decision while performing a complex task. Optimization experts call these "best possible decisions" (like Mt. Everest or the highest topography points in Figures 1-9 and 1-11) *global optima*. Optimization algorithms promise the possibility of reaching global optima for every decision, but this is not how it works in real, complex systems. For example, there is no "perfect move" during a chess match. There are strong moves, creative moves, weak moves, surprising moves, but no perfect moves for winning a particular game. That is, unless you're playing checkers.

In 2007, after almost 20 years of continuously searching the space with optimization algorithms (*https://oreil.ly/L2Gzi*) on powerful computers, researchers declared checkers solved (*https://oreil.ly/q4Dc2*). Checkers is roughly 1 million times more complex than Connect Four, with 500 billion billion possible positions (5×10^{20}). I spoke with Dr. Jonathan Schaeffer, one of the lead researchers on the project, and this is what he told me:

> We proved that perfect play leads to a draw. That is not the same as knowing the value of every position. The proof eliminates vast portions of the search. For example, if we find a win, the program does not bother looking at the inferior moves that yield a draw or a loss. Thus, if you set up a position that occurs in one of those drawing/losing lines, the program might not know its solved value.

So why don't we just solve our industrial problems like checkers? Besides the fact that it took optimization algorithms 20 years to solve checkers, most real problems are more complex than that, and the checkers space is not completely explored, even after all that computation. Remember the tree based optimization methods above? Well, one way that computer scientists devised to measure the complexity of tasks (*https://oreil.ly/fhKcJ*) is to count the number of possible options at the average branch of the tree. This is called the *branching factor*. The branching factor for checkers is 2.8, which means on average there are about 3 possible moves for any turn during a checkers game. This is mostly due to the forced capture rule in checkers. In a capture position, the branching factor is slightly larger than 1. In a noncapture position, the branching factor is approximately 8. Branching factors for some of the most popular board games are summarized in Table 1-1.

Table 1-1. Branching factors for common games

Game	Branching factor
Checkers	2.8
Tic-tac-toe	4
Connect Four	4
Chess	35
Go	250

Then there's uncertainty. One very convenient aspect of games like checkers and chess is that things always happen exactly the way you want them to. For example, if I want to move my bishop all the way across the board (the chess term for putting the bishop on this cross-board highway of the longest diagonal, as illustrated in Figure 1-12, is fiancetto), I can be certain that the bishop will make it all the way to G7 as I intended. But in the real life war campaigns that chess was modeled after, an offensive to take a certain hill is not guaranteed to succeed, so our bishop might actually land at F6 or E5 instead of our intended G7. This kind of uncertainty about the success of each move will likely change our strategy. I'll talk more about uncertainty in a minute.

So for real problems (such as bending spoons in the Matrix), when it comes to finding optimal solutions for each move you need to make, there is indeed no spoon.

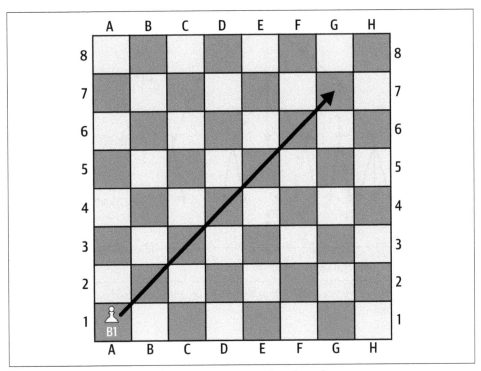

Figure 1-12. Bishop moving from A1 to G7 on a chess board.

Reconnaissance

Reconnaissance just means scouting ahead. You can't explore the entire space ahead of time, but in some situations you can scout out local surrounding areas a few moves in advance. For example, model predictive control (MPC) looks at least one move in advance when making decisions. To do this, you need a model that will accurately predict what will happen after you make a decision.

Most of the AI that performs this kind of reconnaissance uses it in situations with discrete outcomes at each step. This is true for games like chess and Go, but it's also true for decisions in manufacturing planning and logistics. Imagine determining which machines to make products on or which shipment carrier to use for a delivery.

Autonomous AI like AlphaChess, AlphaGo, and AlphaZero can't make good decisions without scouting many moves ahead. These AI use Monte Carlo tree search (MCTS) to navigate large spaces like chess, shogi, and Go, as shown in Figure 1-13.

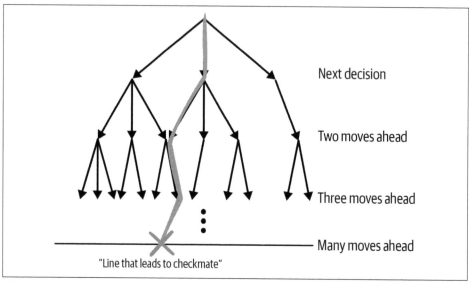

Figure 1-13. A line of moves leading to a winning outcome expressed on a tree of lookahead options.

You can use trees to search many moves ahead. The first set of branches on the tree represent options for your next move and each further branch on the tree represents further future moves. The idea is to keep looking at more future moves until you reach the end of the game. When you do, there will be paths through the branches (called lines in chess) that lead to winning outcomes and others that lead to losing outcomes. If you can make it that far through the search, you'll have lots of winning lines that you can pursue. The average chess game lasts 20 to 40 moves and the tree representing any one of those games has more branches than the number of atoms in the universe. That doesn't mean that you shouldn't use look ahead moves though. There are many ways to pare down the number of branches that you need to examine to get to winning outcomes.

MCTS randomly searches branches on the tree for as long as you have time and compute power to spare. The World Chess Federation (commonly referred to by its French name, Fédération Internationale des Échecs [FIDE]) mandates 90 minutes for each player's first 40 moves, then 30 minutes total for both players to finish the game. AlphaZero uses 44 CPU computer cores to randomly search about 72,000 tree branches for each move. Depending on chance, the algorithm might or might not find a winning line during the search between each of its moves.

Both professional chess and Go players say that the AI has an "alien playing style" and I say that is because of the randomness of MCTS. You see, when the search algorithm finds a line, it chases it and will do absolutely anything (no matter how unorthodox or sacrificial) to follow it. Then, depending on the opponent's play, the algorithm may pick up a new line with seemingly disjointed unorthodox moves and sacrifices. Some of these lines are brilliant, creative, and thrilling to watch but are also at times erratic. Before we move on, let's give credit where it's due: AlphaZero beat the de facto standard AI in machine chess (Stockfish) 1,000 games to zero in 2019 (*https://oreil.ly/ybooO*).

Humans look ahead, but not in this way. Psychologists' research on chess players shows that expert chess players focus on only a small subset of total pieces and review an even smaller subset of tree branches when scouting ahead for options.[4] How are they able to look many moves ahead without randomly exploring so many options? *They're biased.* Many options don't make sense as strong chess moves, others don't make sense based on the strategy that the player is using, others still don't make sense based on the strategy that the opponent is using. I suggest that a promising area of research is using human expertise and strategy to bias the tree search (only explore options that match the current strategy).

What About Uncertainty?

Using optimization algorithms to look ahead depends upon discrete actions and certainty about what will happen when you take an action. Many problems that you work on will have to deal with uncertainty and continuous actions. Almost every logistics and manufacturing problem that I've designed a brain for displays seasonality. Much the same way that tides ebb and flow and the moon waxes and wanes in the sky, seasonal variations follow a periodic pattern. Here's some examples of seasonal patterns of uncertainty:

- Traffic
- Seasonal demand
- Weather patterns
- Wear and replacement cycle for parts

The good news is that this uncertainty is not random. Uncertainty blurs scenarios according to predefined patterns, much the same way that fuzzy boundaries blur the edges of the shapes in Figure 1-14.

---

4 W. G. Chase and H. A. Simon, "Perception in Chess," *Cognitive Psychology* 4, no. 1 (1973): 55-81. *https:// dx.doi.org/10.1016/0010-0285(73)90004-2*

Figure 1-14. Blurry circles.

Each of the shapes is like a scenario for one of the problems you solve. For traffic, there are heavy traffic scenarios (like during commute hours and after an accident) and there are scenarios with lighter traffic. But the boundaries for these scenarios are blurry. Sometimes morning commute traffic starts earlier, sometimes later. But these scenarios and the uncertainty that blurs them do obey patterns. We will need more than optimization algorithms to recognize and respond to these patterns and make decisions through the uncertainty that sits on top of these patterns.

You can spend an entire professional or academic career learning about optimization methods, but this overview should provide the context you need to design brains that incorporate optimization methods and outperform optimization methods for decision-making about specific tasks and processes. If you'd like to learn more about optimization methods, I recommend *Numerical Optimization* by Nocedal and Wright (Springer).

When Should You Use Optimization Algorithms to Make Decisions?

- When you don't have experience or mathematical formulas to tell you what to do
- When the search landscape is very large or where part of the search space is unexplored

- When there are many rules for decision-making (constraints) that need to be followed
- When the value to you of having a better answer (however slight) is significant

Limitations of Optimization

- Optimization algorithms encapsulate no understanding of the system or the skills and strategies required to optimize the system.
- Optimization algorithms require significant time and computational resources to search through options for the decisions they choose.

Expert Systems Recall Stored Expertise

Expert systems look up control actions from a database of expert rules—essentially, a complex manual. This provides compute-efficient access to effective control actions, but creating that database requires existing human expertise—after all, you have to know how to bake a cake in order to write the recipe. Expert systems leverage understanding of the system dynamics and effective strategies to control the system, but they require so many rules to capture all the nuanced exceptions that they can be cumbersome to program and manage.

Let's use an example from an HVAC system like the one that might control the temperature in an office building. The system uses a damper valve that can be opened to let in fresh air or closed to recycle air. The system can save energy by recycling air at times of day when the price of energy is high or when the air is very cold and needs to be heated up. However, recycling too much air, especially when there are many people in the building, decreases air quality as carbon dioxide builds up.

Let's say we implement an expert system with two simple rules that set the basic structure:

- Close the damper to recycle air when energy is expensive or when air is very cold (or very hot).
- Open the damper to let in fresh air when the air quality is approaching legal limits.

These rules represent the two fundamental strategies for controlling the system. See Figure 1-15 for a diagram of how the damper works.

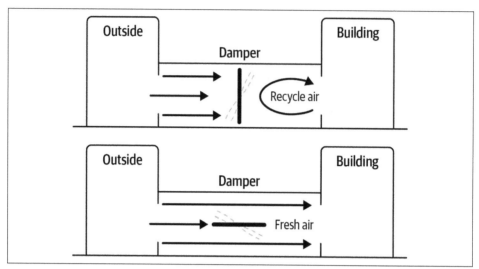

Figure 1-15. How a damper valve in a commercial HVAC system recycles and freshens air.

The first control strategy is perfect for saving money when energy is expensive and when temperatures are extreme. It works best when building occupancy is lower. The second strategy works well when energy is less expensive and building occupancy is high.

But we're not done yet. Even though the first two rules in our expert system are simple to understand and manage, we need to add many more rules to execute these strategies under all possible conditions. The real world is fuzzy, and every rule has hundreds of exceptions that would need to be codified into an expert system. For example, the first rule tells us that we should recycle air when the energy is expensive and when the air temperature is extreme (really hot or cold). How expensive should the energy be in order to justify recycling air? And how much should you close the damper valve to recycle air? Well, that depends on the carbon dioxide levels in the rooms and on the outdoor temperature. It's nuanced—and the right answer depends on the surface of the landscape defined by the relationships between energy prices, outdoor air temperatures, and number of people in the building.

```
if (temp > 90 or temp < 20) and price > 0.15: # Recycle Air
    if temp < 00 and price > 0.17:
        valve = 0.1
    elif temp < 10 and price > 0.17:
        valve = 0.2
    elif temp < 20 and price > 0.17:
        valve = 0.3
```

The code above shows some of the additional rules required to effectively implement two HVAC control strategies under many different conditions.

Expert systems are like maps of the geographic terrain: recorded exploration drawn based on previous expeditions. They hold a special place in the history of AI: in fact, they comprised most of its second wave. The term artificial intelligence was coined in 1956 at a conference of computer scientists at Dartmouth College. The first wave of AI used symbolic (human-readable) representations of problems, logic, and search to reason and make decisions. This approach is often called symbolic AI (*https://oreil.ly/abXyb*).

The second wave of AI primarily comprised expert systems. For some time, the hope was that the expert system would serve as the entire intelligent system even to the point of intelligence comparable to the human mind. Folks as famous as Marvin Minsky (*https://oreil.ly/DBtk8*), regarded as the "Godfather of AI," claimed this. From a research perspective, much of the exploration of what an expert system was and could be was considered complete. Even, so widespread disappointment in the capability of these systems was recorded.

A big reason why expert systems died is the knowledge acquisition bottleneck. This is another insight from my interview with Jonathan Schaeffer. Expert systems use knowledge gleaned from humans, but how do you get the knowledge from the humans in terms that can be easily mapped to code? Not so easy, in general! This is why early expert systems died. They were too brittle. Getting the knowledge was hard. Identifying and handling all the exceptions is harder. Chess grandmaster Kevin Spraggett says it well: "I spent the first half of my career learning the principles for playing strong chess and the second half learning when to violate them."

A long AI "winter" descended amid disappointment that the expert system was not sufficient to replicate the intelligence of the human mind (the field of AI research calls the hypothetical ability of an AI to understand and learn intellectually, as a human could, *artificial general intelligence*, or AGI). Perception was missing, for example. Expert systems can't perceive complex relationships and patterns in the world the way we see (identify objects based on patterns of shapes and colors), hear (detect and communicate based on patterns of sounds), and predict (forecast outcomes and probabilities based on correlations between variables). We also need a mechanism to handle the fuzzy exceptions that trip up expert systems. So expert systems silently descended underground to be used in finance and engineering, where they shine at making high-value decisions to this day.

The current "summer" of AI swung the pendulum all the way in the opposite direction, as illustrated in Figure 1-16. The expert system was shunned in favor of perception, then in favor of learning algorithms that make sequential decisions.

We now have an opportunity to combine the best of expert systems with perception and learning agents in next-generation autonomous AI! Expert systems can codify the principles that Spraggett was talking about and the learning parts of autonomous AI can identify the exceptions by trial and error.

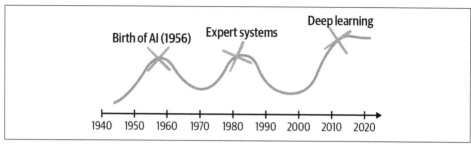

Figure 1-16. Timeline of the history of AI.

If you would like to learn more about how expert systems fit into the history of AI, I highly recommend Luke Dormehl's *Thinking Machines: The Quest for Artificial Intelligence and Where It's Taking Us Next* (TarcherPerigee), an accessible and relevant survey of the history of AI. If you would like to read details about a real expert system, I recommend this paper on DENDRAL (*https://oreil.ly/pzGpe*), widely recognized as the first "real" expert system.

Fast forward to today and we find expert systems embedded in even the most advanced autonomous AI. An expert once described to me an autonomous AI that was built to control self-driving cars. Deep in the logic that orchestrates learning AI to perceive and act while driving are expert rules that take over during safety-critical situations. The learning AI perceives and makes fuzzy, nuanced decisions, but the expert system components do what they are really good at, too: taking predictable action to keep the vehicle (and people) safe. This is exactly how we will use math, menus, and manuals when we design brains. We will assign decision-making technology to best execute each decision-making skill.

When Should You Use Expert Systems to Make Decisions?

- When you have a lot of experience exploring the space, know what to do for many different scenarios, and can express desired actions and in terms of rules and/or strategies

- When you have many constraints that must be obeyed (as with optimization algorithms)

- When you need to explain your decisions but you don't have a mathematical model that you trust enough to use its calculations to determine actions

Limitations of Expert Systems

- Expert systems are limited by knowledge from previous exploration.
- Maintaining the rules—and all the exceptions—in the knowledge base is tedious and error-prone.

Now that I've discussed each method that machines use to make automated decisions, you can see that each method has strengths and weaknesses. In some situations, one method might be a clear and obvious choice for automated decisions. In other applications, another method might perform much better. Now, we can even consider mixing methods to achieve better results, the way that MPC does. It makes better control decisions by mixing math with manuals in the form of a constraint optimization algorithm. But first, let's take a look at the capabilities of autonomous AI.

CHAPTER 2

The Quest for More Human-Like Decision-Making

When a bulldozer driver "cuts" the dirt on a construction site so that it is flat and ready for construction, an automated system lifts and lowers the bulldozer blade to keep the cut flat. The automated system, which is based on technology that the US Navy invented in 1912 (*https://en.wikipedia.org/wiki/PID_controller*), works very well for similar kinds of dirt that it was tuned to handle, but doesn't yield a flat cut when the dirt is too sandy, too wet, or too gravely for what it was programmed to handle. When the operator arrives at the construction site, they retune the controller if they find the material surface to be outside of the default range that the controller will handle well. Bulldozers have to handle all sorts of terrain, but their built-in, automated systems cannot handle a wide range of conditions without manual calibration. The autonomous AI brain learned to control multiple different bulldozer models (this is unheard of in industrial controls!), lifting and lowering the blade for a flat cut across many different types of terrain. It learned by practicing in simulation and responding to feedback. This autonomous AI can be used to take over one function from an automated system while a human retains control of other functions.

Ashe Menon, an executive from NOV, asked me to design an AI brain to improve their CNC processes (*https://oreil.ly/T5xuM*). Ashe didn't want AI to replace people; in fact, he looked out into his community and saw young people doing repetitive, low-wage work who could have been building a career in CNC manufacturing if only he had an AI brain that could help them succeed at their job. He wanted a brain that expert machinists could "download their experience" into. The expert machinists get better results when manually controlling the machines than the results that automated recommendation software can provide. Automated systems, unlike autonomous AI systems, cannot use senses like visual perception or sound to control equipment or processes. The brain that we designed uses the sounds that the spinning tools make as they cut to determine how to control the equipment, just like human machinists do. So this autonomous AI trains humans and helps them make better decisions.

Augmenting Human Intelligence

Of the first hundred brains that I designed, 65 of them were intended to help humans perform better at their jobs by recommending decisions in real-time. In each of these cases, people turned to AI to help them make high-value decisions because they were looking for answers to a changing world, a changing workforce, or pressing problems. Though many fear that AI will replace human intelligence and take people's jobs, I believe that the future of useful AI is a world where AI *augments* human intelligence, with humans using AI to help them make decisions that outperform either humans or AI alone. We see this in chess, where Crampton and Stephens demonstrated that teams of humans and AI playing chess regularly beat both top chess players and sophisticated AI (*https://oreil.ly/TzEB0*), and I believe that you will see this in the AI that you design too.

Concepts, Skills, and Strategies

You will hear these words many times in this book, so let me provide a glossary for these important terms. A *concept* is a notion or an idea that comprises a composable unit of knowledge. There are many types of concepts, but one specialized type of concept is a skill. A *skill* is a concept that is useful for performing a specific task. You can think of a skill as a unit of competence or expertise. A *strategy* is a specific form of skill. Strategies label courses of action that relate to other skills in specific ways. Figure 2-1 illustrates how concepts, skills, and strategies relate to each other. I discuss this in detail in Chapter 4.

A *concept* is an idea or a notion. Concepts are often used to define things. Think of them as nouns, like love, justice, beauty, baseball, machine, drone, etc.

Consider an orbit. Imagine a ball with a string attached. If you grab the string and swing it around in just the right way, the ball starts spinning around your hand. That's an orbit. Motions like using a yo-yo or a hula hoop are very similar. Now try to describe what an orbit is. See? It's hard to define because it's a concept.

A *skill* is a special kind of concept that is *useful for performing a specific task*. You can think of a skill as a unit of competence or expertise. I typically refer to skills as verbs like batting in baseball, playing chess, calibrating a machine, or flying a drone. Thinking about skills as verbs will be useful as you define, label, and compile skills that make up an AI brain.

Now, imagine that you're tasked with designing an AI that controls a space station or a satellite. Even though "orbit" is a somewhat abstract idea, your AI is going to need to master the concept of an orbit to some extent to be successful. And you, as

---

a machine teacher, are going to increase your chances of success if you can teach the concept of an orbit.

A *strategy* is a specific form of skill. Strategies label courses of action that relate to other skills in specific ways. Strategies are also verbs, such as bunting in baseball, the Queen's Gambit in chess, or landing a drone vertically versus landing a drone in a swooping motion. I discuss skills and strategies in detail in Chapter 4, "Building Blocks for Machine Teaching" but it's important to understand how I distinguish them as you read this chapter.

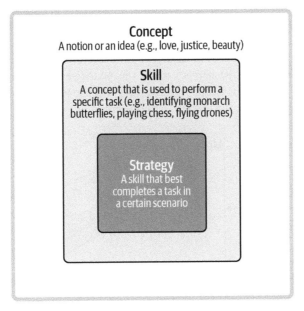

Figure 2-1. How concepts, skills, and strategies relate to each other.

How Humans Make Decisions and Acquire Skills

Each of the limitations of machine automation above could be mitigated by more human-like decision-making. How do we know this is true? When machines don't make good decisions, humans rush in to take over decision-making. I worked with a major airline to design an AI to better transfer bags between planes during layovers. If the bags are not transferred in time, they miss their next flight. Each group of bags that need to transfer from one plane to another can be placed on one of the following transports:

- A conveyor system can transport many bags at a time, slowly.

- Carts drive across tarmac to deliver the bags from the tail of one plane to the tail of another plane. This method is faster but can accommodate far fewer bags.

Each of these transport mechanisms represents a strategy (a strategy is a specialized type of skill, which we'll examine in a later chapter) that airport managers can use to transport a group of bags from one plane to another. If you don't use the right strategy at the right time, bags get missed. This decision is pretty easy when things are going as planned in the airport. The automated scheduling system uses a single expert rule and an optimization routine. If the layover is greater than 45 minutes, put the bags on the conveyor. Otherwise, put the bags on the carts and schedule cart routing.

The problem arises when things don't go as planned. When flights are cancelled due to weather, sick crewmembers, or other unexpected events, the 45-minute rule breaks down. As flights get rerouted, some bags on the carts no longer need to rush and take up valuable space needed to deliver bags for rescheduled flights. Other bags get placed on the conveyor and will miss their flight. When these irregular operations occur, humans rush in to make the nuanced decisions (that a threshold rule could never make well) about which strategy to use for each set of bags based on predictions and schedule adjustments, as represented in Figure 2-2.

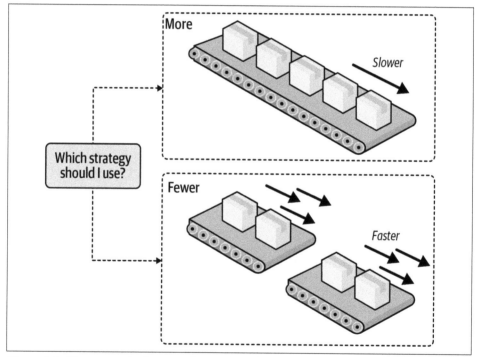

Figure 2-2. Two strategies for transferring bags during layovers.

Humans Act on What They Perceive

We don't know exactly how it works, but humans make decisions based on loops of perception and action. We perceive, then we act. Very rarely do we stop and make explicit calculations like machines when we control complex processes. For example, do you stop and calculate angles during your golf swing or explicitly search through options while driving?

Humans Build Complex Correlations into Their Intuition with Practice

Many times during brain design workshops, people have told me that humans aren't good at managing many variables. I disagree. We don't think visually in more than three dimensions and for most of us it is hard to calculate in multidimensional space, but we don't use either of these methods to make complex decisions. We use our intuition. So, while it's true that we don't calculate in many dimensions well, we do learn to manage many variables while making decisions. It just takes time (a lot of time), feedback, repetition, and exploration of the task landscape to build the correlations of these many variables into our intuition. I have a friend who knits. She tells me that it is important to select the right kind of yarn to match the kind of garment you are making. She doesn't use a lookup table to select the right type of yarn for each knitting project; she uses her intuition from previous knitting projects to make the decision.

Humans Abstract to Strategy for Complex Tasks

The AI researchers on my team had a strong hunch that the best way to train AI was through imitation—a reasonable hypothesis. There are even special algorithms that learn by imitating the actions taken by experts. Imitation is indeed powerful, but every time I interviewed experts, they told me about strategy.

At the steel mill, experts filled whiteboards with different strategies they use to coat steel evenly to the right thickness (this process is called galvanization and prevents rust). Some strategies work best when the steel is thick and narrow and the coating is thick. Other strategies work best when the steel is wide and thin and the coating is thin. Why was I hearing so often about strategies when talking to industrial experts about how they manage their processes? It's because humans use strategies to make complex decisions and to teach each other.

 A strategy is a labeled course of action that describes what to do in a specific scenario.

Here are some examples of strategies from well-known games and industrial processes that I discuss in this book. Notice how the strategies (and the goals; see Chapter 4 for more details) come in pairs. This is because most real and natural systems have a fuzzy trade-off. Table 2-1 illustrates some of these phenomena.

Table 2-1. Strategies in decision-making

Task	Strategy	When to use strategy
Controlling the damper in an HVAC system	Close the damper to recycle air.	Energy is expensive and air is very hot or cold.
Controlling the damper in an HVAC system	Open the damper to freshen air.	Building occupancy is high, air quality is bad, or energy is cheap.
Transferring bags to destination plane during layover	Put the bags on the slower, high-bandwidth conveyor.	Longer layover
Transferring bags to destination plane during layover	Deliver the bags tail to tail with carts.	Shorter layovers
Crushing rocks in a gyratory crusher	Choke the crusher by stuffing it full of rocks.	Rocks are large and hard.
Crushing rocks in a gyratory crusher	Regulate the crusher by keeping it less than ¾ full.	Rocks are small and soft.
Scoring the ball through the hoop in basketball	Shoot a layup.	Very close to the basket
Scoring the ball through the hoop in basketball	Shoot a jump shot.	Farther from the basket

So, the experts were telling me that they use strategy to communicate and teach what to do, but the AI researchers and data scientists were telling me it's better to search for options. Enter the Dreyfus model of skill acquisition (*https://oreil.ly/EUiWc*)!

Hubert and Stuart Dreyfus developed a model to describe how humans acquire skills. These expert systems and computer science pioneers developed their model of skill acquisition for the United States Air Force in 1980 to help fighter pilots improve their emergency response. There are many models that attempt to describe how humans learn, and this model has its critics (other statements and theories from Dreyfus and Dreyfus have also been criticized and refuted), but I've not seen a better model for describing how to acquire skills in a way that's useful for designing Autonomous AI.

Beginner

The first-stage learner, the beginner, learns the rules and goals of the game and begins to practice simple expert rules. The beginning chess player must first learn the goal of the game: you win when you capture (land on a square occupied by) your opponent's king. Then, the beginner learns the rules of the game: which movements each piece can make turn by turn (bishops can move any distance along diagonal unoccupied squares, rooks can move any distance along lateral unoccupied squares). Next, the beginner is usually given one or more strategies to practice. One such common strategy is a point system that assigns a point value to each captured piece (as shown in Figure 2-4). The beginner then practices many games, tallying the points accumulated with the pieces they capture. This system emphasizes a few mental shortcuts: queens are extremely important, so protect them; rooks are more important than knights and bishops. Why does this matter for designing AI? An autonomous AI learns by practicing, just like human beginners, so you can teach it by giving it rules to practice. It will explore and master nuances as it learns.

Advanced beginner

As the advanced beginner practices, they develop these rules into fuzzy skills (concepts) by identifying exceptions to these rules under a variety of different conditions. For example, there are situations in which sacrificing a bishop for a pawn or a queen for a bishop are attractive strategies. There are other situations in which well-placed pawns become much more valuable, much more than their single point value in the point system.

When I first learned how to play Texas hold 'em rules poker, I read *Doyle Brunson's Super System: A Power Course in Power Poker*, 3rd ed. (Cardoza Press), which provided the following expert rule for me to practice as a beginner: play "top 10" hands only and fold everything else. His expert system defines the top 10 hands (AA, AK, etc.) (*https://oreil.ly/88Jmp*) and advises beginning by playing those hands only. Week after week, I did just that. I played only hands from the expert list and folded every other hand. Eventually, I developed preferences for playing hands that were not in the list. For example, depending on the flop (that's the three cards in the middle of the table that all players can combine with the cards they hold to form a poker hand) and the bidding behavior of the opponents, I might gladly play a pair of eights even though it is not a "top 10" hand.

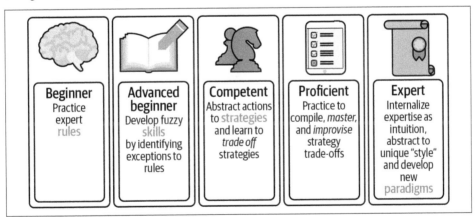

Figure 2-3. The Dreyfus model of skill acquisition adapted for designing AI brains.

As the advanced beginner identifies exceptions to the rules, at first each exception seems like a new conditional rule, which modifies the previous rules. These rules build into concepts and skills as each new exception is integrated into the principle. Over time, the learner uses exceptions to the rules in a more holistic and integrative way, and subjects the exceptions themselves to critical evaluation and further improvisation (thanks for this insight to John Bilorusky).

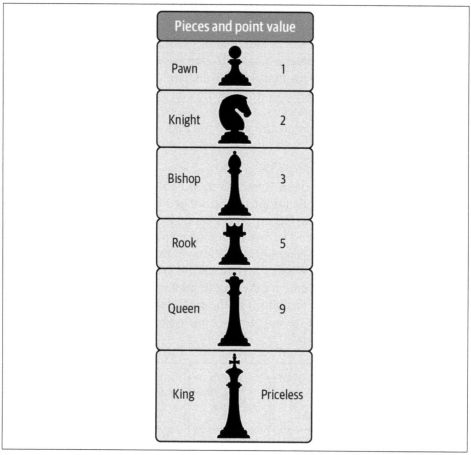

Figure 2-4. Point system for chess.

Humans learn specific skills by practicing. They are taught a rule (such as "protect the queen"), then they identify exceptions to the rule, developing a skill as the principle grows. The rule was never intended to be followed verbatim, just as a starting point for practice.

Why does this matter for designing autonomous AI? Autonomous AI identifies and learns exceptions to the rules during practice, much like humans do. Both human and AI brains inflate rules given for practice into decision-making skills and strategies that weigh both the rules and their exceptions.

Competent

As the learner moves from advanced beginner to competence, they abstract up a level from considering and calculating each move to deploying various learned strategies at various times. They learn strategies and practice when to use them. This is the stage where the chess student, after practicing the point system and gaining a feel for how pieces move and interact, begins to learn known opening sequences and strategies for midgame and mating (the final phase of the game where you capture the opposing king). The coach of a competent student gives more advice about which strategy to use for each board position than advice about which individual moves to make. During this phase coaches and teachers are also keenly aware of checkpoints that suggest transitions between strategies.

Why does this matter for designing autonomous AI? Autonomous AI can learn strategies. This means that we can teach multiple AI brains different strategies (one for each brain) and arrange those brains in a hierarchy that decides which strategy to use under which conditions. See "Autonomous AI Improvises and Strategizes" on page 44 for more details.

Proficient

The proficient learner spends a huge amount of time building their catalog of strategies and learning which conditions are good conditions to deploy each strategy. The proficient learner also begins to improvise on (and across) strategies. This phase of skill mastery is the "10,000 hours of practice" phase. Research shows that 10,000 hours of dedicated practice is required to master a skill. Most critiques of this research that I have read miss the requirement or misinterpret the definition of dedicated practice. Dedicated practice focuses on *practicing the right things in the right way*. I've experienced this myself while practicing the saxophone. Practicing the wrong things in the wrong way will not lead to proficiency. Proficiency requires a tremendous amount of effective practice time and, for humans, it requires a significant amount of determination and dedication.

Why does this matter for designing Autonomous AI? In situations for which we know myriad strategies, we can teach each of them to autonomous AI and let the brain figure out the best situations in which to use each strategy.

Expert

The expert learner has built into their intuition their strategies and preferences about when to use them. Many expert learners transcend their strategies and develop completely new paradigms of play that match their unique style. For example, the author of the 15th-century Göttingen manuscript so preferred the chess playing style that favors building edifices, closed-center positions, and knights over bishops that they developed the Queen's Gambit strategy.[1] This strategy invites opponents to play the aggressive, high-mobility style that Queen's Gambit is designed to crush. The creators of the Queen's Gambit developed a completely new chess paradigm to organize, abstract, and make sense of the large number of strategies that match their chess-playing personality. Some experts also become teachers by codifying new paradigms into building blocks of skill that beginners can practice.

There's a New Kind of AI in Town

Each of the autonomous AI applications that I cite in this book leverage an exciting new form of AI called *deep reinforcement learning* (DRL). DRL allows optimization algorithms to exhibit useful human-like decision-making in some controlled situations. In order to design highly capable brains, it is important to acknowledge the capability of DRL but also to recognize that the principles of brain design transcend any particular technology, including DRL. There are two key components to DRL: reinforcement learning algorithms and deep neural networks. It is important to understand both components separately as well as the benefits that they bring to autonomous AI.

Reinforcement learning acquires skill through practice

In reinforcement learning, an AI brain acquires the skill to perform a specific task through trial and error and by receiving feedback. The brain practices completing the task, gets feedback through a digital simulation (or from the real thing), and learns to take actions that lead to the best rewards.

Reinforcement learning (RL) algorithms approximate learning by trying actions and changing their behavior based on feedback. Reinforcement learning algorithms try actions and receive feedback in the form of a "reward": they translate the resulting actions into an index of success toward the goal for the task. These learners are like young children: infinitely curious (often well beyond their years) and persistent (to the point of being obstinate).

RL algorithms do not apply reasoning to their exploration: they learn based on significant trial and error. Sometimes it takes more trial and error than we hope, but these algorithms efficiently and thoroughly explore large spaces and succeed at tasks by learning complex behaviors that achieve rewards under a huge variety of scenarios. Consider the rivalry between Thomas Edison and Nikolai Tesla. Edison tried in ten thousand experiments to find a light bulb filament that would light up but not burn out quickly. Tesla famously commented that if Edison had reasoned about how electricity works, he wouldn't have needed ten thousand experiments!

---

1 David Shenk, *The Immortal Game: A History of Chess* (Anchor Books)

Along the way, RL algorithms often learn the fundamental dynamics of the task, which can let them succeed in scenarios for which they were not trained. For example, the brain I referenced above that Microsoft built for Siemens practiced so much (it made more than one hundred million decisions in the simulation) that it learned to successfully calibrate real-life machines, even on operations that it had never experienced in training.

For details on how RL algorithms work, I recommend *Reinforcement Learning* by Phil Winder (*https://oreil.ly/LRpg4*) (O'Reilly).

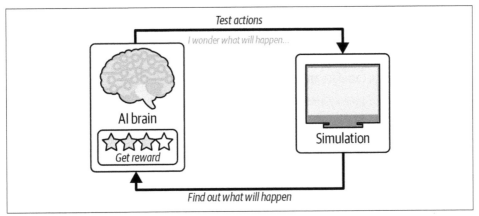

Figure 2-5. Reinforcement learning algorithms "learn" by trying actions, getting feedback, and pursuing maximal future reward.

Explore Versus Exploit

As RL algorithms explore the decision landscape (different algorithms explore in slightly different ways), they spend part of their time exploring (trying new things that they aren't sure will work) and exploiting (relying on decisions that they are confident from experience will work well). This exploration is derived from optimization algorithms (menus). In fact, RL algorithms are specialized optimization algorithms that search for options in sophisticated ways.

But finding good solutions and making quality decisions requires more than exploring. Exploring informs what will happen in different situations. You must also exploit your knowledge to make decisions. This is very much like human students who explore various (and sometimes new) ways to solve problems on homework "problem sets" but rely on tried and true methods to solve problems while taking tests.

Algorithms that explore and exploit can be powerful tools, but it is important that we not rely on algorithms to do all of the exploring for us. One of the fundamental principles of machine teaching is that learning systems explore, but just like humans, their exploration is most effective when guided by a good teacher. Good machine teachers design AI that explores unknown areas. Leveraging the exploration of these algorithms is useful for discovering new solutions and skills and for the validation and refining of existing solutions and skills.

We need to be careful not to abdicate our responsibility to understand the limitations and tendencies of each decision-making technology, even if it is a learning algorithm. That's why I've spent so much time discussing the strengths and weaknesses of math, menus, and manuals in this chapter. As digital calculators became commonplace, many of us ceded our responsibility and ability to mentally check calculations. Learning algorithms may tempt us to do the same for exploration, discovery, and decision-making itself. The best machine teachers understand the limitations of autonomous AI components and design AI that explores and learns well.

Neural networks can correlate any relationship between variables

A neural network is a system of interconnected nodes that imitate neurons in our brains. The nodes accept different weights (or values of importance) based on the effect that the weight of each node has on the output of the entire network. The network learns how to represent complex relationships between network inputs and outputs as the weights of each node evolve. When there are multiple layers of these nodes in the network, this approach is called *deep learning*. So, a neural network devises (or learns) outputs by correlating success in a task with certain conditions and assigning more weight to relevant nodes in the network.

There are two critical implications for neural networks in autonomous AI. The first is that they can approximate any function. This means that they can learn anything. This doesn't mean that it is easy to learn anything, or that a neural network is guaranteed to learn anything, but it is possible. The universal approximation theorem (*https://oreil.ly/vWZJE*) proves this. The graphs in Figure 2-6 illustrate different ways to approximate functions.

Without neural networks, you needed to choose a mathematical model that might fit the relationship between input and output best. Now, with neural networks, we can draw any line that matches the relationship, whether we have a mathematical formula that describes the relationship or not (see Figure 2-7).

The second key quality of neural networks for autonomous AI is that they can "store" learning. They do this by building a nuanced relationship between inputs and outputs. So, whether the relationship is between pictures and a classification of whether the picture is a cat or a dog, or the relationship is between what's happening in a supply chain and where to store incoming goods in the warehouse, a neural network can memorialize what's been learned about this relationship. Neural networks can also be stacked together with other neural networks, programming logic, and other algorithms.

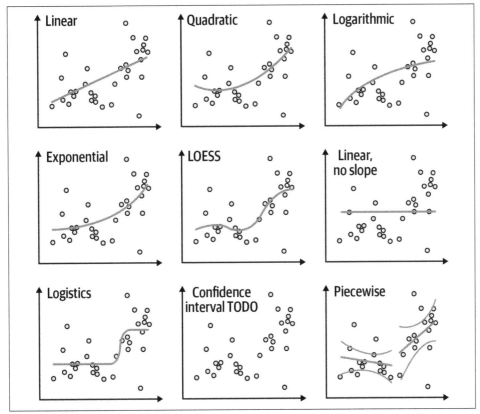

Figure 2-6. Various curve fitting methods apply different formulas to create a line that describes the relationship between input (x-axis) and output (y-axis) variables. For example, linear curve fitting uses lines in the form of $y = ax + b$ (straight lines), quadratic curve fitting uses lines in the form of $y = ax^2 + b$, etc.

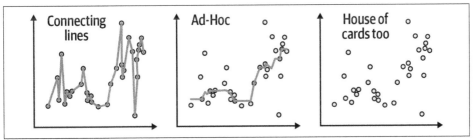

Figure 2-7. Neural networks can model any function like the pictures in this figure. Functions like these are very difficult to describe with mathematical formulas.

Autonomous AI "stores" its learning in a matrix of neural networks and automated decision-making systems which can build and respond to complex, nonlinear relationships. The universal approximation theorem assures us that brains, with practice, can theoretically learn to control any system. The reinforcement learning algorithm manipulates the neural network weights as the brain learns which action responses lead to maximum future rewards for each environment state. To learn more about neural networks, I recommend *Neural Networks and Deep Learning* by Aurélien Géron (*https://oreil.ly/mPxh7*) (O'Reilly).

When Should I Use Deep Reinforcement Learning?

- When you need more human-like sequential decision-making
- When you are no longer able to improve the system and process performance of your automated intelligence

Limitations of Deep Reinforcement Learning

- DRL can take a lot of practice to learn.
- DRL can struggle to obey many rules (constraints) as it makes decisions.
- Writing functions that describe penalties and rewards is difficult.
- DRL agents are black boxes that don't explain their actions.

The Superpowers of Autonomous AI

Arthur C. Clarke said that "Any sufficiently advanced technology is indistinguishable from magic."[2] New technology can revolutionize how we do things. When you apply it to the right problem or situation, it can seem like magic compared to previous solutions. The automobile, with its "horsepower" inside the combustion engine, must have seemed like magic compared to a horse drawn carriage.

The Gemini and early Apollo space missions used human calculators to chart out the trajectory of the spacecraft and plan how to control the rocket into orbit. The IBM computer that performed its calculations using tiny transistors thousands of times faster than the fastest humans must have seemed like magic to many.

In the same way, the things that modern AI can do seem like magic compared to earlier methods machines have used to make decisions, like when engineers at Siemens successfully taught an AI to auto calibrate CNC machines 30 times faster and more precisely than expert operators (*https://oreil.ly/fnYUi*). Sending expert operators out to manually calibrate CNC machines is costly and time consuming, but experts and programmers could not find a way to autocalibrate machines using existing

---

2 *The Limits of the Possible* (Orion, [1962] 2000).

methods. As the spinning tools (they look like drill bits) cut the metal inside CNC machines, friction causes them to lose accuracy. After cutting a certain amount of metal, the machines need to be recalibrated. To calibrate a machine, an expert operator performs a standard cutting operation like a circle, takes measurements during the operation, then adjusts the machine to remove the error. They repeat the process many times until the machine error is less than 2 microns. The AI not only calibrated the machines 30 times faster than experts, it calibrated to superhuman accuracy and worked for many different types of machines and cutting operations.

Autonomous AI Makes More Human-Like Decisions

The key differentiating factor of autonomous AI brains is that they can flexibly and adaptably respond to what they perceive is happening, much more than automated systems can. This allows autonomous AI to make more human-like decisions and address a variety of common problems in manufacturing, logistics, and other areas.

 An AI brain is an instance of autonomous AI that has learned to perform a specific task.

This does not mean that autonomous AI brains will replace human decision-making. Sometimes autonomous AI is used to directly control equipment, like drones or robotic arms, in order to perform tasks that are difficult for humans. This was a problem for Sberbank, which needed a machine that could identify and grasp bags of coins and place them on a table for counting—a much more difficult task than you might expect. People at the bank were suffering repetitive stress injuries from lifting bags from the delivery carts onto the table where they counted the currency. The problem with automating this process is that bags of coins are flexible, which makes their features harder to see and which makes them much harder to grasp than rigid objects. Automated systems cannot translate visual input into real-time control without extensive custom programming. AI and robotics researchers built the bank an autonomous AI (*https://oreil.ly/y34cz*) that practiced identifying and grasping bags in simulation and learned to grasp bags autonomously. It succeeds 97% of the time in real life and it was designed using the principles in this book.

Autonomous AI Perceives, Then Acts

One unique quality that sets autonomous AI apart from automated systems is its ability to learn from "what it sees and hears" and make supervisory decisions. For example, when human operators control kilns that cook limestone as the first step in the cement-making process, they use their senses. They supervise and control the process based on how the kiln flame looks: its shape, its color, and the haziness of the air around it. When an AI can do the same, this kind of "sensory perception" moves it toward higher-level executive functioning (but only in the context of machine and process control).

While automated systems cannot make supervisory decisions based on visual and auditory perception, autonomous AI can. DRL, which uses reinforcement learning algorithms to train neural networks, is the only control system technology that can input visual, sound, and categorical perception and act on this perception to control the system.

The Difference Between Perception and Action in AI

I get a lot of questions about the difference between machine learning and AI. This distinction is nuanced, with many conflicting opinions. Instead of directly addressing the algorithmic difference between AI and machine learning, I like to reframe the discussion around two key components of autonomous AI and how they relate to machine learning and AI. Here's a simple distinction that will help you as you design autonomous AI: machine learning perceives things and AI makes decisions. Many machine learning technologies sense and perceive complex relationships, while AI technology is able to make decisions (see Figure 2-8). When you are an AI brain designer, it's far more important to understand which technologies perceive and which technologies act than it is for you to know the historical difference between ML and AI.

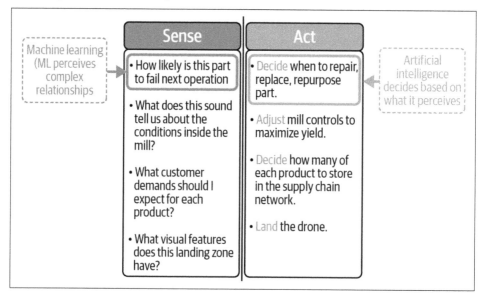

Figure 2-8. Table of examples showing the difference between machine learning perception and AI decision-making for several scenarios.

Autonomous AI Learns and Adapts When Things Change

I once met with a room full of MPC experts who quizzed me (it was perfectly friendly, I promise) about the benefits of DRL compared to MPC. After over 60 minutes of conversation, one of the researchers gave me this example that helped me explain. Have you ever borrowed your friend's car and screeched the tires (accelerated too quickly) because the accelerator on their car was touchier than yours? I drive an old Honda Pilot with a really mushy gas pedal. You have to press the pedal far down to get it to accelerate. MPC control systems (and most other control systems) have a single behavior when it comes to the variable that they control. The distance that you have to press the pedal to get additional acceleration is called a gain. Touchy gas pedals have a high gain and mushy gas pedals have a low gain. Either way, a gain-based control system will never change its behavior. It will either be touchy or mushy.

Autonomous AI can learn to change its behavior based on the circumstances. It can be a mushy gas pedal when it needs to be and a touchy gas pedal when it needs to be.

Autonomous AI Can Spot Patterns

Humans often use pattern recognition from previous experience to make decisions. Supply chain and logistics professionals have described to me many times how they make decisions about how much of each product type to make and how to deliver each product type by matching patterns. One company I consulted with makes water sports equipment like kayaks and canoes and built an AI to help them make better plans and schedules (*https://oreil.ly/DIpVM*). They produce and ship the boats to large box stores like Walmart, Target, and Costco, which sell them. Here's the challenge: each of those stores provides a forecast for how many boats of each type and color they want. But these forecasts are never completely accurate and they never will be. So, the best way to deal with this is for planners to match patterns based on past experience. The patterns are similar to the following made up examples:

- Costco tends to ask for more canoes than they actually need during the off-season.
- Target tends to underestimate the amount of blue boats they need during peak season.
- Walmart overestimates how many kayaks they need in urban areas but underestimates how many they need in rural areas.

Much like humans, AI brains can match patterns like the ones above—even complex patterns that involve many variables.

Autonomous AI Infers from Experience

One of the key motivations for developing RL algorithms was to handle situations where some system changes cannot be measured. Of course, key states need to be measured in the environment, but autonomous AI can infer and respond to some changes in the environment by building correlations with other state variables. Pepsi built an AI that does this (*https://oreil.ly/Jh9jr*). This AI (which performs as an expert operator making Cheetos snack foods) responds to the moisture level of the incoming corn and controls the manufacturing equipment differently based on the way it responds to changes in moisture, even though this moisture level is not measured.

Autonomous AI Improvises and Strategizes

DRL is the only technology of any kind that has demonstrated the ability to learn strategy. Early chess-playing machines utilized programmed strategies, but brains learn strategy as they gain experience. The AlphaChess AI program learned and regularly used the 12 most common opening move sequences in chess *on its own* without being taught.

If brains can learn chess strategies, they can also learn strategies to control high-value equipment and processes. For example, a piece of equipment called a gyratory crusher is commonly used to crush rocks as the first step in many mining processes. The goal is to crush as much rock as possible (measured in tons per hour) to the particle size that will fit through the holes in a large shaking sieve. A gyrating steel arm rotates inside the cone and crushes the rocks against the steel cone. The rocks then fall through the bottom of the funnel.

If you stuff the crusher chock-full, the resulting compression forces crush even the largest, hardest rocks, but it takes more time for the rocks to move through the crusher. If you fill the crusher two-thirds to three-quarters full, you can move more material through the crusher per hour, but the crusher doesn't generate as much compressive force. The first control strategy efficiently crushes large, hard rocks. This second control strategy is perfect for increasing throughput when the rocks are softer and smaller. An autonomous AI can learn to move between these two strategies to maximize throughput, as shown in Figure 2-9.

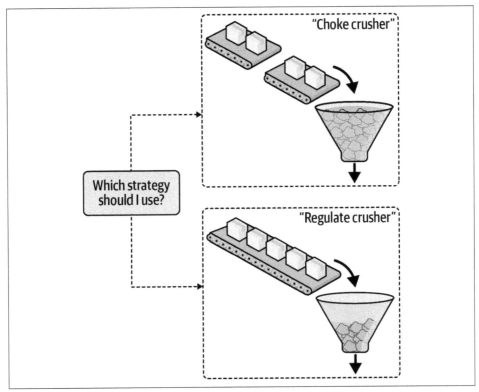

Figure 2-9. Choke the gyratory crusher when the rocks are large and hard. This ensures that they get crushed efficiently. Regulate the crusher when the rocks are softer and smaller. This maximizes the throughput of crushed rocks.

Autonomous AI Can Plan for the Long-Term Future

In some complex situations, the optimal move in the short term is shortsighted, not optimal in the long term. Let me give you an example: squirrels store up nuts and save them for later. Bears store energy as fat, not because they need it now but because they will need it later when they hibernate during the winter.

Researchers at Microsoft Project Bonsai experienced this forward thinking in an amusing way while teaching the Jaco robotic arm to grasp and stack one block on top of another. This seven-jointed robot arm was folding in on itself while performing the task, so the researcher set a reward for maximizing the distance between the block and the shoulder of the robotic arm and a stiff penalty for bringing the block closer to the base and shoulder.

After more practice, it began to wind up, bringing the block closer to its shoulder—*at great short-term penalty*—to strike or throw the block. This machine agent learned that it could achieve much greater rewards *in the long term* by winding up and throwing the block, enough to cancel out the penalty for winding up. Of course, what the researcher really intended was to reward the agent for keeping the robot wrist far from the shoulder. Once they changed the parameters of the reward to be more specific, this disincentivized the throwing behavior and prompted the robot to learn the intended behavior of extending its arm.

You might just be thinking, why not just reward the AI for the distance to incentivize this behavior from the beginning? That's a great question. Why did the brain learn to throw when it was penalized for winding up and what might it do if it was not penalized for winding up? We got lucky. Either way, if we tried this again, the AI would probably explore a lot of movements that don't include a wind up. Best to teach winding up explicitly as a skill.

So far in this chapter, we've demonstrated that the human-like decision-making capabilities of autonomous AI can outperform automated machine intelligence. The rest of this book will describe how to design autonomous AI, but let's finish off this chapter with a discussion of when to use autonomous AI.

Autonomous AI Brings Together the Best of All Decision-Making Technologies

Please do not confuse DRL with autonomous AI. Just because DRL has unique decision-making capabilities does not mean that it can do the job of autonomous AI all by itself. Every automation technology has unique decision making capabilities. PID controllers are extremely reliable, MPC controllers are fantastic at following rules while making high-quality decisions, and optimization algorithms are the best way to make a decision if you don't have prior knowledge of the decision landscape.

Machine teaching combines decision-making techniques, designing the right technology to perform the right skill for the right task.

When Should You Use Autonomous AI?

You don't need to replace every control system, optimization algorithm, and expert system with an AI brain, and you don't need autonomous AI for every application. Autonomous AI is an investment. Here's when you should consider it.

When the superpowers matter most
> You now know how to compare the decision-making capabilities of brains with automated systems and humans. Now you need to decide whether or not this difference in performance matters. Almost every brain I've ever designed is for a system or process where a 1% improvement in the key performance indicators

leads to over $1 million USD in savings or increased revenue for one facility. That matters.

When humans need to take over the decision-making process
When humans have to take over, it's a surefire sign that you need more human-like decision-making.

Here are a few final tips regarding when to use autonomous AI:

- Look for high-value decisions.
- Look for decisions that require human intervention.
- Look for complex decisions that require complex perception.

Table 2-2 explores the relative value of different decision-making capabilities in a variety of situations.

Table 2-2. Comparison of decision-making capabilities for machine intelligence and humans

	Control theory (math)	Optimization (menus)	Expert systems (manuals)	DRL	Autonomous AI	Humans
Changes behavior	No	No	Limited	Yes	Yes	Yes
Fuzzy control	Limited	No	No	Yes	Yes	Yes
Nonlinear control	Limited	No	No	Yes	Yes	Yes
Advanced perception	No	No	Limited	Yes	Yes	Yes
Understands concepts	Limited	No	Yes	Limited	Yes	Yes
Explores efficiently	No	Yes	No	Yes	Yes	Yes
Predictable and deterministic	Yes	Yes	Yes	No	Limited	Yes
Can make decisions across multiple types of tasks	No	No	No	No	No	Yes

Autonomous AI Is like a Brilliant, Curious Toddler That Needs to Be Taught

The documentary film *AlphaGo* tells the story of Alphabet subsidiary DeepMind's AlphaGo AI defeating reigning champion Lee Sedol in 2016 in a five-game series of Go, long considered one of the most strategically complex games ever created (even more so than chess). AlphaGo learned and discovered a system of fuzzy rules and strategies. With this understanding, AlphaGo competed with, and defeated, human champions. As it tries and learns, the AI is infinitely curious. It never needs a nap and will never quit because of frustrated emotions.

Using Games to Demonstrate AI

Even before the term *artificial intelligence* was coined, computer scientists used games as an intelligence test for algorithms. Perhaps the game most commonly used to benchmark AI is chess, but AI has been used to play checkers, shogi (Japanese chess), most Atari games, Starcraft, Defense of the Ancients 2, and many others.

Consider just how amazing it is that an algorithm can learn to play a video game with no prior knowledge or understanding, just by looking at the screen and the scoreboard, trying actions, and receiving feedback (*https://oreil.ly/pkDyN*). Let me give you an example. When I first started experimenting with decision-making AI, I worked down the hall from Tod Frye, the computer programmer who adapted *Pac-Man* for Atari 2600. The game *Pac-Man*, originally developed and published in Japan by Namco, invites game players to control a yellow disc-shaped character tasked with consuming objects on screen by moving onto them. Players earn points by chomping pellets and fruit but can lose their life (end their turn) if they touch a ghost without first eating one of the larger, circular "power pellets" found around the edges of the screen (see Figure 2-10).

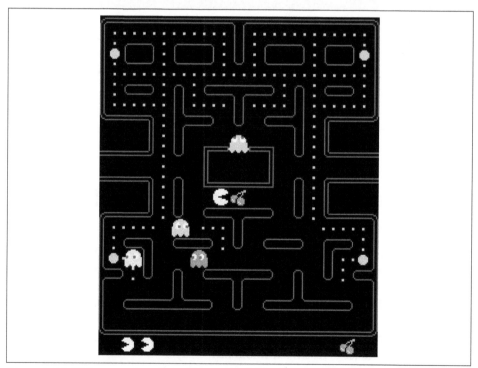

Figure 2-10. This screenshot shows the original arcade version of Pac-Man by Namco, not the Atari 2600 version (https://oreil.ly/UCi7p), which is what OpenAI used.

Imagine you are an AI learning to play this game, with no understanding of what will happen when you interact with each object. You don't know what *Pac-Man* looks like, you don't know what a ghost is, you don't know what fruit is, you don't know what a pellet is. You also don't understand basic concepts about the world that we take for granted: what a game is, or a level, a life, or death. When humans play *Pac-Man* for the first time, we instinctively understand that the yellow chompy thing is eating, but as an AI, you don't know what eating is, so you miss the reference.

You are rewarded for seeking the highest possible score over time and you learn by responding to careful observation. You observe that the score increases when you come into contact with pellets. Your score goes up even more when you come into contact with fruit. If you chomp all the pellets on a level, you go to the next level, but you don't know what a level is, so you observe this phenomenon as the ever increasing opportunity to earn more points by coming into contact with round, white objects (pellets). Then, there are ghosts. You learn from experience that if you come into contact with ghosts on three separate occasions, your opportunity to earn points in the game is permanently capped (you lose the game).

The amazing thing is that AI brains learn how to play most Atari games this way without any understanding of most of the concepts that we use to orient ourselves to a new task. They even achieved superhuman competence at most games! But there's a problem. Learning effective strategy, even for a simple game like *Pac-Man*, is a lot more challenging without the concepts that we rely on when playing games. I can easily think of three intuitive strategies for playing *Pac-Man*.

- One strategy is to avoid ghosts. To execute this strategy, you move away from ghosts to open areas of the maze that allow you the most room to move without ghosts nearby.
- The second strategy is to trap ghosts. This strategy is a variant of the "avoid ghosts" strategy. You lure or draw ghosts to the corner of the screen, then enter the tunnel which transports you to the opposite end of the screen. This gives you time to eat pellets and fruit before the ghosts catch up to you in your new location.
- The third strategy is to eat ghosts. In this strategy, you eat a power pellet, then pursue ghosts to eat them.

Now imagine how hard it is to discover and use these strategies when you don't even know what a fruit or a tunnel or a trap is!

This might be part of the reason why AI succeeded in learning some Atari games without help but struggled to learn other games that require separate skills and strategies, like *Pac-Man* and *Montezuma's Revenge*, which require the player to match multiple skills and concepts to scenarios that they perceive.

PART II

What Is Machine Teaching?

We're entering an era of teaching intelligence skills and strategies.

In the first era of computing (before the groundbreaking work of mathematician Alan Turing on computer programming and reusable algorithms), you needed a unique machine for each calculation or type of decision you wanted to make. So, you might build one automaton to write a word but need to build another automaton to ride a bicycle and yet another to play a tune on a piano. In fact, you needed separate machine rolls to play each song on a player piano.

Along comes Turing who builds a master machine that can accept separate programs that contain instructions for each task. Now, I don't need a separate machine for each task; I can simply write a new set of instructions. Turing's Enigma machine accepted programmed instructions on how to break Nazi German codes. This development ushered in the age of algorithms.

Table II-1. Eras of machine intelligence

Era of intelligence	Scope of intelligence	Examples
Machine intelligence	Build a new machine to provide intelligence for each task.	Automaton, IBM Voting Machine
Algorithm intelligence	Write a new algorithm to provide intelligence for each task.	Turing computer, player piano, software
Teaching intelligence	Teach the learner each new task.	AlphaGo, Tesla AI

Since then, almost every new software application (or example of machine intelligence) is labeled an algorithm, even now that algorithms can learn. In the algorithms paradigm, each and every brain that we design would be a "new algorithm," but in the teaching paradigm, it's just the result of one of the many, many possible learning schemes developed by the teacher. Algorithms tell you exactly how to do things, skills make you practice different ways to do things well under all sorts of conditions. Teach the AI what you already know and let it learn what you don't know yet.

 Machine teaching is the practice of guiding the exploration of learning systems based on what we already know about how to accomplish tasks.

In Chapter 3, I discuss how teaching is how AI learns best, just like teaching is how humans learn most efficiently, and in Chapter 4, I explain that skills are the building blocks that machine teachers use to construct autonomous AI. Brain designs are learning plans that use skills as landmarks to guide learners as they practice (explore) how to succeed at tasks.

- Chapter 3, "How Brains Learn Best: Teaching Humans and AI"
- Chapter 4, "Building Blocks for Machine Teaching"

How Brains Learn Best: Teaching Humans and AI

Recent research suggests that the brain builds structures on the fly in 11 dimensions (*https://oreil.ly/TH2C8*). Apparently, the brain assembles neurons into structures of various shapes and complexity as it processes information and makes decisions. There seems to be a link between learning and the design of structured intelligence. This matches my experience with brain design, and it matches what we know about teaching. There is intelligence in the design of the human brain (the arrangement of the neurons), and that design is dynamic based on the thought process. Similarly, there is intelligence in the design of AI brains, and better designs learn better. This chapter lays the groundwork for what a brain design is and how to use one to guide learning.

Learning Multiple Skills Simultaneously Is Hard for Humans and AI

I hope that you agree at this point that complex tasks often require multiple skills and strategies, and that those skills and strategies are likely dictated by the dynamics of the task itself. Chess strategies work *within* and *because of* the game's own rules. Basketball strategies work within and because of the dynamics of basketball. Here's the problem: it's proven quite difficult for humans and AI brains to practice multiple skills simultaneously.

The "Ray Interference" paper, published by Google DeepMind in 2019 (*https://oreil.ly/c4UPH*), asserts and empirically proves that AI brains that store learning in neural networks get confused and take a long time to learn multiple skills simultaneously. Games like *Pac-Man*, *Montezuma's Revenge*, chess, and Go require many different skills and strategies to succeed. If the task requires multiple strategies, the paper explains, the brain will learn each skill incompletely and sequentially, with long learning plateaus in between because it doesn't know where one skill begins and another ends.

The author's prescriptions for avoiding this confusion are to not store learning in a neural network (which is a bad idea for multiple reasons that I will explain below), use clever algorithmic learning tricks (which aren't always feasible), or *teach skills explicitly*.

Teaching Skills and Strategies Explicitly

If I can teach my AI the skills and concepts that I already know, I can help ensure that the AI succeeds. It might discover the skills and strategies that I already know, but it might not. There's no way to tell until it tries. Even if my AI does learn these skills on its own, I've wasted valuable time and money letting my AI discover things that I could have taught it. For example, DeepMind's AlphaChess AI discovered the 12 most common opening sequences in chess—some of which were innovated over a thousand years ago (see Figure 3-1). One thousand years! Why would we pay millions of dollars in computation costs for AI to learn strategies as well known as those?

The same thing happened with Go: AlphaGo learned a greedy strategy that any beginning player would be taught. Then, the AI discovered more sophisticated known strategies. Then, much like more advanced humans, it began trading off and improvising strategies in sophisticated ways.

The whole point of teaching is helping students learn faster by telling them a bit of what you already know. Imagine if I taught my young son to play basketball by bringing him to a hoop, handing him a ball, and offering him ten cents for every time he gets the basketball to go through the hoop. He'll try and try and try—and probably become discouraged and quit before he finds a way to get the ball through the hoop consistently.

In fact, this method of teaching would be cruel. Why would I ever "teach" my son how to play basketball without telling him about the jump shot and the layup (Figure 3-2)? These tested methods of launching the basketball through the net require practice, especially to get it right from various distances and speeds. But they provide a known set of skills to structure the practice without forcing players to reinvent (or rediscover) the wheel.

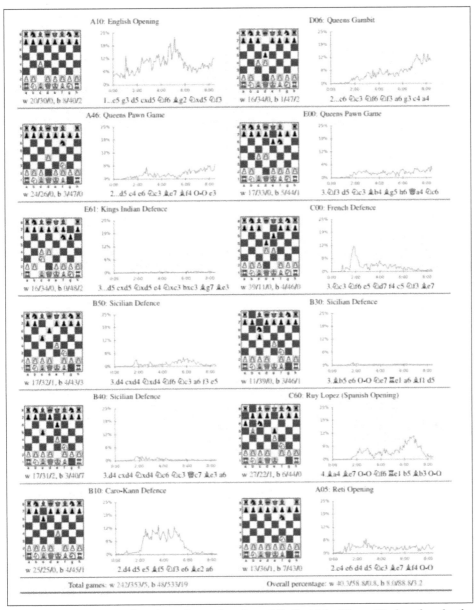

Figure 3-1. Histogram that shows how often DeepMind's AlphaChess AI played each of the twelve most common opening sequences.

Figure 3-2. The steps of a basketball layup shot and a jump shot.

To shoot a layup, the player approaches the hoop, jumps from one leg in stride and extends the ball in their hand toward the hoop. The layup shot is a good strategy when the player is close to the basket, to ensure high chances of making the shot. I would likely teach this skill step by step through demonstration, then (most importantly) instruct my son to: (1) shoot layups when close to the basket, and (2) practice layups on both sides of the hoop.

The jump shot is used to make shots from farther distances. I would likely teach this skill by breaking it down into phases (we will discuss this later) and having my son practice the phases separately. I would then instruct my son to (1) shoot the jump shot when farther from the basket, and (2) practice jump shots from various distances. See Figure 3-3 for some examples of where on the court you might use each strategy.

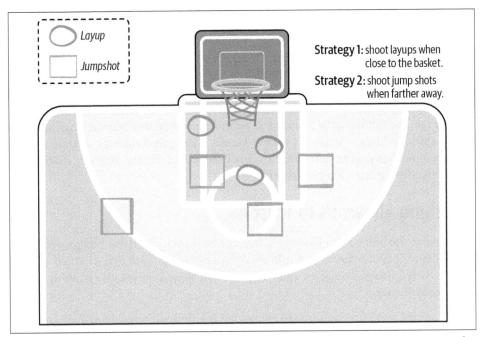

Figure 3-3. Top view of basketball court showing two prominent scoring strategies. Both strategies should be practiced from different locations.

I know what some of you are thinking: *Kence, by doing all this teaching, aren't you biasing the AI's explorative practice and preventing it from discovering something creative?* Yes, teaching does indeed bias exploration based on what the learner already knows about successfully completing the tasks; no, good teaching does not prevent learners from exploring creatively and discovering new paradigms. For example: Michael Jordan, generally considered the best basketball player of all time, innovated many widely imitated techniques. Did learning the jump shot and the layup stifle Jordan's genius? No way! In fact, learning the jump shot allowed him to explore ways to refine it for specialized situations without having to relive and rediscover its entire evolution.

Let's take another example: the composer Wolfgang Amadeus Mozart is widely considered a genius of Western music. Mozart lived and composed in the Classical period, just after the Baroque period. Did learning harmonic conventions from the Baroque period (from Bach and other composers) prevent him from innovating Western music theory? Just the opposite, actually: Mozart was able to stand on the music theory he had learned, then innovate from there.[1] On the other hand, if you

---

1 Russian psychologist Lev Vygotsky describes this phenomenon in his theory of zones of proximal development and in his work on scaffolding.

reinvent or rediscover the wheel, you have to go through the entire evolutionary process because there's no existing knowledge to build on.

The fact that AIs playing chess and Go against themselves discovered some of the same decision-making policies that humans use suggests that these strategies couldn't simply be artifacts of human thinking: *they tap into fundamental dynamics dictated by the structure of the game itself.* The same is likely true for the jump shot. As a strategy, it leverages the fundamental anatomical relationships between human fingers, hands, arms, and shoulders to make it easier to launch a basketball through a circular hoop. If human anatomy were different, that anatomy would dictate different strategies as most effective for launching basketballs.

Teaching Allows Us to Trust AI

Remember the brain from Chapter 1 that controls rock crushers? I suggested to my co-designer, a data scientist at a mining company, that a *black box* AI could practice on a virtual crusher simulation and come up with some very creative ways to operate the crusher better.

Black box AI is AI that outputs decisions that are difficult to explain, audit, or trace. The decision may be very good, but you don't know much about how the AI arrived at that decision. One drawback of neural networks is that they often produce black box AI and there is limited visibility into why the AI did what it did. I explained to him that if you want an AI that can "tell you what it's doing" in terms humans understand, you should have it practice known skills separately, then practice how to combine them. He replied, "I really, really like this decomposition approach. While I understand that a monolithic concept might come up with really novel strategies, the people and process concerns require decomposition."

Allowing a black box AI to practice without any instruction about which skills to practice would be like SCG saying to its boardmen: *Go ahead, try whatever you want and use whatever method works best.* That may work for video gamers and home bakers, but not for real decisions that have to produce a consistent product, win or lose real money, or preserve the safety of real people's lives.

Pitak and the team at SCG told me they had come across strategies that could produce fantastic results when used at the right time but could also damage equipment when used in the wrong way or in the wrong scenario. One of those strategies is called overshoot. You run the reaction at a higher temperature and pressure than normally advised. When you temporarily exceed guidance under just the right conditions, the reaction runs faster and better. If you use the overshoot strategy at the wrong times, you pointlessly stress the reactor because you don't increase the speed or quality of the reaction. This is similar to sitting with bad ergonomics. Things that are under repetitive stress eventually break. That's why these strategies are reserved for experts who are trained to use them properly.

Now, imagine a black box AI practices on a virtual chemical reactor, discovers these strategies, and begins using them. You have no way to know whether it is carrying them out as safely as an expert would. You couldn't allow that in a workplace; you'd have to take it offline for the sake of your employees' safety and your valuable equipment.

What if, instead, you design an AI (like the one in Figure 3-4) that learns Strategies 1 and 2, practices them separately, and then practices when to use each strategy? You'd have a way to validate that this AI can indeed behave like an expert operator. Every time it makes a decision, it "tells" you not just what it wants to do, but which strategy it is using to make that decision. Now you can follow its logic.

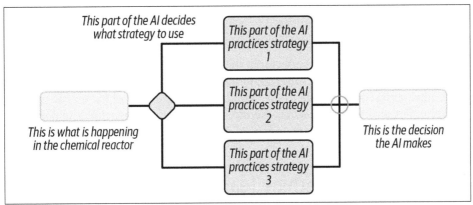

Figure 3-4. An AI that learns separate strategies for controlling a chemical reactor.

 This process of breaking tasks down into separate skills and strategies to practice, then building them back up into complete tasks by practicing how to use the skills together, *is teaching*.

One of my favorite movies of all time is *The Karate Kid* (1984). In this movie, set in Los Angeles, Mr. Miyagi, a karate master from Okinawa, Japan, teaches the karate blocking system to a teenager named Daniel using a really interesting method. On the first day, Mr. Miyagi invites Daniel to his house and shows him how to wax a car using a very specific circular arm motion. Then he instructs Daniel to wax his collection of cars. This is the exact circular motion required to perform *soto uke*, the inward middle-forearm block, but Daniel doesn't know that. The next day, Miyagi teaches Daniel a specific technique for painting fences—which happens to be the exact up-down motion required to perform *age uke*, the rising block—and then asks him to spend all day painting a fence. The third day is house painting with a side to side motion, and on the final day of his initial training Daniel sands a wooden deck with the motion required to perform the circular block *kagite uke*.

Daniel, angry that he "hasn't learned any karate" but only has "done yard work for his karate master," threatens to quit his lessons. Miyagi calls him back and demonstrates how the motions he's practiced are used together in blocking. In a very short practice sequence (*https://oreil.ly/0tQyQ*), Daniel is able to assemble the skills into a coherent blocking system.

AI researchers did something very similar when teaching an AI to grasp and stack blocks with a robotic arm (*https://oreil.ly/mvnsH*). They taught each of the skills separately: moving the arm laterally, extending the arm, orienting the end effector (hand) around the block, grasping the block, and stacking the block. After mastering each of these skills, the AI learned how to combine the skills extremely quickly (22,000 practice iterations compared to a similar Google experiment where the brain took 1 million practice iterations to learn the task).

So, it turns out that this architectural skill of designing autonomous AI is about teaching: breaking down tasks into component skills, orchestrating how they relate to each other, and sequencing them for practice. This approach, which we call machine teaching, has enabled mechanical, chemical, aerospace, and controls engineers with no previous AI experience to design AI brains that use their expertise to make high-value industrial decisions.

The Mindset of a Machine Teacher

There is a big difference between teaching and doing. It's the difference between defining a sequence of skills for someone to practice and learning how to do something and programming an algorithm to make all the decisions. It's also the difference between helping others succeed and being the star of the show. Teaching is an underrated skill, and when it comes to brain design, architecting autonomous AI is much more like teaching than programming and requires the curiosity of a learner more than the knowledge of an expert. Teaching is the difference between the ability to do something and setting up a system that will learn how to do it through structural practice.

Teacher More Than Programmer

Most of us associate the skill required for designing advanced AI with programming, but as I mentioned above, teaching is required to train even machine systems that can learn. Teaching is a skill, but there is tension even for teachers at the university level who are expected to research and rarely trained on how to teach.

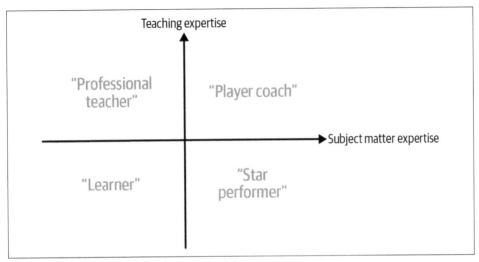

Figure 3-5. Quadrants of teaching and subject matter expertise.

The Last Dance (*https://oreil.ly/Av1sC*) is a 2020 American sports documentary mini-series that revolves around the career of Michael Jordan, with particular focus on his final season with the Chicago Bulls. The series depicts Michael Jordan as a star performer with high expectations for himself and his teammates. Over time he seemed to develop some coaching skills to bring out the best in others, but his primary persona was the star performer. Star performers don't make good brain designers. Data scientists, be careful. Some of the data scientists I've worked with have too many "star performer" characteristics in them to be good brain designers. The temptation will be to write your own algorithm that dictates exactly what the AI should do and how it should learn. A good brain designer needs to be willing to learn and able to teach (outline skills for practice and self-discovery).

The player-coach started off as a subject matter expert but gained significant interest and expertise in coaching over time. Though Michael Jordan was the star of *The Last Dance*, Phil Jackson was my favorite character. He won two championships as a player with the New York Knicks. This gives him tremendous credibility as a basketball expert. There is a whole episode of the series that shows how fascinated Jackson was with coaching and how much he studied under one of the great coaches in the game. I also consider Steve Kerr a great example of a player-coach. He is an eight-time NBA champion, having won five titles as a player: three with Michael Jordan and the Chicago Bulls, two with the San Antonio Spurs, and three with the Golden State Warriors as a head coach. Player-coaches can make the absolute best brain designers: subject matter experts who can teach and have lots of street cred with other subject matter experts.

The professional teacher might not be a subject matter expert at all. Their expertise is teaching itself. They are curious and inquisitive and ask great questions. They not only absorb information quickly but can break down what they learn into component parts and quickly organize those parts based on what they hear. This is my experience as a brain designer. So, I have to rely on my skills as a teacher and my willingness to learn.

One quick word for those of you who are in the learner category: you have limited subject matter expertise in the area for which you will design brains and you have limited expertise in teaching. Learn to teach. The rest of this book will provide a framework for interviewing subject matter experts and teaching what they know to AI.

Learner More Than Expert

My favorite aspect of brain design is the wide variety of different processes and systems I've designed AI for. I'm certainly no expert in bulldozers, extruders, drones, gyratory crushers, drilling equipment, warehouse logistics, or robots, but I love a challenge, learn fast, and ask good questions. If you take a similar approach, armed with the framework in this book, you'll design some amazing brains of your own.

What Is a Brain Design?

I love maps, especially old maps. There's something intriguing to me about the visual representation of geographic information. Maps tell us about familiar territories and which areas are yet unexplored. Systems and processes are kind of like geographic landscapes. Some of the decision landscape has been explored and recorded in maps (think process guidelines, procedures, and specifications), but some of the decision landscape is unexplored territory. Learning how to perform a task (acquiring a skill) is like exploring an area of the decision space. Teaching tells you what people already know about how to acquire that skill (navigate the decision space), and brain designs are maps of the decision space that guide exploration. Figure 3-6 provides an example of how to view learning and AI design as exploration and navigation.

Some people navigate primarily by cardinal directions (north, south, east, west) and others primarily by landmarks. Others still seek turn by turn directions for each trip they take. When I'm traveling to a place that I've been to before, I use landmarks. The landmarks provide checkpoints that let me know I'm moving in the right direction and I improvise turn by turn instructions between landmarks.

Figure 3-6. Example map.

A brain design is a mental map that guides exploration with landmarks. It provides checkpoints toward a goal on the landscape. As it learns, AI explores the spaces between landmarks.

How Decision-Making Works

Before showing you how to use brain designs, we need to discuss in more detail how humans and machines make decisions.

Exploring without a map

When humans start practicing a skill or when machines use math, menus, and manuals to make decisions, they have very limited information about the space they are searching for solutions. Imagine we're searching for the highest point of elevation on a landmass, but we don't have a map. We don't know where the boundaries of the landmass are, we don't know what the geographic features are, and we most certainly don't have step by step instructions on how to reach the highest point of elevation on the landmass.

The one thing that we do know is the elevation of the point where we stand (as shown in Figure 3-7).

> (Elevation 465 ft above sea level)

Figure 3-7. A point on a map representing the state of a system. When humans and machines make decisions, we have limited information about the space that we're searching for solutions. Just like this single point on a map, all we see when we're making decisions is the situation we're currently in.

Let's assume for a moment every step that you take travels the same distance. Each time you make a decision, you get feedback on the new elevation for where you now stand (as shown in Figure 3-8).

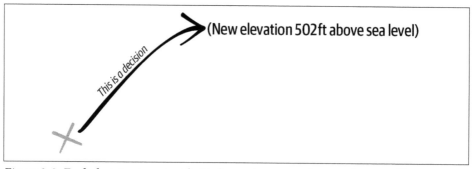

Figure 3-8. Each decision is a step that takes us to a new place on the map. This step takes us from 465 ft elevation to 502 ft elevation.

Each automated decision-making method makes the decision about which step to take slightly differently. Remember the PID gains from math, menus, and manuals? Each of those gains (the P, the I, and the D in PID, for example) are numbers, mathematical codes for how the controller should respond to feedback. So, when making the next decision (taking the next step), math consults its model of the world and calculates the next move based on its gain values. This manifests in our example as moving along directional paths, such as the dashed lines in Figure 3-9.

Optimization systems make the next decision by testing out potential next moves, measuring the altitude of each potential destination, then taking the step that leads to the highest elevation. You need to decide how many options to test before deciding. For example, should you test 4 times at 90 degree angles, 8 times at 45 degree angles (that's what's shown in Figure 3-9), or 360 times at 1 degree angles.

Expert systems prescribe either exactly what move to make or landmarks to watch out for based on previous exploration experience. Opening sequences in chess prescribe the exact first few moves to make because the landscape is very treacherous and there are many early moves that could result in quick losses. The opening sequences look like the four prescribed initial decisions marked by the curving path of arrows in Figure 3-9.

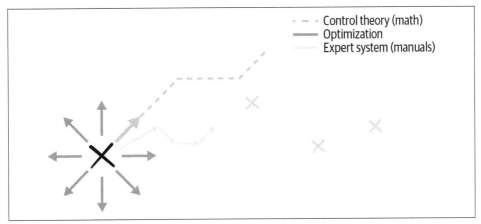

Figure 3-9. Math makes directional decisions based on (mostly) straight-line mathematical gains, optimization takes test steps and altitude measurements before making each decision, and expert systems provide prescriptive steps and landmarks based on previous exploration.

Learning systems navigate better with skills as landmarks than rote instructions

Humans use both skills and rote instructions to make decisions, but they navigate complex spaces better using skills as landmarks. That's the fun part. Learning systems don't need to be spoon-fed every decision they make. Whether humans or AI, learning systems explore well through self-discovery. The most efficient way to skill them up is to guide their exploration, not micromanage them.

So, what is a skill?

Figure 3-10 shows us two important landmass features that the explorer can't see. The high mountain peak is to the east; that's helpful to know. There's also a big mountain range between the explorer and the goal peak. A skill provides guidance for practicing, exploring, and completing a complex task.

In this case, we provide two skills. The first skill is to travel east. This is a far cry from step-by-step instructions for how to reach the goal. It provides valuable, easy to retain information about landmass features without requiring exact coordinates or limiting exploration of creative routes.

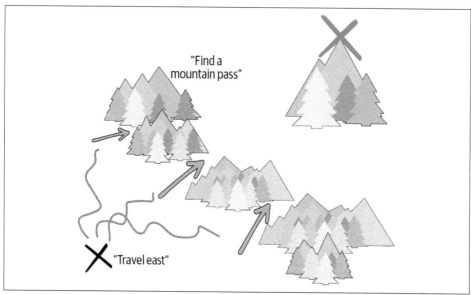

Figure 3-10. The skills "travel east" and "find a mountain pass" guide exploration of known geological features that you cannot see, like the mountain range and the peak that you will hopefully find.

The second skill is to find and travel through a mountain pass. Mountain passes are low points between mountains, so traveling through one comprises the exact opposite of the long-term goal: find the highest altitude point on the landmass. But, because of what we know about the landmass from previous exploration, it provides an invaluable clue. Without this skill, the explorer will ascend one of the lesser mountains in the central mountain range and declare success on the overall task. Optimization experts call this a *local maxima* (a peak that's high, but not the highest on the landmass) and for this landmass, that's a big mistake.

There are also three different mountain passes. The skill doesn't presume to dictate which mountain pass the explorer should navigate. We don't know enough about the terrain between the origin and the mountain range to tell exactly what route to take as we travel east, never mind which mountain pass we will think best after we explore and navigate that space.

Why can't you just give me a map?!

This whole exploration thing can be frustrating to the human explorer and the observer. Why can't I just get a map of the entire terrain, then I'll figure out the best way to get to the highest peak? Not so fast! The *only way* to get a map that detailed is to explore and record the entire landscape. Remember checkers? Computers scoured that decision-making landscape for 20 consecutive years and recorded 500 quintillion (billion billion/18 zeros) points. Checkers is incredibly simple compared to any real-life problem. That's why you can't just get a map of the space to make decisions for it.

Autonomous AI Profile: AlphaGo

AlphaGo was designed and built by DeepMind in 2016.

My favorite AI paper is *Mastering the Game of Go without Human Knowledge* (*https:// oreil.ly/q8u2b*). The paper, published in *Nature*, and the AI that it describes sparked many imaginations about what was possible with Autonomous AI. What an impressive scientific feat: building an artificial intelligence decision system that beats the best player in the world at a game with eight times more options than chess.

The claim was that the system learned all this from scratch (tabula rasa), but it wasn't just learning how to make chess or Go moves by practicing against a reward, and it wasn't really mastering the game without human knowledge. Using the framework I present in this book, it's easy to see that AlphaGo benefitted from quite a bit of machine teaching.

Though the modules are fused together deep in the learning algorithm and neural network, this autonomous AI comprises three skills:

- Recognize board positions.
- Guide lookahead with intuition about moves.
- Look ahead to test possible moves.

AlphaGo and AlphaChess use supervised learning to identify board positions. Both chess and Go have an enormous number of possible board positions. The supervised machine learning algorithms executed the skill of identifying board positions by training on data from thousands of recorded chess games. This is similar to what humans do when they study historical games to better understand the significance of various board states.

Deep reinforcement learning (DRL) doesn't learn to make the chess moves. It learns intuition about which moves are likely to be effective. Then MCTS performs lookahead reconnaissance influenced by the intuition. This is much more like the way humans look ahead to move possibilities. There are too many possibilities for MCTS to search every option in a reasonable amount of time, so the intuition narrows the search significantly.

The fact that AlphaGo and AlphaChess used separate modules to teach separate skills is no slight against this powerful AI. Rather, it's a sign of its sophistication. *Machine teaching allows us to devise, collaborate on, and test architectures like these very quickly.* With the right technology, we can quickly snap together designs as well, even if we're

---

not neural network experts, AI algorithm programmers, or professional software developers.

Skills let your learner learn

After you factor in the incomplete information on the maps of most decision spaces, the cost to scout ahead, and uncertainty, it turns out that *teaching skills is a more efficient way to help learners find good navigation paths* than giving them step-by-step instructions. Skills guide the exploration, even when most of the features of the landmass are still unknown.

Acquiring Skill Is like Learning to Navigate by Exploring

Lev Vygotsky, known for his work on the psychological development of children, posited two theories that help us better understand the function and purpose of brain designs: zones of proximal development and scaffolding.

Zones of proximal development

Vygotsky defined the zone of proximal development as "the distance between the actual developmental level as determined by independent problem solving and the level of potential development as determined through problem solving under adult guidance or in collaboration with more capable peers."[2] He is saying that there is a gap between what we can learn from self-discovery and exploration and the more advanced skills that we could acquire with the help of someone who better knows the landscape (a teacher or a capable peer). Brain designs enable autonomous AI's more advanced skill acquisition by providing maps for exploring decision landscapes.

Scaffolding

Scaffolding describes the process of teaching and learning concepts sequentially in an order that better facilitates skill acquisition. Learning to ride a bike is a good example. At first, a child rides a bike with training wheels to help the bike stay upright. Next, the child rides without training wheels and an adult may run alongside the bicycle helping the child to steer and balance. Finally, the adult steps aside after the child learns to balance well on their own.

If the mighty human mind needs teaching and scaffolding, then so too do limited algorithms that can change behavior but have limited reasoning capabilities and even more limited prebaked concepts of the world to rely on when learning specific tasks. No modern human can say they've gained all of their current skills without

---

2 Vygotsky, L.S. *Mind in Society: The Development of Higher Psychological Processes* (Harvard University Press, 1978).

the benefit of teaching (that is, through self-guided practice alone). That's why brain designs are so important.

A Brain Design Is a Mental Map That Guides Exploration with Landmarks

Decisions (actions you take) are like routes across geographic terrain. You must explore the terrain to understand the geography, as in the video game *The Legend of Zelda: Breath of the Wild* (*https://oreil.ly/cRrto*). Some areas are easier to explore than others. Take for example, the landmass in Figure 3-11. This terrain is safe and easy to explore any way you want. If you are looking for the location marked with an X, you can approach it from many directions using many routes.

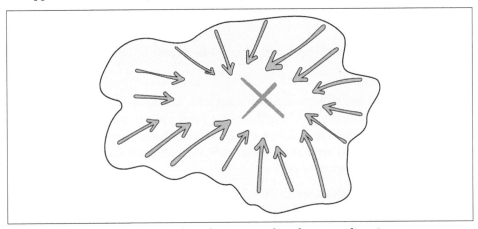

Figure 3-11. Landmass that is safe and easy to explore from any direction.

Take Figure 3-12 as a counterexample. This landmass dictates very specific exploration in order to arrive at the point marked X from any of the arrows. The arrows represent the current state of any system or process, and the X marks the state you want the system to be in after you make a series of sequential decisions. The route represents the sequential decisions that will take you from origin to destination. There are many ways to explore this landmass that would never lead to the destination (many invalid routes assuming that you can only travel over land). A useful guide for exploration would communicate two critical exploratory steps in sequence:

1. Explore different ways to get to the confluence where the land masses meet.

2. Explore different ways to get to the point marked by an X.

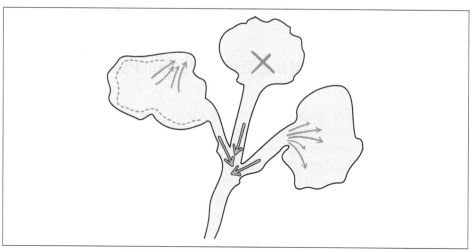

Figure 3-12. Landmass with peculiar geography that dictates how effective exploration proceeds.

Note that these are not step-by-step instructions for how to reach the target. They are skills, strategies to practice reaching the target from various starting points. So, this brain design, at a high level, looks a lot like the brain designs we discussed earlier in the book for baking and for making plastic at SCG. Each point on the map represents an outcome for your system or process.

There's a much older Atari game called *Lunar Lander*. Many who never played it know it because it became a benchmark for autonomous AI. In this game, you control the side thrusters and the bottom thruster of a spacecraft. Your objective is to land it quickly but safely between two flags that mark the landing zone, shown in Figure 3-13.

There are many paths that you can take through the decision landscape to get from the current state of the craft to the landing state. Note that the state of the craft includes the horizontal and vertical position, angle, velocity, and angular velocity (spinning) of the craft. From the origin state in Figure 3-14, a pilot could take path 1 through the state space by tilting first, moving horizontally, then landing; or path 2, which swoops down to land in one motion.

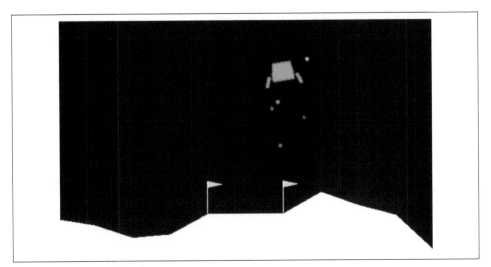

Figure 3-13. Lunar Lander game.

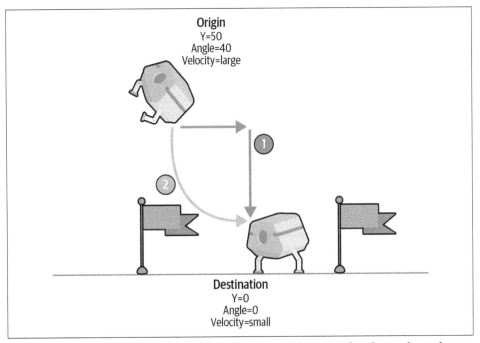

Figure 3-14. Two routes the craft can take from its starting state (height, angle, and velocity) to landing state: tilt and move horizontally, then descend vertically, or swing into landing state in a single swooping motion.

Figure 3-15 shows two brain designs that allow an AI or even a human pilot to practice landing from different starting states using the routes prescribed in the brain design.

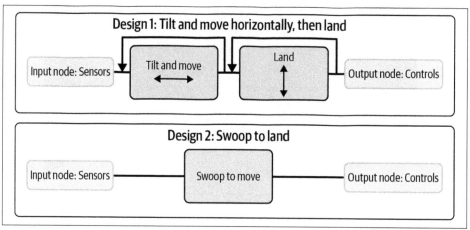

Figure 3-15. Two brain designs that guide exploration for different strategies of landing a spacecraft.

So it turns out that maps are a great analogy for decision-making. Remember, the whole idea is not that we learn to make better decisions ourselves (though that might be a nice side benefit). The goal of this book is to teach you how to design an AI system that can make good decisions for completing specific tasks. The design of this brain is best compared to a mental map with landmarks. For algorithms that learn (change behavior and adapt to feedback), this mental map guides the algorithm's exploration and self-discovery of the decision-making landscape. Even for systems that calculate decisions (math), systems that search, but don't change their behavior (menus) or expert systems (manuals), this brain design provides a helpful palette for you as a brain designer to organize and combine techniques. In the next chapter, I will define the building blocks for brains and provide a framework for organizing these building blocks into brains.

CHAPTER 4

Building Blocks for Machine Teaching

My eight-year-old son, Christien, loves to play with LEGO blocks. He can play for hours building cars, jets, and landscapes. I enjoy building things together with him. Sometimes, when we are building, we need just the right piece to complete a section. So, we search through large bins, trolling for just the right piece for the job. When we find a block that performs the right function, the whole structure comes together nicely.

The same is true for AI brains. Autonomous decision-making that works in real life doesn't magically emerge from a monolithic algorithm: it is built from building blocks of machine learning, AI, optimization, control theory, and expert systems.

Here's an example. A group of researchers at UC Berkeley, under Pieter Abbeel, taught a robot how to walk. This robot, Cassie, looks a little like a bird with no torso (just legs). The AI brain that they built to control the robot (*https://oreil.ly/FUbCC/*) snaps together decision-making modules of multiple different types and orchestrates them in a way that makes sense with what we know about how walking works. It combines math (control theory), manuals (expert systems), and machine-learning AI modules to enable faster learning of more competent walking than any of those decision-making techniques could on their own.

You can see from Figure 4-1 that this brain uses different modules to perform different functions. It uses PD controllers to control the joints. As you learned in Chapter 2, PD controllers are quite good at controlling for a single variable like joint position based on feedback. The gait library contains stored expertise about successful walking patterns (I'll discuss exactly what a gait is in a minute). This module is an expert system (remember manuals from Chapter 2) that allows lookup of codified and stored expertise. The module labeled "Policy" is a DRL module that selects the right gait pattern to use and how to execute that gait pattern. You can read the details of how this brain works in the Cassie team's research paper (*https://oreil.ly/dkKZJ*).

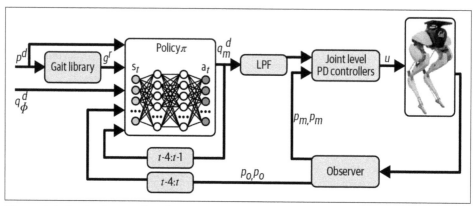

Figure 4-1. Brain design of AI that controls the Cassie walking robot.

Each of these modules works at different time scales and uses different decision-making technology, but neither of these characteristics explain why this brain has multiple modules. The reason for different brain modules is to perform the multiple skills necessary for walking. One quick and easy way to determine that you need multiple modules, though, is to look for decisions that happen at different timescales and assign them to skills. For example, PD controllers operate at a very high frequency (think 10 decisions per second) as they move the joints. But how quickly does body position change during the execution of the walking gait? Not quite as quickly. When we're walking, we change gaits when the surface or walking conditions change, even less frequently than adjusting to a new body position to execute the gait.

Table 4-1 outlines the skills that the research team explicitly taught the brain through their modular design. The first skill is about understanding what a gait is. A gait is a repeating cycle of phases in a complex walking movement. Simple robots have simpler gaits, but bipeds with ankles and toes (such as humans) use approximately eight gait phases when we walk. Before you get carried away thinking about whether AI has true, human-like understanding, let me explain to you what I mean. Without this gait library expert system, the AI would have no understanding of what a gait is, how a gait relates to walking, or how to use gaits to walk. But this expert system defines and stores gaits that the AI will use to walk the robot. So, in a primitive way, this brain does indeed understand gaits.

Table 4-1. Walking skills used by the AI brain controlling the Cassie robot

Walking skill	Technique used to perform skill
Understand gait	Expert system (menus)
Select and execute gait	Deep reinforcement learning
Translate gait to joint control	Low pass filter (math)
Control joints	PD control (math)

The second skill is to select which gait to use at any particular time and to make sure that the pose of the robot obeys the gait. A robot pose is much like a human pose: the shape of the robot frame when its joints are set to specific positions. This is a job for DRL! You can think of each gait phase (Figure 4-2) as a strategy to be used at just the right time to complete the task successfully. DRL is great for learning strategy and adapting behavior to changing conditions.

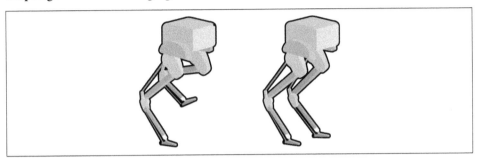

Figure 4-2. Examples of robot poses related to walking.

Next, we need to translate the poses to low-level control of the joints. This third skill is not a decision-making skill. It doesn't take any action on the system. It's a translator between the pose and the joint position command to give to the PD controller. The technology that is a perfect fit for performing this skill is a *low pass filter* (*https://oreil.ly/LSTDV*). Often used in audio applications, low pass filters are great at blurring or smoothing signals so that the joints move smoothly between poses instead of jerking around. After using low pass filters to articulate the joints, we can finally use our tried and true PD controllers to apply feedback and make sure that the joints execute the motions of successful walking. The brain design captures the fundamental skills required for walking and allows the learning algorithm to acquire walking behavior in a structured way with practice. Figure 4-3 shows what the brain design looks like translated into our visual language for brains.

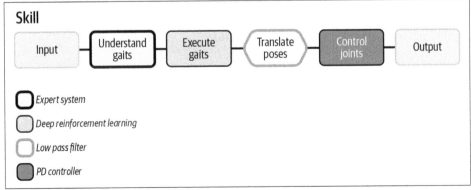

Figure 4-3. Brain design diagram of the Cassie robot brain from Abbeel's team.

Case Study: Learning to Walk Is Hard to Evolve, Easier to Teach

Walking on two legs is a complex movement that is difficult to describe and execute. Roboticists have done a lot of work to reverse-engineer walking and teach robots to walk. Most of this work uses complex mathematics to calculate control actions, then apply them to each robot joint. A second approach leverages AI algorithms to learn control policies or to search for the right way to control each joint for walking (this includes optimization algorithms like evolutionary algorithms and DRL). Neither of these approaches allow a human to teach even the most well-understood knowledge about walking.

See the funny looking purple robot in Figure 4-4? This is a training gym for teaching AI how to walk on two legs (*https://oreil.ly/Yyg4L*). This environment simulates a two-legged robot with four joints: two upper joints that work like human hips and two lower joints that work like human knees. This robot has no ankles or feet.

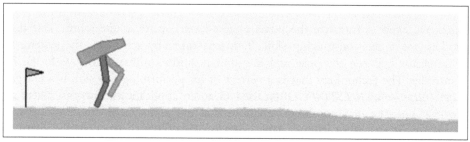

Figure 4-4. Simple, simulated two-legged walking robot for AI to practice controlling.

Remember, in DRL, the agent practices the task and receives a reward based on how well it performs the task. The basic reward that comes with this gym environment gives points for how much forward progress you make but penalizes 100 points if you fall over (your purple hull touches the ground). One AI researcher (*https://oreil.ly/E8JRX*) uses the picture in Figure 4-5 to describe four movement strategies that agents will learn on their own with this reward.

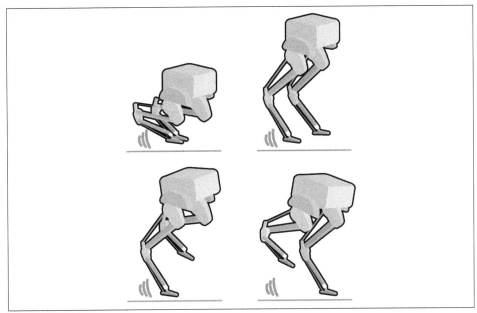

Figure 4-5. Four self-learned movement strategies that do not qualify as walking.

The double balance looks like someone rapidly tapping the ground on their tiptoes. While kneel balancing, the AI kneels on one knee, then uses the front leg to reach out and drag the body forward in a pawing motion. The rear balance strategy puts the weight of the body on the back leg and moves forward by pawing the front leg. This is similar to the kneel balance, but in a standing position. At first glance, this looks a little like walking but the legs never cross in the characteristic scissor motion. Finally, the front balance extends and stiffens the back leg and paws forward with the front leg. Again, the legs never switch.

So, Why Do We Walk?

Walking is defined by an *inverted pendulum* gait in which the body vaults over the stiff limb or limbs with each step and where at least one leg remains in contact with the ground at all times. Basically, this means that when you walk, you vault (like a pole vaulter (*https://oreil.ly/MRxxp*)) over your planted leg, lift the opposite leg, then repeat the process. So that's a bit of how we walk, but here's why: walking is the most energy-efficient way for bipeds (animals with two legs) to move around. It's not the fastest way to move around or the easiest way to move around, but walking uses the least amount of energy for each distance that you travel.

So am I telling you that none of the motion strategies above even meet the criteria of walking? Exactly, none of these strategies for moving around on two legs meet the definition of walking. So, while these agents have learned to move by experience alone, they have not learned to walk. If brains can learn by practicing and pursuing reward, why don't these agents learn to walk? It turns out that DRL becomes conservative when you penalize it harshly, much like human learners do. The AI receives severe punishment when it falls over but a much smaller reward to incentivize it to take its first steps. In contrast, the AI has to get a lot of things right to get the full reward of walking, so it settles for things that are more certain ways to get rewards without punishment. These things (which are more like crawling) let the brain get the reward of moving forward with a lot less risk of falling and without having to learn to balance.

The AI training gym comes with a PID controller that is tuned to perform the walking motion. The controller walks successfully, but will only succeed at certain walking speeds. Mathematical calculation provides a very precise definition of which action to take under each condition but results in a jerky mechanical walking motion. When I saw the PID control example, it gave me an idea. The PID controller separates the motion into three walking gait phases. After seeing this, I used my first two fingers (index and middle fingers) as "walking legs" to identify and name the three walking skills that I wanted to teach. My goal was to go beyond the motion strategies that emerged from trial and error only and the rigid walking motions of the PID controller: I wanted to teach the AI how to walk.

Table 4-2 shows how each heuristic strategy specifies effective joint motions that comprise the walking gait.

Table 4-2. Simple walking gait phases that we can teach as strategies

Gait phase	Heuristic strategy (hips)	Heuristic strategy (knees)
Lift swinging leg	Flex swinging hip (curl swinging leg), extend planted hip	Flex swinging knee, extend planted knee (keep planted leg straight)
Plant swinging leg	Extend swinging hip, flex planted hip/flex	Extend swinging knee (curl, then straighten swinging leg)

Strategy Versus Evolution

The AI research conference NeurIPS (Neural Information Processing Systems), formerly NIPS, hosted a reinforcement learning competition in 2017 and 2018 where the challenge was to train AI to control a human skeleton and 18 lower-body muscles to make it run and walk. A couple freeze-frames of the winning AI are pictured in Figure 4-6.

Figure 4-6. The winning entrant of the NIPS '17 competition actually runs!

I designed and trained AI for this competition. It was extremely frustrating to watch my AI brain do things like the movements shown in Figure 4-7, none of which are used in walking, when (being a bipedal walker myself), I already had quite a bit of knowledge about walking that I wanted to teach.

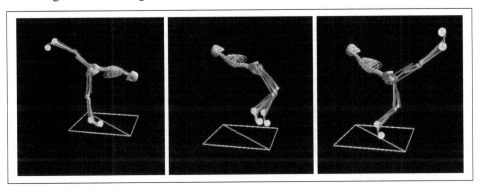

Figure 4-7. My skeleton performing three motions that are not used to walk: leaning forward and extending one leg backward (this is yoga, not walking), jumping up and falling backward, and kicking one leg out (this looks more like bad can-can dancing than walking)

My brains performed horribly at the competition tasks, but what I learned helped me develop the brain design techniques in this book and solve a lot of real-world problems. Table 4-3 shows some other behaviors that my AI brain spent a lot of time exploring, and the corresponding things that I desperately wanted to teach it instead.

Table 4-3. Behaviors that my AI spent a lot of time exploring that will never lead to walking

Don't do this	Reason	Do this instead
Hop	When walking and running, both legs do not operate in unison.	Move legs in a scissor-like motion.
Fall forward	Walking involves vaulting over a planted leg.	Swing one leg forward, then plant it.
Stand on one leg, while swinging the other leg around	Walking requires planting your swinging leg, so that you can vault over it and move forward.	Swing one leg forward, then plant it.

Even the 2017 competition winner, NNAISENSE (*https://oreil.ly/sIqFo*), feels my pain. Here's the warning they share on the website with the code they used to create the AI (*https://oreil.ly/yhA2A*):

> [Reproducing] the results using this code is hard due to several reasons. First, the learning process (mostly in Stage I: Global Policy Optimization) was manually supported — multiple runs were executed and visually inspected to select the most promising one for the subsequent stages. Second, the original random seeds were lost. Third, the whole learning process required significant computational resources (at least a couple of weeks of a 128-CPUs machine). You have been warned.

Translation: we had to capture the brain doing things correctly like lightning in a bottle and stitch behaviors together, and even then it took extreme amounts of practice and computing power.

This is not surprising, since it took humans approximately 2 million years to learn to walk fully upright through evolution (*https://oreil.ly/P0fon*). In "The Origin of Strategy" (*https://oreil.ly/5leWY*), a groundbreaking article on business strategy, Harvard Business School professor Bruce D. Henderson asserts that strategy creates intelligent, creative, and planned interruption of incremental evolution. In biology, competition drives natural selection to differentiate, but incrementally and at a very slow pace. This is how the poison dart frog developed bright-colored, toxic skin to deter predators, and how the Roraima bush toad developed the behavior of curling up and jumping off mountain cliffs, which makes it look like a rock rolling downhill.

Strategy disrupts and diverts evolution and its long periods of drift toward equilibrium. Much like the scientific revolutions that we discussed in Chapter 1, strategy punctuates these periods. Stephen Jay Gould and Niles Eldredge describe a very similar phenomenon in their 1977 journal article "Punctuated Equilibria" (*https://oreil.ly/eqcyP*).[1] We see this in business all the time. The Blockbuster movie rental chain dominated the home entertainment market by allowing you to browse titles in-store and borrow your selection for a few dollars. Then, Netflix offered to send the

---

[1] Gould, Stephen Jay, and Niles Eldredge. "Punctuated Equilibria: The Tempo and Mode of Evolution Reconsidered." *Paleobiology* 3, no. 2 (1977): 115–51. *http://www.jstor.org/stable/2400177.*

movie directly to your home and later enabled you to stream it directly to your TV. You don't have to leave your home, but you don't get access to all the most recent releases either. Then, Redbox offered a new and interesting twist to location-based movie rentals when they created vending machines where you can self-serve and rent the titles you want. Walking gaits are strategies that humans discovered over millions of years. We can shortcut learning to walk by introducing these strategies to the agent. In the next section, I'll show you how I used strategies to bootstrap learning for my AI brain.

Without strategy, it's going to take evolutionary timescales or extreme luck to learn to walk.

Teaching Walking as Three Skills

So, I decided to teach my brain the same three skills that the PID controller used in the reference example: the skills that I validated by walking my fingers across a table.

Defining skills

To teach each of these three skills, I had to limit the range of motion for the hip and the knee for each skill (strategy). For example, you can't lift one leg (balancing on the other leg) unless you keep the planted leg stiff. You can't keep the planted leg stiff unless you extend the knee and flex the hip. This is where it helps to try it out by walking your fingers on a hard surface. See Table 4-4 for details on the action ranges I used.

Table 4-4. Simple walking gait phases that we can teach as strategies

Gait phase	Range of motion (hip)	Range of motion (knee)
Lift leg	Flex (close) swinging hip, flex then extend (open) planted hip	Flex (curl) swinging knee, extend (straighten) planted knee
Plant leg	Extend (open) swinging hip, flex then extend planted hip	Extend (straighten) swinging knee, extend (straighten) planted knee
Swing leg	Flex (close) swinging hip, flex then extend planted hip	Flex (curl) swinging knee, extend (straighten) planted knee

Figure 4-8 illustrates the outcome of these efforts. This is what walking looks like. The AI made a lot of mistakes and took a lot of practice, but it didn't spend any time doing things that don't resemble walking! By the way, this step of defining the actions each skill requires is crucial. I cover it in detail in Chapter 5, "Teaching Your AI Brain What to Do". You can find the complete code for teaching this brain on a GitHub fork of OpenAI Baselines (*https://oreil.ly/pWn67*).

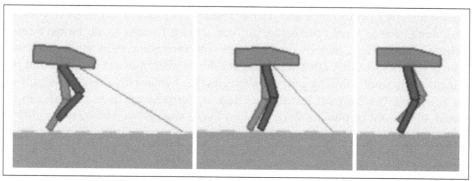

Figure 4-8. My AI brain executed the three skills I taught it: lift leg, plant leg, swing (opposite) leg.

Setting goals for each skill

Next, I set a goal and success criteria for each of the three skills. We will talk more about setting goals for your AI brain in Chapter 6. Each gait phase has distinct goals that facilitate walking.

Table 4-5. Distinct goals for each gait phase

Gait phase	Goal
Lift leg	Push off with enough *velocity* to vault over the planted leg.
Plant leg	Plant the leg with enough *impulse* (force at the moment of impact) to support the weight of the robot.
Swing leg	This is the gait phase that generates most of the *forward motion*.

You can see that each of these gait phases have radically different goals. The first gait phase is about pushing off and picking up enough speed to vault over the other leg when you plant it. In the second phase, velocity doesn't matter nearly as much. Walkers succeed in the second phase when they plant their leg with enough force to support the weight of the body. Otherwise, the walker will collapse to the ground. The final phase has yet another primary objective: forward motion. This phase is the big mover of the three gaits. During the first and second phase, the body doesn't move forward very much even when the phases are very successful. Do you see how each gait phase performs a different functional skill with different goals?

Is Reward Really Enough?

Some of the pioneers of reinforcement learning published a paper in 2021 arguing that providing a reward is all that is truly required, not just for AI to learn specific behaviors but to succeed generally at many tasks (Silver, Baveja, Precup, and Sutton, "Reward Is Enough," *Artificial Intelligence* 299 [2021], *https://doi.org/10.1016/j.artint.2021.103535*).

Let's process this assertion through the walking example that we've discussed. The overarching goal of walking is efficient forward motion. You can express that goal as `distance traveled / energy used`. That's a pretty elegant reward, but practicing toward this reward can still lead to learning at evolutionary time scales.

If we introduce the skills of the gait phases and the goals that match with each skill, now we can construct a reward that is much more likely to lead to success at the task. Now, we have a reward structure that looks something like this:

```
if lift_leg: # first gait phase
  goal = maximize_velocity
if plant_leg: # second gait phase
  goal = target_impulse # generate enough impulse to carry the body weight
if swing_leg: # third gait phase
  goal = maximize_forward motion
```

But even now, this reward structure doesn't completely describe the skills that comprise the walking task. For example, you can't just maximize forward motion. You actually need to limit your forward motion to actions that lead to a successful first gait phase after the `swing_leg` phase.

For this reason, I prefer to think about the walking task as a set of skills that each have their own goals and constraints. These skills relate to each other in specific ways, and walkers need to practice each of them to succeed at the overall task. So my conclusion is that every task indeed has goals (at very least directions that lead to success) but that, no, reward is not enough for teaching and learning complex tasks.

Organizing the skills

Next, I snapped these skills together into a brain design. The gait pattern for walking cycles the skills in a sequence: lift leg, plant leg, swing leg, lift (the opposite) leg, plant (the opposite leg), swing (the opposite) leg, etc. Figure 4-9 shows what the brain design looks like.

This brain design separates the brain into the skills that it will learn and orchestrates how the learned skills will work together. Each brain design is a miniature AI that will practice and learn how to perform that skill. Three skills execute the gait phases and one skill switches between gait phases. In the next section, I define and categorize the building blocks that you will assemble into your brain designs and provide a framework for organizing those skills together.

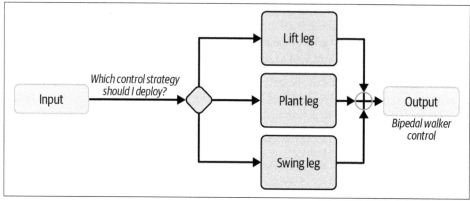

Figure 4-9. A brain design diagram that lists and orchestrates the skills needed to perform the walking task successfully.

Concepts Capture Knowledge

A concept is a notion or an idea that comprises a composable unit of knowledge. There are number of concepts that I wanted my walking AI brain to learn from practicing the skills that I taught it:

Balance
I want the brain to learn how to keep the robot from falling over.

Symmetry
I want the brain to learn that the walking gaits are roughly symmetrical movements.

Oscillation
I want the brain to learn that walking legs oscillate in periodic motion.

These concepts are hard to describe, but as humans we rely on them to walk properly. In my brain design, my teaching plan relies on teaching gait motions explicitly as skills and the AI learning the additional concepts by pursuing rewards as it practices. The AI brain will not succeed consistently unless it learns balance, symmetry, and oscillation even though I haven't explicitly taught any of these concepts.

Skills Are Specialized Concepts

Skills are concepts too, but they are specialized concepts that take action for performing tasks. Skills are units of competence for completing tasks successfully. They are the building blocks for complex tasks. If you perform the right skill at the right time, you succeed. For example, the sequence of skills in our walking AI is important. To walk successfully, you need to lift the robot's leg, then plant the robot's leg, then swing the robot's opposite leg. Otherwise, the robot will not push off with enough velocity (that's the goal of the first walking skill), not plant its leg with enough force to support its weight (that's the goal of the second walking skill), and not achieve efficient forward motion as it vaults over the planted leg (that's the goal of the third walking skill).

This is true for all complex skills, whether it's Pac-Man, Montezuma's Revenge, chess, basketball, or the many industrial examples I provide in this book. Let me give you one more example. Remember the AI brain that I designed to control HVAC systems on the Microsoft Headquarters Campus? Figure 4-10 shows some data from controlling the cooling for those seven buildings.

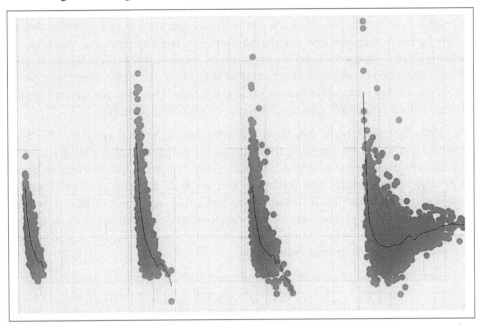

Figure 4-10. Data plot of variables for HVAC chiller system that show different control policies required for each of four temperature ranges.

Can you guess how many skills are required to control this system well?

The data is telling us that the system behaves completely differently in each of four temperature regimes. So, when the experts told us that four skills were required, they were simply reporting on how the system behaved in their experience. This exploratory data analysis told us the exact same thing.

We taught these skills explicitly by creating different modules in the brain that practiced each of these distinct temperature ranges separately. The brain learned by exploring each of these regimes and building more nuanced correlations between input variables and output actions than any single mathematical model could.

Brains Are Built from Skills

The mindset of algorithmic intelligence suggests that brains are built from algorithms. If you need a new brain for a new task, write a new algorithm. But the mindset of teaching intelligence tells us that brains are built from skills. If you need a new brain to accomplish a new task, identify and teach skills. Regardless of which learning paradigm you use to simulate learning, the brain will need to acquire skills to succeed. So how does an AI brain build and acquire skills?

Building Skills

Have you ever tried to articulate a concept that was hard to describe? Here's a few examples: love, justice, beauty. Each of these concepts are abstract and best defined by giving many examples and counterexamples (sunsets and roses and smiles can be beautiful, but a sardonic smile is not beautiful, it's disturbing). Sociologist Herbert Blumer described these kinds of concepts as sensitizing concepts.[2] Sensitizing means laying out a set of parameters that we can use to evaluate whether the concept applies. Blumer would define love, justice, and beauty as sensitizing concepts.

The skills that your brain will learn are a lot like sensitizing concepts. We learn sensitizing concepts by receiving feedback on the parameters that evaluate whether the concept applies. For example, one parameter that many use to evaluate beauty is how something makes you feel when you see it. If it makes you feel happy or sad, it might be beautiful. If it makes you feel afraid, angry, or disgusted, it likely isn't beautiful. We then discover the boundaries around these concepts by comparing many examples against the defined sensitizing parameters for the concept. The same is true for skills that your brain will learn.

For example, the skill of an effective (American) football offense is fuzzy. You must be able to score against 3-4, 4-3, player-to-player, and zone (coverage) defenses. Each of those defenses are sensitizing criteria for a team's skill at executing American football offense. The same is true for industrial processes and factory automation. One of the most challenging aspects of managing industrial processes is that there are multiple, often competing goals, and many more scenarios to succeed under. One goal in manufacturing is throughput (how much you make) but another competing goal is efficiency. I can make a lot of products but might also spend a lot of energy to do it. I can make products very efficiently (labor and energy) but might sacrifice throughput to gain that efficiency. For this manufacturing skill, throughput and efficiency are both sensitizing criteria.

---

2 Herbert Blumer, *Symbolic Interactionism: Perspective and Method* (University of California Press, 1986).

Expert Rules Inflate into Skills

The process of learning skills fits well into Blumer's prescription for learning sensitizing concepts: start with a set of examples and then add examples and counterexamples from there.

 You can think of an expert rule as the starting point for learning a skill.

A rule provides a set of examples the same way that the definition of a line provides a set of points. The form y = mx + b (the equation for a straight line) gives us a set of points for the line. So, if a = 1 and b = 0, then the set of points on the line will be (0,0), (1,1), (2,2), etc. The rule provides solid examples that are both true to the concept and easy for the beginner to understand. With practice and experience, the beginner starts to identify exceptions to the rule. These exceptions are also true to the concept and provide a much more nuanced understanding of the concept.

A rule is the starting point of a skill. A skill is developed by identifying exceptions to a rule and aggregating them into a fuller, more nuanced description of the concept. This concept is defined by parameters in two dimensions in Figure 4-11, but concepts can be defined by parameters in any number of dimensions.

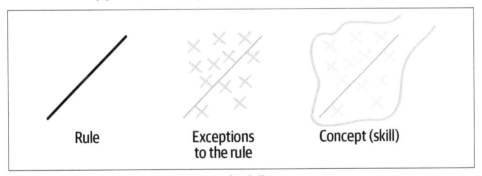

| Rule | Exceptions to the rule | Concept (skill) |

Figure 4-11. A rule as the starting point of a skill.

Table 4-6 shows a few examples of skill concepts that can be expressed as an expert rule but also fleshed out in more detail by discovering exceptions. Most of these examples have already been discussed in the book; we'll look at the naval fleet planning example momentarily.

Table 4-6. Skills, the rules that approximate them, and the rule exceptions that more fully describe them

Skill	Rule	Example exceptions
Bidding (as in Texas hold 'em poker)	Play "top 10" hands only, fold everything else.	Unless you have a lower pair and believe (usually by the bidding) that no one else has a top 10 hand.
Baggage handling (airport logistics)	Use the conveyor for bags whose connecting flight is scheduled 45 minutes out or more.	Unless predictions suggest that some flights will be canceled for weather. In that case, use the conveyor for bags whose connecting flight is likely to be canceled, even if it is scheduled to leave within 45 minutes.
Basketball scoring	If you are close to the basket, shoot a layup, not a jump shot.	Unless you are closely defended by a larger defender. In that case, shoot a jump shot (consider a fadeaway).
Rock crusher	Choke the crusher for large, hard rocks, and regulate the crusher for small, soft rocks.	Unless you have a low customer demand for ore. In that case, produce the required ore as efficiently as possible, which may include choking the crusher for smaller, softer rocks than you otherwise would.
Naval game fleet planning	Use a tank (ship with oversized armor and weapons) to attract and sink the enemy fleet.	Unless, the enemy has a large swarm of ships. In that case, use multiple medium-large ships to split the swarm, then attract and defeat each swarm section.

As humans and AI practice skills, they identify exceptions to the rule which provide a more accurate and nuanced picture of how to perform the skill, much the same way that we gain a more nuanced understanding of what love, justice, or beauty are after many experiences and of examples counterexamples.

Take a look at the data points in Figure 4-12. I don't know what concept or skill this represents, but it looks quite nuanced and complex. One way to approach this skill is to find a single straight line that seems to best represent this concept. This technique of fitting a line to a set of points is called linear regression. Figure 4-13 shows a linear regression line drawn over the points of data.

There are benefits to this simplifying approach. These simplified representations provide portable replicas of the concept that are easy to manipulate and transfer. In the context of designing autonomous AI, where the concepts are skills that the AI will learn, the simplified representations are expert rules. Humans simplify concepts to expert rules for three main reasons:

- Expert rules provide a starting point for practicing skills.
- Expert rules are easy for beginners to understand and follow.
- Expert rules are easy for teachers to communicate.

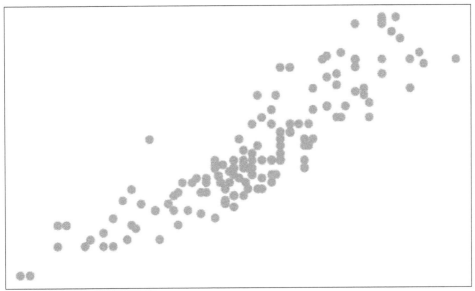

Figure 4-12. A set of examples that might represent a concept. You may be able to approximate this concept with a straight line, but the reality is much more nuanced than the straight line.

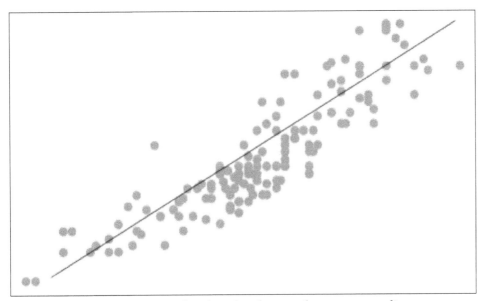

Figure 4-13. A linear regression that describes this complex concept as a line.

This idea of deflating concepts to simplified expert rules is the basis of expert systems. In the same way that vacuum sealing food makes it more portable, deflating concepts into expert rules makes them easier to teach. Promising, but I discussed the drawbacks already in Chapter 2. Is there a way to leverage the simplifying benefits of expert rules and still embrace the full nuance of the concept?

Yes! In the next section, and then in much more detail in Chapter 7, I'll show you how to use expert rules as abbreviations for the concepts that you'd like to teach. This allows you to define which skills are important for the learner to master (instead of leaving it up to the learner to discover both the skills and how to accomplish them) and allows the learner to discover unique and creative ways to perform these skills by practicing them.

Teach expert rules, and let the learner inflate the concepts through practice

A set of expert rules defines the skills in the AI brain, but instead of writing hundreds of additional expert rules to capture exceptions to describe the nuances of each skill, we allow algorithms like DRL to inflate the skill by practicing: identifying and adapting to the nuances. The structure of the skills provides some of the explainability and predictability of expert systems with the creativity and flexibility of DRL agents. Often human learners also benefit from seeing a few beginning examples of how to inflate a concept; then they can take it further on their own.

Let's return to the example of the gyratory crusher. The structure of the expert rules, which reflect the two operating modes of the machine, outlines three skills that should be taught and learned. The first skill is the strategy of choking the crusher when the mine produces larger, harder rocks. The second skill is the strategy of regulating the crusher when the mine produces smaller, softer rocks. The third skill decides when to choke the crusher and when to regulate the crusher. This act of using subject matter expertise to define these three skills is itself teaching. Then, if we train each of three separate DRL agents on one of the three skills above, the combined brain will not only tell the engineers which next action to take to control the crusher but also which skill it is using at each decision point to make that decision. Figure 4-14 shows how the skills can be expressed as expert rules (to both people and AI), then practiced to fully inflate the skills in a neural network based on sensitizing feedback.

As the AI learns (in the case of DRL, anyway), it captures the policy in a neural network. The teacher defines the skills to learn. The learning algorithm learns each skill. Machine teaching leverages what you already know about how to perform the skill to structure the AI. Machine learning builds the AI (in this case a set of neural networks).

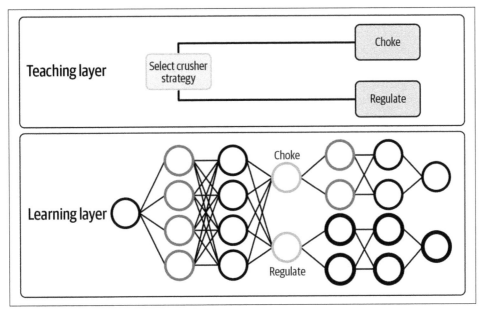

Figure 4-14. Diagram of skills to control a mining crusher.

As a brain designer, strive to express known skills in the form of expert rules. Then, allow the AI to practice, master, and trade off with other skills.

Next, I'll outline the three different types of concepts that you'll use in your brain designs. Perceptive concepts help the brain understand what is happening. Directive concepts help the brain decide what to do. Selective concepts assign perception and decision-making work to other brain modules.

Perceptive Concepts Discern or Recognize

Reacting to a changing environment starts with gathering information about what's happening in that environment. Machines gather information with mechanical sensors. For example, a thermometer is a type of sensor that measures temperature and a barometer is a type of sensor that measures atmospheric pressure. People that design factories and industrial systems don't use the same thermometers and barometers that we use at home, but they are good examples. We also have sensors on our bodies. Our eyes are complex light sensors, our ears are sophisticated audio sensors (like microphones), etc. See Ravi Teja's blog post, "What is a Sensor? Different Types of Sensors and their Applications" (*https://oreil.ly/Y5CiN*) for a more complete list and description of industrial sensors.

The sensors gather the information, but the information has to be processed and translated into a format that can be used to make decisions. For example, our eyes are more than just sensors that receive light. The rods and cones in our eyes process the light and translate it into electrical signals that our brains can use to make decisions. Our ears perform a similar function after receiving a sound. Machines need more than sensors to make decisions.

Perceptive concepts process information that come in through the sensors and send relevant information through to the decision-making parts of the brain. For example, auditory processing disorder (APD) is a neurodevelopmental disorder impacting sound perception in humans. The ears hear just fine, but difficulty interpreting sounds obscures information. There are five common perceptive skills commonly used in autonomous AI design.

See and hear

Bell Flight designs and builds helicopters and other vertical takeoff and landing (VTOL) vehicles. Have you ever seen the V-22 Osprey (*https://oreil.ly/GCSFi*)? It looks like a plane, but when it takes off, it tilts its rotors up and takes off (straight up) like a helicopter. After it is in the air, it tilts its rotors back and flies like a plane. There is an autonomous version, the V-280 Valor, that flies without a pilot. Bell also makes freight- and passenger-carrying drones.

Autonomous drones and larger rotorcraft like the V-280 use global positioning systems (GPS) to calculate position and control. But if GPS is blocked by buildings, autonomous systems must fly and land by sight, much like human pilots would. Calculating systems like the ones that fly by GPS are based on control theory (math) and cannot process visual information from video feeds and camera images.

So, Bell built an autonomous AI to land by sight. This brain has two modules: the first is a machine learning module that processes the image data and extracts features about the landing zone. Imagine a model that can input an image of the landing zone and output things like coordinates for the center of the landing zone, as well as the pitch, yaw, and roll of the drone in 3D space. This is the perceptive concept and it helps the brain see.

The second module is a DRL module that has practiced landing the drone in simulation many times, on many different landing zones using the visual information that the first module passed to it.

Predict

We make predictions to help us make decisions all the time. When I decide which checkout line to wait in at the grocery store, I look at the number of people in each line (length) and the number of items that various people have in their carts, and make a rough assessment of the speed of each checker. I don't look at every cart in every line and I have no way to measure the actual speed of each checker or the actual number of items that each customer in each line needs to check out. I'm sampling data from many variables that I have observed before, using my experience to predict which line will get me through the checkout most quickly, then acting on that perception and choosing a line.

I worked with a manufacturing company that wanted to better predict how long their cutting tools would last. Spinning tools cut metal to make all kinds of different parts that we use every day. They wear and break depending on how fast they spin, how much friction they experience, and how much you bend them in each direction. If you retire the tool too early, you've wasted money, but if the tool breaks while cutting a part, you might have to throw away the part you were working on, wasting even more money.

Figure 4-15 shows three scenarios of part wear. In scenario 1, the tool is run at low speeds but high load for the first part of its life and low speed, high load for the second part of its life. The tool experiences high friction for its entire lifetime. Even though this tool is always run at either high speed or high load, it has the longest lifetime of the three tools. The tool in scenario 2 fails soonest when it is put under very high speed and friction even though it starts its life under low speed, load, and friction. The tool in scenario 3 starts its life at very high speed, and even though it is later used at low speed, load, and friction, it fails soon after the transition. This example isn't intended to model any particular physical scenario, but I want to demonstrate two things to you: predicting wear is difficult, and scenarios determine wear patterns.

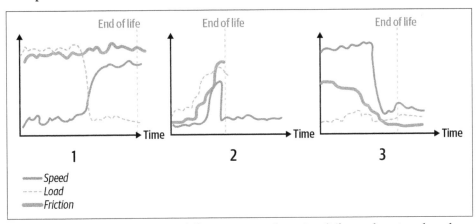

Figure 4-15. Three parts wear in different ways and survive different durations based on what they experience over their lifetime.

The two most common complex predictions I see in industry are wear predictions like the one above and predictions about how much market demand there will be for products. Market demand is complex, seasonal, and depends on different variables for different products. The demand for some products is highly seasonal, for example snowshoes and sunscreen. Crude oil contains gasoline, diesel fuel, and jet fuel, so oil refineries operate differently to make more or less of each depending on the demand. Europe consumes more diesel in the winter to heat homes and more jet fuel during the summer travel season.

There Is No Perfect Prediction

One of the common misconceptions that I encounter while designing AI is the belief that a better prediction eliminates the need for better decision-making. Prediction is powerful, but there is no perfect prediction. This means that even better, more nuanced decision-making is required, not less.

I see this happen in supply chain applications most often. Supply chain logistics networks store and move goods from the factories that make them to the people that buy them. The fundamental challenge in logistics is moving the right amount of goods to the right place based on where and how many people want to buy them. But since no prediction is perfect, each prediction has error (sometimes called bias) in it. Sometimes this bias is included in the prediction on purpose to help the receiving company better manage their supply chain.

Imagine that three major U.S. discount big box retailers (Walmart, Costco, and Target) each provide a forecast (prediction) to a manufacturer of how many of each product SKU they will need, as shown in Table 4-7.

Table 4-7. Example of how the bias in predictions makes decision-making more difficult

Prediction	Bias	Decision-making
How many coats does *Walmart* need?	*Walmart* tends to overforecast (asks for more than they need) during the peak season.	*Walmart* overforecasts during the peak season. How much should I discount this forecast to get the right production level for them?
How many coats does *Costco* need?	*Costco* tends to underforecast (asks for less than they need) during the off season, but only for raincoats (not overcoats).	How many more overcoats should I produce during the off season than this forecast from *Costco*?
How many coats does *Target* need?	*Target* tends to overforecast during the peak season, but only for overcoats (not raincoats) and underforecast during the off season for all products.	How many fewer overcoats should I produce during the peak season and more of all products should I produce during the off season than this forecast from *Target*?

Even with high-quality predictions, the supply chain demands sophisticated pattern matching and response to uncertainty to determine how much of each product to produce for each box store at a given time. Humans learn this over time with lots of practice. Autonomous AI powered by machine learning can learn how to handle prediction errors as well.

Detect

Have you ever played the childhood game "one of these things is not like the other?" In this game, you look at multiple objects (see Figure 4-16 for an example) to determine which one is different (somehow doesn't match the pattern). When you play this game, you're looking for anomalies.

Figure 4-16. Some of these objects look similar but belong in different categories.

Detecting anomalies is an important perception skill that informs decision-making. One company that I worked with wanted to use AI for cybersecurity to stop cyberattacks like the distributed denial-of-service (DDoS) attack (*https://oreil.ly/yynn0*) in 2018 that used over 1,000 different autonomous bots to disrupt the GitHub code repository site (*https://oreil.ly/EvTCA*) for over 20 minutes. In a DDoS attack, hackers purposefully generate fake traffic to a website—so much traffic, in fact, that the website can't function. The first step in countering a DDoS attack is detecting one. It's hard to tell whether a sudden spike in traffic is due to a legitimate spike in customer demand (this would be a very good thing) or the beginning of a DDoS attack (a very bad thing). My prescription was that the AI should have one module that learns to detect anomalies in web traffic and classify them as either a traffic spike or DDoS attack and another module that accepts the first module's conclusions and passes them to the decision-making module, which takes action to stop attacks but lets valuable, legitimate traffic through.

Classify

Sometimes it helps to classify things into categories before making a decision. In the grocery shopping example above, in addition to predicting, I am classifying things that

I see: slow lines, quick lines, long lines, short lines, full grocery carts, empty grocery carts, no grocery cart (just a few handheld items), and overstuffed grocery carts. You get the picture. Maintenance technicians often do the same thing after taking a machine offline for repair. They classify the machine into states, then take different actions to bring the machine online based on what state it's in. This is like what you might do when moving a bicycle from a fixed position. If the bicycle is facing downhill, don't worry about which gear you're in, just push off. If the bicycle is on flat ground, shift to a lower gear, then push off. If the bicycle is on a hill, stand up and pedal. You'll need the extra force to get started no matter what gear you are in. Before making this decision, you need to perceive the slope of the path you are headed down.

Filter

There is a fascinating part of the steel-making process called coking where you introduce carbon into molten iron in the presence of limestone. There are hundreds of variables to consider while controlling the blast furnace where this process occurs. That's difficult even for human experts who've built decades of experience into their intuition. So, instead of considering the full scope of variables at each decision point, the engineers devised an index that packs a huge amount of information into a single number. This number tells the operators most of what they need to know to control the furnace well. Yes, you lose a lot of information when you process data like this, but that's what filters are for: showing you the information that you need to see while weeding out the information that won't help you decide. This index was likely carefully constructed and tested before using it as feedback on real furnaces. You should take care in how you filter data for decisions as well.

 Data scientists, this is another area where we desperately need your help. Devising composite indices that effectively filter many variables in a way that facilitates decision-making is very challenging.

Directive Concepts Decide and Act

Directive concepts make things happen. They decide and act. Whether the decision-making is learned, programmed, or even random, these concepts make the decisions about what the system will do next. I go into a lot of detail on how to use directive concepts in your brains in Chapter 5, "Teaching Your AI Brain What to Do".

Why Separate Perception and Action?

As we learned from the 2013 DeepMind work training AI to play Atari games, autonomous AI can learn what it's looking at and simultaneously learn what actions to take to earn rewards. We also know from DeepMind's 2019 work and from human experience that learning multiple skills simultaneously is hard. This is similar to how simultaneous interpretation (*https://oreil.ly/zdhum*) is much more difficult than consecutive interpretation. The following are three reasons why we recommend learning perception and action as separate skills in separate modules:

1. Learning perception and decision-making simultaneously is hard. We're forcing the AI to learn what it's looking at and what it should do at the same time.

2. Separating perception and action provides explainability. You get visibility into what the AI perceives and separately what decision it decided to make.

3. Separating perception and action facilitates troubleshooting. A black box is hard to troubleshoot, but separate perception and decision modules make it easier to tell whether the problem lies with bad perception or bad decisions.

Selective Concepts Supervise and Assign

Every job needs a supervisor, right? Unless you're an ant, you need a supervisor to take a high-level view of the work and assign tasks and jobs to team members and crews. Each crew serves a different purpose or needs to be activated in different situations according to their specialty or training. Selective concepts are the supervisors for the brain. They are specialized directive concepts. Their role is to assign the right decisions to the right concept. Once a directive concept is called into service, it makes the decision for the brain.

Figure 4-17 shows an example of an AI that controls heating and cooling in large commercial buildings (such as an office building). The HVAC system uses ice to store energy and water to cool the air in the building. Ducts pass the air across water that cools it. The chiller uses energy to make ice during the times of day when energy is cheaper. The ice stores the energy to cool the building without using energy when energy is more expensive. To control the chiller you switch it into the right mode (make ice, melt ice, pass the water directly through without cooling, etc.).

The most difficult thing about controlling the chiller is the fact that buildings behave differently during the day and during the night. During the day, the flow of people entering and leaving the building drives cooling demand. At night when there are few people in the building, running machines require most of the cooling. These day and night scenarios are so different that you'd train a separate day crew and night crew to control the building at different times. Sometimes it's easy to determine when to send the day crew home and call in the night crew; other times it's not.

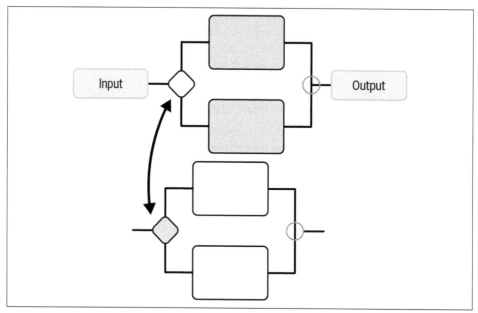

Figure 4-17. AI brain that controls chillers for building heating and cooling. One concept trains on day scenarios, another concept trains on night scenarios; a supervising selective concept assigns control to either the day or the night concept.

We can distinguish two kinds of concepts here: *programmed* and *learned*. Design programmed concepts into your brain when it's clear which concept should make the decision. Use learned concepts when it's hard to tell which concept should be called to make the decision in a brain.

Programmed concepts

The rule of thumb is that if someone can describe how to assign each crew to the right task as a set of rules, then program the selector. For the buildings with employees that mostly come exactly at 9 a.m. and leave exactly at 5 p.m., you can program the selector like we did. Here's what the selector code looks like in Python:

```python
if time >= 9 and time <= 5: # It's daytime, assign the day crew
  assign = day_concept
else: # It's nighttime, call in the night crew
  assign = night_concept
```

Programming is step-by-step teaching where you specify every decision to make along the way. If you are confident that you know and can simply express instructions for how to supervise the concepts in your brain, design with a programmed selector.

Learned concepts

But when the decision of which crew to assign to a task is fuzzy, it's better to teach an intelligent supervisor to assign the right crew. A learned selector is a reinforcement learning module that practices assigning tasks to the right concept at the right time. It experiences rewards and penalties based on whether it makes the right assignment. Learned selectors work really well when the policy for which concept to assign tasks is nuanced and depends on a lot of different factors.

So, a learned selector is perfect to supervise the brain that controls chillers for a building where employees arrive and leave at very different times. To decide whether to assign the day crew or the night crew the selector needs to consider lots of factors that affect when people arrive and leave. For example, on Tuesday and Wednesday afternoons employees tend to stay later to beat traffic. On Thursday and Friday afternoons many employees leave early to beat traffic, or even earlier on Fridays before holiday weekends.

Learning allows the brain to explore how best to supervise the concepts in a brain. If you don't know the best way to supervise concepts in a brain under all circumstances, or if you know but writing the instructions would take too much time and effort, design with learned concepts. One of my clients told me that they knew there were two strategies for operating their equipment but that they know how to use only one of the strategies well. I designed a learned selector into the brain. The learned concept figures out how to perform the second strategy, the learned selector figures out when to use the second strategy.

The distinction between programmed and learned concepts applies to directive concepts as well as well as selectors. For example, you can use math, methods, or manuals to perform action skills. If performing a skill (remember, skills are concepts that perform a specific task) is nuanced and requires identifying many exceptions to a rule under different circumstances, learn the directive concept.

Brains Are Organized by Functions and Strategies

So if the building blocks of brains are concepts that perform skills and subtasks, how do you organize these skills as you design a brain? *Sequences* and *hierarchies* are the two major paradigms for organizing skills in brains.

Let's return to the mapping analogy. Remember, a point on a map represents a good outcome in your process where you will arrive if you make good decisions. Brain designs are mental maps with landmarks that help you explore the landmass. Be careful not to confuse the mental map with the landmass (terrain) itself. Even with the mental map and landmarks, you'll need to practice reaching goal destinations from various starting points. Just because you have defined a skill that a task requires, doesn't mean that you are proficient at it. I know that shooting a jump shot is the best way to score in basketball from 18 feet out, but I'm not a great jump shooter yet. You still need to practice and your brains will need to practice the skills that you teach them, too.

Sequences or Parallel Execution for Functional Skills

Customers often tell me that for their task, you need to perform the skills in a particular sequence. They report that experience and evidence suggest (even demand) that they perform skills in a certain order. Note, I'm not talking about a sequence of steps here, but a sequence of skills. For these tasks, if you perform the skills in the right sequence, you will reach the goal. If you perform the skills in the wrong sequence, you will get hopelessly lost and never find the location on the map that represents success at the task.

Figure 4-18 gives us a perfect example. The mountain pass provides an obstacle that sequences the skills. One skill: making your way across the mountains, from various starting points on the left side of the island, must be completed first. After you make it through the mountains, the second skill of reaching the target becomes possible. This reminds me of the technology trees in the video game *Civilization*. You must develop steam power before you invent the locomotive train. This is also related to Vygotzky's concept of zones of proximal development that we discussed earlier in Chapter 3. Discovering steam power makes it more likely that you'll invent the locomotive. The skills are related.

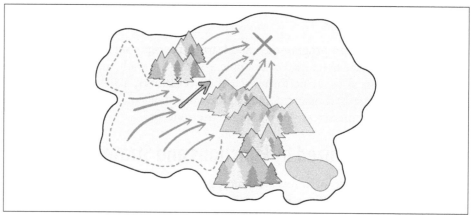

Figure 4-18. A decision landscape where two skills must be executed in sequence to reach the goal. Head through the mountain pass, then explore the flatland to reach the goal.

There's a mathematical term (*https://oreil.ly/npkzf*) for tasks with decision space landmasses that look like this: they are called funnel states. Funnel states are mathematical bottlenecks like doorways that you must go through in a problem to get to desirable goal states (like the red X marks in each of our landmass diagrams). To navigate these kinds of spaces, you need to use different skills in sequence. Each skill is a function that takes the right navigation action at the right time. Here's a real example.

Let's explore the autonomous AI that Microsoft researchers built to teach a robot to grasp and stack blocks (*https://oreil.ly/UjK3b*) from the People and Process Concerns section of Chapter 1, in more detail. The researchers designed a brain with five directive concepts to execute skills and a learned selector to supervise the concepts:

Reach
    This movement extends the hand out from the body.

Move
    This movement sweeps the arm back and forth and up and down.

Orient
    This movement put the robot hand in the right position to grasp the block.

Grasp
    This movement squeezes the fingers to grasp the block.

Stack
    This movement picks up the block and places it on top of another block.

Each skill is a function that uses specific joints to perform a subtask. This is important because limiting the actions that each skill takes as it performs its function prevents the brain from having to explore many movements that couldn't possibly accomplish the goal. For example, orienting your hand around a block (putting your hand in position to pick it up) involves rotating your wrist. Now, imagine if your arm is in the perfect position and all you needed to do was turn your wrist to put your hand in position to grab the block, but you jerk your elbow! Now your hand is in a position where you can't grasp the block, no matter how you turn your wrist.

Figure 4-19 illustrates some of these skills for our block-moving robot example. The reach skill extends the robot arm by activating the shoulder, elbow and wrist. The move skill moves the arm laterally back and forth and up and down by activating the shoulder joint only. The grasp skill closes the hand by activating the fingers only.

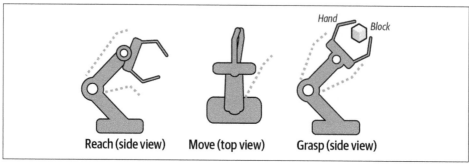

Figure 4-19. Three skills for a robot arm.

Functions separate the actions into groups that are relevant for the skill.

Table 4-8. Functional skills for controlling a robotic arm and hand to grasp and stack blocks

Skill	Actions
Reach	Elbow, shoulder, wrist
Move	Shoulder
Orient	Wrist
Grasp	Fingers
Stack	Shoulder, fingers

Try this out for yourself. Identify an object within reach that you can grasp. Reach out your arm (moving mostly your elbow, and also your shoulder and wrist as needed) but only extend your arm straight out from your body. Now use your shoulder only to laterally move your hand toward the object. You might be able to grasp the object at this point, but don't. You're so close! Now move your arm around from the elbow. See how frustrating that is! Your elbow movements just moved your hand away from the object that you were previously able to grasp. Now imagine watching your AI brain use joints that ruin the skill sequence over and over in 1,000 different ways instead of turning the wrist and grasping after the arm is in position. This is exactly what will happen to you if you allow an AI to practice a task without teaching functional skills explicitly.

Sequences live in the selector

See the sequence? For the robot arm example above, the skills must be performed in a sequence. Imagine what will happen if you try to grasp the block, then move your hand into the right position or if you try to stack the block before you've grasped it!

First, before I talk about the different types of functional skills and how to represent them, let me tell you where they live. Sequences live in selective concepts. The selective concepts that supervise the brain and assign which skill to perform next must obey all of the sequence rules that I present in this section. For each example, I include a brain design diagram that outlines the sequence that the selector must obey as it makes its assignments (as shown in Figure 4-20).

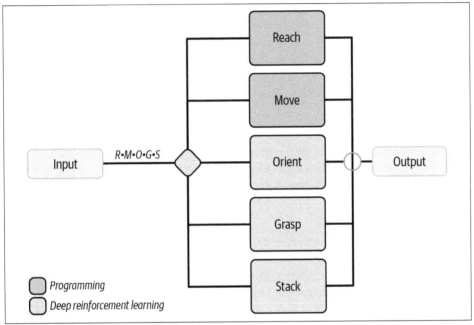

Figure 4-20. Brain design for grasp and stack robotic task with sequence definition living in the selector.

So, how do you make a selector obey a sequence as it assigns tasks? There are two ways to accomplish this. Programmed selectors can accept selection rules that enforce sequences. Alternately, you can enforce sequences in learned selectors using action masking (*https://oreil.ly/FZCG0*). Action masking is a technique that sets the probability of unwanted actions to zero in the learning algorithm. This is the technique I used to enforce the sequence of the walking gait for the bipedal walker brain.

We borrow some mathematical language symbols from a field called task algebra to describe the rules about how skills relate to each other. These symbols, collected in Table 4-9, represent the landmarks that provide clues to the sequence of skills. Each of the skills in the sequence is a function. When the function has served its purpose, move on to the next task function in the sequence.

Table 4-9. Symbols from task algebra that we will use to describe relationships between skills

Operator	Name	Example	Description
—∘	Sequencing	A —∘ B	Skill A must complete before Skill B can execute.
⊗	Exclusive choice	A ⊗ B	Both Skill A and Skill B are enabled and can be executed in any order, but not at the same time.
&	Conjunction	A & B	Both Skill A and Skill B are enabled.
X[ ]	Hierarchy	X[A, B]	Skill X assigns Skill A or Skill B to execute. The assigned task must be completed (Skill A or B) before Skill X is considered done.

Some readers will find this kind of mathematical representation refreshingly precise and others will find it intimidating. Don't worry, I'll provide plenty of examples.

The task algebra for the robotic arm example above is R —∘ M —∘ O —∘ G —∘ S. This means that the brain will always reach first, then move, then orient the robot hand around the block, then grasp the block, then stack the block.

Fixed order sequences

R —∘ M —∘ O —∘ G —∘ S is a fixed order sequence. The sequence doesn't change, regardless of the starting point or the destination on the landmass. Sometimes we know why this is true (physics or chemistry tells us), but sometimes we don't have the science to explain it—yet we know that the sequence holds true because experience over time proves it. In this case the fixed-order sequence of skills is effective but seems a bit too rigid. For example, I can easily imagine many ways that you could move the arm first, before reaching, or alternate between reaching and moving the arm to get the arm into position for orienting the hand. A more flexible brain design allows more options for how the brain sequences the reach and move tasks, for example:

R ⊗ M —∘ (O —∘ G —∘ S)

R ⊗ M means that you can perform the reach and move skill as many times as you want in any order, which is a more natural movement. Then after reach and move are complete (the hand is in position to grasp the block after the correct wrist movement), the orient, grasp, and stack skills must be executed in exactly that order, as shown in Figure 4-21.

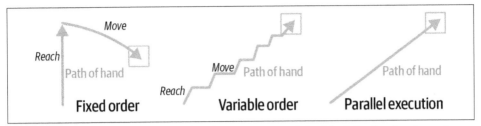

Figure 4-21. The path of the robot hand moving toward the block for fixed order task sequences, variable order task sequences, and parallel execution of the reach and move functions

Parallel execution of functional skills

Sometimes skills can be executed independently but in parallel. The most smooth and natural hand motion for reach and move likely results from parallel execution. See Figure 4-21 for an example. If you reach first, then move R ⊸ M, the motion looks very mechanical. The robot reaches the entire distance, then activates the move skill to sweep over to the block. A variable order sequence R ⊗ M alternates between reaching and moving, which looks smoother but is still a jerky motion. Activating reaching and moving simultaneously at each time step (R & M) leads to the smoothest path toward the block. The reach skill controls one set of joints and the move skill controls another set of joints, so that each action to control the arm joins the decisions from the independent reach and move skills. I think that the original definition of the reach skill (with the shoulder, elbow, and wrist) is a better brain design.

Not every set of skills can be executed successfully in parallel. We can only teach these skills in parallel (practice them separately, then combine them for parallel execution) if we slightly change the definitions of the skills. Recall how the reach skill uses the shoulder, wrist, and elbow and the move skill uses the shoulder only. To teach and execute these skills in parallel, each skill needs to use a mutually exclusive set (*https://oreil.ly/pk641*) of joints. This means that no joints are shared between skills. So, if we changed the reach skill to use the elbow and wrist only, then we can teach and execute reach and move in parallel.

You might look at the resulting paths toward the block and wonder why we should use fixed order or variable order sequences for skills that learn this grasp and stack task. Keep in mind that the research project used fixed order R ⊸ M very successfully to complete the tasks and that the motion looks quite smooth as this seven-jointed robot learns and executes the skills (*https://oreil.ly/7dFlW*). That's one of the great things about brain design: there are multiple (maybe even many) valid brain designs that provide good landmarks for autonomous AI to acquire skills that enable them to complete tasks well, just like there are many teaching strategies that can guide human students to successfully learn the jumpshot.

Variable order sequences

Just like the reach and move skill sequence for R ⊗ M, other task sequences can be completed in any order. In the Nintendo game *Breath of the Wild* that I discussed earlier, the first four puzzles can be solved in any order, but the subsequent skills must be performed in a sequence. You need a paraglider to get off the plateau (completing the first "level" of the game). The task algebra for the opening skills in *Breath of the Wild* is:

```
(Gain Spirit Orb from Ja Baij Shrine ⊗ Gain Spirit Orb from Keh Namut Shrine
⊗ Gain Spirit Orb from Oman Au Shrine ⊗ Gain Spirit Orb from Owa Daim Shrine)
⊸ Climb Tower ⊸ Fly Glider
```

Figure 4-22 shows a landmass that requires skills to be performed in variable order. Sometimes you will need to travel around the lake first, then through the mountain pass to get to the goal state; other times you will need to travel through the mountain pass first, then travel around the lake. Perform the tasks in any order that helps you succeed.

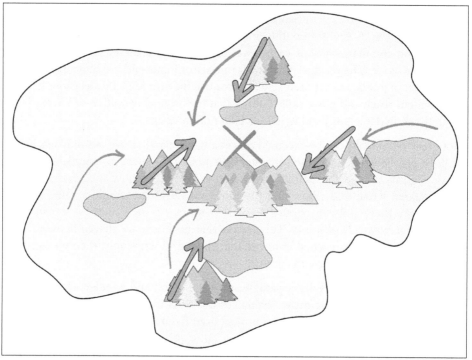

Figure 4-22. Landmass where exploration functions ("travel through the mountain pass" and "travel around the lake") should be used in variable sequences.

From any point on the outskirts of the island, you will need to navigate around lakes and through mountain passes in sequence, but the sequence will vary depending on which point you start from. The task algebra looks like this:

```
Travel through the mountain pass ⊗ Travel around the lake
```

Let me give you another real robot example, this time with variable order sequences. In this example, the brain is controlling the two-armed Baxter (*https://oreil.ly/tkgAA*) robot to lift a table. This brain was also built by researchers at Microsoft. But here's the catch: the robot needs to follow a human's lead. Most of us have done this before. We team up with another person to lift a table: one person leads and the other follows.

Figure 4-23. Baxter robot lifting a table in simulation. There is a simulated, invisible force standing in for the human on the other side of the table. Baxter is trying to learn to lift the table by following this force's lead.

We divide the task and teach it as two separate skills, shown in Table 4-10: lift and level.

Table 4-10. Skills and goals for a robot lifting a table

Skill	Goal
Lift	Move the table's center of mass vertically upward. If you lift one end of the table only, this goal cannot be satisfied.
Level	Return the angle of the table to 0 degrees (perfectly level). You need to level the table only if the table is tilted.

For the lift and level tasks, there is clearly a sequence, but the sequence is variable. If the table is not level, you need to perform the level skill before you can successfully lift the table vertically. But if the table is level, you should start lifting (there is no leveling to do). The task algebra for these skills looks like this: Lift ⊗ Level. The tasks must be performed in sequence, but the sequence is variable. A good sequence might look like (Lift —∘ Lift —∘ Level —∘ Lift —∘ Level —∘ Lift) but will vary depending on how the other lifter leads. Note that these skills cannot be taught as parallel execution (taught separately, then combined) because they are not completely independent.

Hierarchies for Strategies

Strategies are different from functions. Functions are skills that must be performed in some sequence or executed in parallel. Strategies are skills that map to a scenario, not a sequence. Use strategies on landscapes that force you to choose the right skills for the right scenario.

Take a look at the landmass in Figure 4-24. Unlike the lift and level skills in the table-lifting example, both strategies are completely valid ways to traverse the island from left to right. But one of the strategies looks significantly more attractive depending on where you start and where the target is. If you start closer to the top or the bottom of the island, going around the bodies of water will require less distance traveled. If you start closer to the center of the island (vertically), then you can reach the goal sooner by traveling between the bodies of water.

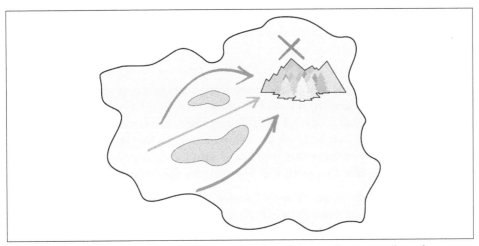

Figure 4-24. This landmass allows you to travel from left to right using either of two strategies: pass between the two bodies of water or around the bodies of water.

That's how strategies work. You need to read the situation correctly to choose the right strategy. In his iconic 1985 talk "Can Machines Think" (*https://oreil.ly/GnKBc*), Richard Feynman tells the story of how Douglas Lenat used strategy to win a prominent game competition. In this wargame competition, participants designed a navy fleet of miniature ships with different amounts of armor and weapons. Mock naval battles had rules governing the maneuverability, survivability, and destructive output of a variety of vessels, and players use a combination of tactical maneuvering and chance (as many games do) to determine the outcome of ship-to-ship combat, with the last navy standing declared the winner.

> During the month of June 1981, the EURISKO program was set the task of exploring the design of naval fleets conforming to a body of (several hundreds of) rules and constraints as set forward in Traveller: The Trillion Credit Squadron. EURISKO designed a fleet of ships suitable for entry in the 1981 Origins national wargame tournament, held at Dunfey's Hotel, in San Mateo, Ca., over July 4 weekend. The Traveller tournament, run by Game Designers Workshop (based in Normal, Illinois), was single elimination, six rounds. EURISKO's fleet won that tournament, thereby becoming the ranking player in the United States (and also an honorary admiral in the Traveller navy). This win is made more significant by the fact that the program's creator, Professor Douglas Lenat of Stanford University's Heuristic Programming Project, had never played this game before, nor any miniatures battle game of this type.

Lenat's heuristic program (heuristic is just another term for strategy) devised a strategy to build one gigantic ship that contained all of the available armor and weapons. This is a well-used strategy in many battle video games; gamers would call this ship a "tank" (a large unit that can both inflict and absorb a huge amount of damage). These units are usually very slow, but their firepower and damage absorbing bulk can help them succeed, as Lenat's gigantic ship did.

Discovering strategies

Well, the next year, the wargame's rules were changed to prevent a single huge ship from winning the competition. OK, game over, right? Nope. That year, Lenat's competition entry used a navy of 100,000 tiny ships to overwhelm the competition and win for a second year in a row. Each ship delivered a tiny amount of damage, but there were so many of them that they added up to a victory. Video gamers use this strategy in battle games frequently too. They call this the "swarm."

I'm not a video game player (mostly because I don't play them well), but I used to enjoy a strategy game called *StarCraft II*. In this game, you control a galactic space army. Depending on the race of the space army you control (Terran, Protoss, or Zerg), different strategies become attractive. The Zerg is a "swarm" race; its military units are collectively stronger by being part of a group. It's easy to defeat an individual Zerg unit but, you'll be overwhelmed by a swarm. That's how most Zerg players win the game.

When designing brains, look for extremes. The extremes help you identify strategies. Scenarios and strategies always come in pairs, so I always ask experts, "What is the opposite of this strategy you just told me about?"

Strategies for Social Good

I strive to design Autonomous AI for social good, not just to improve industrial productivity or make better business decisions. Strategies are important to political and social initiatives and AI that learns to navigate strategy can make social decisions. Researchers at Salesforce.com built an autonomous AI that they call the AI Economist (*https://oreil.ly/dP2gs*). This AI uses a simulated society with independent agents (think laborers, managers, consumers, etc.) to practice economic policy. Much like Lenat's AI-devised naval fleet strategy, the AI Economist devised economic policy. It discovered socialism and capitalism on its own, then it developed a novel economic policy that improves the trade-off between equality and productivity by 16% over baseline policies (*https://oreil.ly/JxgHx*). Autonomous AI can discover new strategies too.

Strategies help us navigate complex spaces. They work in factories, but also for economic policy and political parties, so they can be used to promote justice and freedom. The book is intended to help us learn how to think about skills and strategies. I also hope that it prompts us to consider how we can use strategy for good.

Strategies wax and wane in effectiveness over time

These kinds of strategies aren't just useful in games. Businesses use the swarm strategy as well. Amazon built a reputation as an online shopping giant, a megalith that sells everything from underwear to high-end electronics from its website. It even bought the grocery-store chain Whole Foods. It wins by scale and by controlling a massive, efficient supply chain. Amazon's global dominion is reminiscent of the Galactic Empire in the Star Wars science fiction series: a huge intergalactic government with massive resources. They even built a space weapon the size of a planet: seemingly unbeatable.

Well, along comes Shopify (and the Rebel Alliance). Shopify provides technology for almost anyone to build and maintain an ecommerce store. OK. Now we're powering up a swarm of small, nimble ecommerce stores; the Zerg of ecommerce, if you like. Here's another thing about the Zerg. The Zerg ecosystem grows in power over time and is almost unbeatable late in the game. You have to beat them early in the game in order to win. In an article titled "Shopify: A StarCraft Inspired Business Strategy" (*https://oreil.ly/w6hZm*), Mike, an "ex-activist investor," illuminates these very insights and suggests that over time, the Shopify strategy will gain ground over the Amazon strategy.

Strategies capture trade-offs

One ship versus many, tank versus swarm, small and fast versus big and slow—there's always a trade-off. I've learned some of my most valuable lessons about trade-offs by studying the game of chess. I am not a proficient chess player, but I am fascinated by the strategy of the game. One book in particular that has served as a source of inspiration is Jeremy Silman's *The Complete Book of Chess Strategy*.

In his books, Silman, a teacher and coach of chess masters, evaluates positions according to the "imbalances," or differences, which exist in every position, and advocates that players plan their play according to these. A good plan according to Silman is one which highlights the positive imbalances in the position. He's saying that the differences in chess board scenarios present opportunities for various strategies to have more impact on the game than others.

But there were so many strategies listed in the encyclopedia! I needed a pattern to help me organize and make sense of so much chess strategy. In this context, a trade-off is an organizing pattern for strategies.

Let's start with the phases of the chess game: the opening, the mid-game, and the endgame. Each of these phases has different objectives and therefore different strategies that map to them. The objective of the opening is to survive. The objective of the mid-game is to gain advantage, and the objective of the endgame is to mate the opponent's king.

I still needed another scheme to help me better organize all the strategy I saw in the encyclopedia. Another Silman book, *The Amateur's Mind*, gave me the organizing pattern I was looking for. It was a trade-off. Looking for strategies that define trade-offs for a task will help you identify patterns among many strategies and design brains that balance important objectives. We'll talk about how to do this in detail in Chapter 6.

- One strategy is extremely aggressive. It favors mobility (the ability to move pieces quickly) and therefore favors bishops over knights. Bishops are very mobile and can travel across the board on the long diagonal superhighway (called fiancetto). Bobby Fischer favored this strategy.

- The opposite strategy is fundamentally defensive. It favors controlling the center of the board and builds edifices of pieces to block and own the center of the board. It favors knights over bishops. Knights can move more easily through crowded center areas of the board. A group of chess masters so preferred this style that they developed the Queen's Gambit (*https://oreil.ly/WJuSM*) to lure a player into playing the aggressive, offensive strategy and punishes their hubris. The Queen's Gambit accepted takes up the challenge. The Queen's Gambit declined sees the danger and takes action to mitigate this strategy's advantages.

As depicted in Figure 4-25, strategies often come in pairs, but executing strategy usually requires effective navigating of the areas between the extremes.

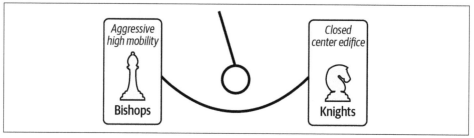

Figure 4-25. Pendulum of strategy

The most important insight is that you can't just play whichever strategy you want. The board scenario (position of your pieces and your opponent's pieces) tells you when it is most advantageous to use each strategy. There are strategies at almost every point on the continuum that help navigate from most any type of board position.

Here's an example from horse racing. The movie *Ride Like a Girl* tells the story of Michelle Payne, the first woman to win the prestigious Melbourne Cup race. Her father teaches her how to read the competitors during a race to effectively navigate between strategies. The first strategy is to hold the horse back and stay with the pack. Her father then explains that when horses tire during the race, the pack parts and a clear but temporary opening appears. If you wait until the opening appears to make your move, you will charge ahead of the pack. If you try to make your move before the opening appears, you will not be able to break away from the pack.

Selective concepts navigate strategy hierarchies

Strategies live in hierarchies. The selector (remember, selectors are supervisors) decides which strategy to use in each situation, and the strategy decides what to do. The task algebra for the hierarchies above looks like this: `Selector[Strategy 1, Strategy 2]`. Here are the task algebra representations of each of the strategy examples that I presented earlier in the chapter:

```
Select Navigation Strategy[Travel Between Lakes, Travel Around Lakes]

Select Naval Fleet Strategy[One Huge Ship, 100000 Tiny Ships]

Select Chess Strategy[Offensive, Defensive]

Select Horse Racing Strategy[Hold Horse Back, Charge Ahead of Pack]

Select Crusher Strategy[Choke, Regulate]
```

As you design brains, you will need to identify hierarchies of strategies and sequences of functional skills so that you can apply AI design patterns that teach skills effectively (that is, they guide the learning algorithm to acquire the skills to succeed). Just like a skilled teacher or coach, you need to be much more concerned with providing landmarks to guide exploration than with figuring out how to prescribe each action (perform the task yourself). In the next chapter, I will describe how to listen to detailed descriptions of tasks and processes for clues that illuminate which building blocks you should use to design a brain that can learn that task. If you practice, you will be able to quickly and easily identify sequences and hierarchies and sketch out effective brain designs. Next, I'll provide some visual language for expressing brain designs and an example that combines many building blocks that we introduced in this chapter.

Visual Language of Brain Design

You will collaborate with many stakeholders during and after the brain-design process, so it helps to have a common language to describe brain designs. I often whiteboard brain designs together with subject matter experts. I sometimes ask other brain designers to review my preliminary designs and give me feedback. After I am finished designing a brain, I pass the brain design to the group that will build the brain.

Let's not reinvent the wheel in determining an effective design workflow. Workflow diagrams in the style shown in Figure 4-26 already provide a useful and well known visual language for systems that process information, output decisions, and choose which modules to activate.

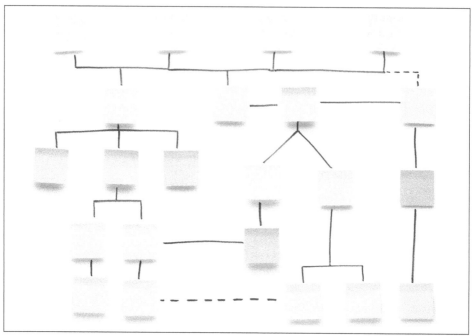

Figure 4-26. Stylized workflow diagram example

Perceptive concepts process information, directive concepts output decisions, and selective concepts choose which directive concepts to activate, so I use workflow diagrams as the visual language for brain designs, with the symbols outlined in Table 4-11 used as the building blocks to create diagrams such as the one shown in Figure 4-27.

Table 4-11. Symbols to use in workflow diagrams

Symbol	Meaning in workflow diagram	Function in brain design
Oval	Terminal (beginning or end of a workflow)	Input to the brain, output from the brain
Hexagon	Processor	Perceptive concept
Rectangle	Action	Directive concept
Diamond	Decision between branches of the workflow	Selective concept

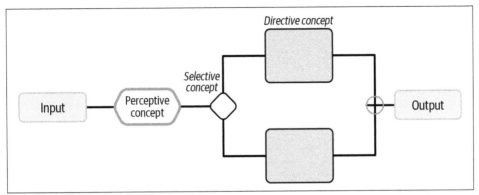

Figure 4-27. Brain design diagram labeling the workflow symbols I use to describe inputs, outputs, perceptive concepts, directive concepts, and selective concepts

How Do You Teach a Machine?

Machine teaching is a process of using teaching techniques to help machines perform useful tasks quickly, reliably, and explainably. Teaching breaks down tasks into skills, orchestrates how those skills relate to each other, and sequences the practice of those skills for the learner. Each skill requires that certain actions be taken to perform the skill, and each skill has goals that guide the learner. In Part III, I will show you how to set actions for your brain, set goals for your brain, and teach skills to your brain. Then, I will provide advanced teaching techniques to help you guide your brain toward expert skill acquisition. Here is the outline of this part of the book:

- Teaching your AI brain what to do
- Setting goals for your AI brain
- Teaching skills to your AI brain
- Giving your AI brain the information it needs to learn and decide

Understanding the Process

Curiosity and *understanding* are mandatory requirements for teaching. Anytime I design a brain, I gather the subject matter experts, data scientists, software engineers, and business process owners and have them walk me through the entire process from end to end. *I ask questions that help me understand the process, its goals, the current method for controlling the process, and the limitations of that method.* This is the first and most crucial exercise you'll perform to design brains.

Meet with Experts

At least one person who earns their living making the decisions that you want your brain to learn should be present for your subject matter expert interview. I respect the engineers who designed the process, the data scientists who analyze the process, and the software developers who integrate the process. But the people who make these decisions day in and day out are most intimately aware of the skills, strategies, goals, nuances, and trade-offs that your autonomous AI will need to learn in order to succeed. The best practice is to interview stakeholders together. Business owners will have the best view of process goals and measurements of success, while engineers and data scientists will often have the best information on the current decision-making method and its limitations. Software developers will have crucial information on how your AI will need to integrate with other systems.

Your subject matter expert interview will help you determine which actions your brain should take and which skills you will need to teach your AI brain for it to learn to achieve the process goals.

Ask the Right Questions

Good machine teachers ask great questions, but they also ask only the questions necessary to understand what to teach and how to teach it. I call this asking the right questions. There are two extremes to avoid while asking questions. The first is not asking enough questions, which assumes that you can figure out the solutions to problems without consulting the experts. This is closely related to the mindset of data science colonialism, which I talk about in Chapter 1. I've witnessed consultants who march into meetings with experts and declare certain techniques as the solution for the experts' problems after barely asking any questions, or after asking questions but clearly missing the nuances of the challenges those experts face.

Unfortunately, I've witnessed countless more well-meaning consultants who seem to be trying to understand absolutely everything about the process. This may seem wise, but it carries some of the same arrogance as data science colonialism. Experts have spent most of their lives learning everything they know about the process. I don't need to know everything about the process; I need to know the actions the AI should take, the process goals, and the skills that the AI should learn. I'm the expert in AI design, they're the expert on the process. The second extreme to avoid while asking questions is asking endless questions that go far beyond what we need to effectively teach AI.

Here are some questions that I commonly use in my expert interviews:

- What makes it difficult to control the process?
- In what situations does the current method not yield good results?

- What are the steps in the process?
- (After someone describes a step in the process) OK, what happens next?
- When does this strategy not work well?
- Are there ever situations when this skill does not work well?
- If I were an expert operator, would you give me the freedom to make that decision?
- Is that a constraint or an expert rule?

Case Study: Let's Design a Smart Thermostat

Seeing an end-to-end example of AI brain design will help you grasp the machine-teaching process. As I show you each step, I will apply it to this brain. By the end of this book, you will see a complete feasible design for a smart thermostat.

A traditional thermostat requires you to determine what temperature you want it to be in your space. I don't know exactly what temperature I want it to be in my space. Usually, the thermostat also requires you to explicitly turn on either the heating or cooling. Smart thermostats automate some of these heating and cooling control tasks. We can do a lot better than traditional thermostats with autonomous AI as well, so let's design a smart thermostat together.

- Chapter 5, "Teaching Your AI Brain What to Do"
- Chapter 6, "Setting Goals for Your AI Brain"

Teaching Your AI Brain What to Do

In Chapter 3 I discussed how every *decision* is an *action taken* to get closer to a goal. This is true for all kinds of decision-making environments. Table 5-1 shows a few examples, most of which I've introduced in earlier chapters.

Table 5-1. Examples of decisions, goals, and goal states

Activity	Decision	Goal	Goal state
Chess	Which move to make (which piece to move and to which destination square)	There are a variety of goals related to specific strategies, but the overall goal is to pin the enemy king so that it cannot move.	Any board position where the enemy king is pinned in checkmate
Airport baggage handling	Choose a method to move each bag from one plane to the next, plus follow-on decisions (if a cart, which cart trip will take a given bag?)	Deliver as many bags as possible to a connecting flight before it departs	Maximum possible number of correct bags at correct gates before flight departs
Naval game fleet planning	How many ships to build and how much armor and armament to build into each ship	Sink all enemy ships	Any naval battle arrangement where all enemy ships have been sunk
Drone flight	How fast to spin each rotor and which direction to tilt each rotor	Travel to destination using minimal energy	Safe landing at destination location, maximum battery charge level
Rock crusher	How fast to run conveyor, how to adjust crusher arm and casing	Crush enough rock to produce enough final product to satisfy demand	Throughput profiles that contains minimal bottlenecks and delivers required ore to downstream machines
Jazz improvisation	Which notes to play over the song structure	There are many, many strategies for sequencing notes to manipulate tension and release, but the goal is to produce various emotions in listeners.	Listener is stimulated, satisfied or otherwise moved emotionally

To teach your AI brain what to do, you will need to determine which actions it will take, set the conditions that will trigger each decision, and set the decision frequency for actions that will be taken at regular intervals.

Determining Which Actions the Brain Will Take

Imagine a world in which you could see things that needed to be done, but could not do anything about them. When you think about it that way, it's easy to see that the purpose of perception is to get the information that we need to make decisions.

Perception Is Required, but It's Not All We Need

The rise of data science and deep learning propagated a fallacy that a very effective prediction could replace or serve as effective decision making. As I discussed in Chapter 4, there is no perfect prediction; it's impossible to tell exactly what will happen. That's why the best decision-makers (including autonomous AI) learn to synthesize perceptive viewpoints (different predictions; seeing things from different angles) and factor the bias of each viewpoint to make better decisions and mitigate risks. The same is true for all forms of perception.

A data scientist once told me that he had taken predictions made by machine learning models and used them effectively as decisions on a real-life process. This is a categorical mistake. A driver might spot an obstacle along the road, but seeing it is not, in itself, the same thing as making a decision about how to drive. Sometimes the things that we perceive point so strongly to specific decisions that a simple prescriptive rule can make the decision effectively (e.g., "avoid obstacle").

For example, if the weather forecast predicts a 90% chance of rain, the decision of whether to take an umbrella is simple. The weather forecast is a prediction. It doesn't make the decision, but a rule like "if you're really sure it's going to rain, bring an umbrella" can make the decision from the prediction. On the other hand, if the forecast predicts a 53% chance of rain, the decision about whether to take an umbrella when you leave the house requires more nuanced decision-making than the prescriptive rule can provide. Table 5-2 explores a few decisions that can be made with prescriptive rules.

Table 5-2. Examples of decisions, goals, and goal states

Decision	Perception	Prescriptive rule
Whether to take an umbrella when you leave the house	Weather prediction	If the predicted chance of rain is high (greater than 90%, for example), take an umbrella; if low (less than 10%, for example), do not take an umbrella.
Whether to apply the brakes while driving	Visual identification of an object in front of the car	If there is an immovable or otherwise hazardous object directly in front of the car, apply the brakes.

Decision	Perception	Prescriptive rule
Which type of basketball shot to shoot	Proximity to the basket; obstacles between you and the basket	If you are within 5 feet of the basket and there are no defenders between you and the basket, shoot a layup.

One of the missing ingredients in early AI was perception, so it makes perfect sense that machine learning–driven perception is getting a lot of attention. Just remember that while perception is often required, it doesn't replace skillful decision-making.

Sequential Decisions

If a decision (about the action that my autonomous AI takes in an environment) moves me to a different state in the environment, why do I need to take multiple steps to get to a goal state? Why can't I just teleport from my current state to the goal state? Take a look at the decision landscape in Figure 5-1. Can you see how it's impossible to reach the goal from the starting state in one straight-line decision step? (See "How Decision-Making Works" on page 63 if you want more details on how straight lines on a map represent decisions.) It takes multiple steps from the origin state to reach the goal state.

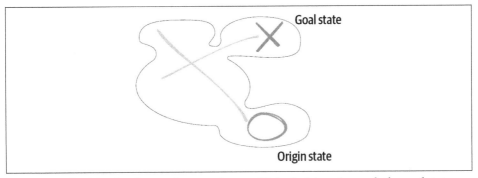

Figure 5-1. Decision landscape that requires multiple decisions to reach the goal state.

This happens in real life all the time: for example, the AI that Siemens built to calibrate CNC machines (described in Chapter 2). Human experts follow a calibration procedure that adjusts the machine, takes measurements to see how accurate the machine is, then repeats these two steps until the machine's accuracy meets the specification:

```
do {
    adjust;
    measure;
} while( machine_accuracy < specification );
```

While working on this AI (full disclosure, I didn't design this one), the scientists and I wondered whether it was possible to make one single adjustment (calibration step) to bring the machine's accuracy within specification. There was no way to know without knowing the landscape of the state space. As I described in Chapter 4, the only way to learn that is to interview subject matter experts who have explored the space previously, or to explore and record the topography (like the example of solving the game of checkers discussed in Chapter 1). My hypothesis is that the expert operators take multiple steps to calibrate the machines, instead of one giant calibration step, because the landscape dictates it.

After you walk through the process in your subject matter expert interview, you should have an opinion about which actions the brain should take. The actions should produce measurable change in the environment state and the system should be able to accept the actions from the brain. There are two ways for your brain to integrate with the systems that it will control:

Decision support
> In the decision support paradigm, your AI brain provides recommendations that assist humans in their decision-making.

Direct control
> In the direct control paradigm, your AI brain programmatically connects to the system it controls and its decisions are automatically carried out.

Triggering the Action in Your AI Brain

After you decide which decision actions your brain will take, you need to determine when the brain will take action. There are two paradigms for triggering action in your brain: you can tell it to take action at regular intervals, like a metronome, or in response to specific events, like an alarm.

Regular intervals
> I practiced playing the saxophone for many hours with a metronome. You set the metronome to the speed that you want to practice, and the metronome clicks beats at regular intervals. In the same way, brains that make decisions at regular intervals take action and receive feedback on a fixed periodic cycle.

Specific events
> Sometimes you only want to take an action (make a decision) when specific events occur. For example, when a fire alarm sounds, I need to decide whether there is a fire or whether a test or false alarm is occurring. In the same way, many processes only require action when specific events occur. I designed a brain for one manufacturing company that only calls for decisions from its operators when product quality measures drift below certain thresholds. The alarm sounds, the operators make their decision, then the process continues under automated control.

Setting the Decision Frequency

Decision frequency only applies to actions taken at regular intervals. How frequently you tell the brain to make decisions will depend on how long it takes the system to react by performing the action. Each action should produce measurable results in the state of the system. For example, imagine you are teaching a brain to control a robot with wheels through a maze. If the brain sends commands to the robot at 100 hz (100 times per second), the robot will not have moved enough for accurate sensors to tell that it moved at all. If the brain sends commands to the robot every 5 seconds, the robot will have moved much further and overshot the goal state, as shown in Figure 5-2. If you make decisions too quickly, they will not produce measurable changes in the system. If you make decisions too infrequently, you will not be able to maintain good control of the system. It's kind of like the resolution for decision-making. Images that are low in resolution (like infrequent decisions) look pixelated because there are not enough pixels to faithfully represent the features of the images. Likewise, with the frame rate of videos, 60 frames per second (fps) appears smooth to the human eye, but if the frames are too infrequent (less than 24 fps), the video looks choppy.

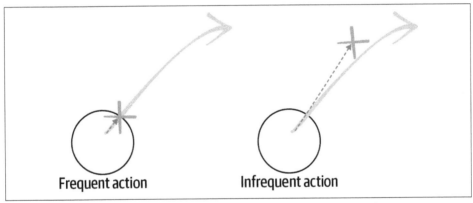

Frequent action   Infrequent action

Figure 5-2. Top view of wheeled robot (think about iRobot's vacuum) that is given commands to follow a trajectory too frequently and too infrequently. When given commands too frequently, the robot barely moves between actions; too infrequently, and the robot overshoots the trajectory.

Handling Delayed Consequences for Brain Actions

Sometimes you don't see the full consequences of your actions until later. When you make a move in chess, the full consequences of a particularly weak move aren't fully realized until much later. Now imagine that you are running a warehouse. Goods are delivered, and you decide where in the facility to store them. The metric that measures the strength of your decisions is how long it takes to retrieve goods from the warehouse when trucks arrive to pick them up. You won't be able to measure this until long after you've stored the goods.

Quality measurements commonly cause this kind of delay in manufacturing. Some feedback on the manufacturing line is given frequently and automatically by sensors. Operators measure other feedback manually and less frequently. One chemical process I observed waited for feedback from chemical lab tests. Another required operators to sample and manually test food products. Table 5-3 lists some examples of common feedback delays in manufacturing and logistics.

Table 5-3. Examples of delayed consequences for actions

Process	Delay	Reason for delay
Chemical manufacturing	Chemical reactions take varying amounts of time to complete.	Chemical reaction time
Chemical manufacturing	Time passes while heat passes from one tank of liquid to another.	Heat transfer
Manufacturing	Operators test a product sample every few hours.	Quality measurements
Logistics	Trucks pick up goods at the warehouse days, weeks, or even months after they arrive.	Demand for goods
Logistics	Goods and feedback on logistics decisions arrive over time.	Transportation time

Rule of thumb for delayed consequences in AI brains

If the full consequences of the brain actions appear within the order of 10 control actions, an AI brain that uses DRL can correlate the delayed result with the previous actions taken. See "Autonomous AI Can Plan for the Long-Term Future" on page 45 for details.

For example, if a brain takes actions every 15 minutes but the most infrequent quality measurements are taken manually in a lab every three hours, the full consequences of each decision register within 12 actions. That's within the order of magnitude of 10, so the brain will likely learn this control across the delay. But what if the consequences come after more significant delay? If the brain takes actions on the same process every second, the full consequences of each decision register after 10,800 (3,600 seconds × 3 hours) actions. This delay is on the order of magnitude of 10,000, not 10, so DRL is unlikely to learn across this delay.

If the delay is out of bounds for unassisted DRL, you have two options:

- Redesign the brain to change the decision frequency, the trigger type, or the brain feedback.

- Consult reinforcement learning experts about algorithm or neural network settings that might support learning despite significant delay in reward.

Actions for Smart Thermostat

Let's define the actions and action frequency for our smart thermostat.

Table 5-4. Actions our smart thermostat will need to take

Action	Trigger	Frequency
Turn on/off air conditioner	In the event that the setpoint is lower than the current temperature	N/A
Turn on/off furnace (heater)	In the event that the setpoint is higher than the current temperature	N/A
Adjust thermostat setpoint	Regular interval	15 minutes

In the next chapter, I will show you how to set goals for your AI brain.

CHAPTER 6

Setting Goals for Your AI Brain

Goals come in pairs.

In order to discover and set goals for your AI, you must understand that there are always going to be trade-offs. I learned this by interviewing hundreds of subject matter experts about their systems and processes, but one particular example cemented it for me. A group of optimization experts asked me about the differences between DRL, gradient descent algorithms, and evolutionary algorithms for industrial decision-making. I explained the differences (see Chapter 2) and then they told me about a problem that they were working on with an industrial process.

The process manages a chemical reaction that produces a valuable chemical product. The price of this product fluctuates significantly with market demand. The catalyst that drives the chemical reaction is also expensive and fluctuates with market demand. They have different goals and strategies, and how they deploy those strategies depends on the market.

There's Always a Trade-off

Here's the first goal/strategy pair: When the demand for the chemical is high, its price is also high. So at times when the price of the catalyst is relatively low, the goal is to make as much chemical as possible and the strategy is to consume catalyst as quickly as possible.

Then I asked the process expert about the opposing strategy, the companion strategy that trades off against this one. This surprised one person in the meeting, who told me that the optimal strategy was always to maximize production. However, my question did not surprise the process expert, who then told me about the second strategy, which is the exact opposite of the first strategy. The second goal/strategy pair is: When the price of the output chemical is low and the cost of the catalyst is comparatively high, the goal is to maximize the efficiency of the operation. You want to nurse the catalyst, consuming as little as possible to maintain the reaction at a slower pace while you wait for market conditions to change.

How did I know that there was another strategy? Goals and the strategies that pursue them map to scenarios. So, like goals, strategies almost always come in pairs.

Learning to program optimization algorithms trains practitioners to focus on one goal, program it into the objective function, and use that goal to drive the search for the optimal decisions. Sure, there are many algorithmic methods for trading off goals, but as a brain designer, you will need to learn to identify pairs of goals and strategies for various scenarios, as shown in Table 6-1.

Table 6-1. Parameters that describe variation in baseball swings

Scenario	Goal	Strategy
Market demand of chemical product is high, price is high, and value of catalyst is comparatively low.	Maximize process production	Consume as much catalyst as possible (run the reaction as quickly as possible)
Market demand of chemical product is low and price is low.	Maximize process efficiency	Consume as little catalyst as possible (run the reaction as slowly as possible)

Can you think of a brain design that might work well to teach these strategies to an AI brain? Figure 6-1 represents my initial thoughts for a brain design, based on what I'd heard thus far about the process.

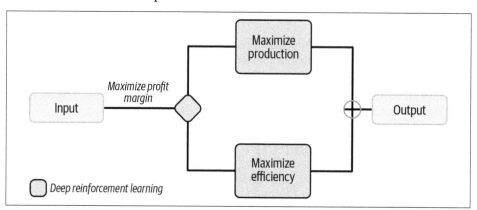

Figure 6-1. Brain design to teach strategies for control of a chemical manufacturing process

In this brain design, one brain module learns how to maximize production, one brain module learns to maximize efficiency, and a third brain module learns to assign decision-making control between brain modules (choose which strategy to use in each scenario).

Western music is a constant, wandering trade-off between tension and release. Tension is when the music sounds dissonant; notes tend to clash with one another and produce feelings of stimulation or anxiety or even discomfort. Release is when the music sounds consonant (notes tend to sound pleasant together and produce feelings of resolution, happiness, and pleasure). Music that contains only release is bland and boring: this is the common complaint about "elevator music," which is intended to provide relaxation in stores and commercial buildings. Music that contains only tension is grating and hard to listen to.

Masterpieces of music swing back and forth between tension and resolution in creative and interesting ways. Just when you start to feel uncomfortable, you land on a pleasant resolution. Before you become disinterested, an interesting twist of tension captures your attention. In fact, without tension, resolution wouldn't feel quite as pleasant at all.

As I discussed in Chapter 4, masterpieces of chess strategy (games that display formidable skill by both players) swing back and forth like a pendulum between two major schools of strategy. In this case, the chess master is not swinging back and forth between opposing strategies to entertain or move an audience even though audiences are most certainly moved by the storyline arc that results from the combating strategies. The chess master swings back and forth between competing, opposing strategies to navigate the decision landscape of chess and emerge victorious from a match.

Just like the skillful composer of music and the chess master, skillful AI will swing back and forth between these goals and succeed at tasks. In order to discover and set goals for your AI, you must understand that there's always a trade-off.

Throughput Versus Efficiency

This chemical process is an example of the most common trade-off I see in industrial processes: throughput vs. efficiency. *Throughput* is the amount of product that you can produce and sell from a manufacturing line. *Efficiency* is the amount of resources you spend to produce that amount of product. In this example, throughput is the amount of chemical you produce (perhaps measured in tons per hour), and the efficiency is the amount of money that you spend on catalyst to produce that amount of product. Table 6-2 lists some additional throughput/efficiency trade-offs.

Table 6-2. Throughput versus efficiency trade-off for various processes

Process	Throughput	Efficiency
Chemical production with catalyst	Amount of chemical produced	Cost of catalyst per ton of chemical used to run the reaction
Rock crushing in gyratory crusher	Amount of rocks crushed to specification per hour	Cost to run crushing equipment to crush each ton of rock to specification

Process	Throughput	Efficiency
Warehouse logistics (location scheduling)	Amount of goods that can be retrieved for customer orders	Cost to retrieve each customer order from the warehouse
Fast food restaurant production	Amount of food sold in the restaurant	Labor cost to produce the food in the restaurant plus the cost of food per dollar of food sold
Watercraft production	Amount of canoes and kayaks produced in injection moulding process	Cost of materials and labor to change molds per dollar of revenue from selling watercraft

Don't Stop the Process

One common question about efficiency is: why don't I just shut down the reaction (that's the most resource efficient thing to do)? The goal is to *run* the reaction efficiently. Shutting down the reaction is not running the reaction at all. Efficiency is the nonzero (positive) amount of resource required to run the process.

Supervisors Have Different Goals Than Crews Do

Note that the supervisor selector concept has a different goal than the directive concepts in the brain design. In the same way that supervisors are responsible for taking a comprehensive, bird's-eye view of how things are going, selector concept goals unify the goals of the directive concepts. For many processes, the unifying goals are financial. The selector concept in the chemical process is responsible for maximizing the profit margin of the process. Profit margin is calculated with the following equation:

```
(revenue from chemical sold - cost to produce chemical) / revenue
```

In this simplified example, the cost to produce the chemical is the cost of the catalyst used to drive the reaction.

 You can also validate goals and strategies by reverse engineering the goals and thinking about what will happen if you use the wrong strategy in the wrong scenario.

Table 6-3 proves how matching the wrong strategy to the wrong scenario will lead to decreased profit margins. This is what happens when a selector concept makes the wrong decisions about which strategy to apply. This is also what happens when you don't consider both scenarios and goals for each pair of strategies. If we optimized the chemical process for the first goal and strategy only, we'd be doing *the exact opposite* of what is optimal when market demand for the chemical is low, the price is low and the price of catalyst is comparatively high.

Table 6-3. Reverse engineering goals by examining what will happen if you apply the wrong strategy for each scenario for a chemical process

Scenario	Strategy	Goal	Effect on unifying goal
Market demand of chemical product is high, the price is high, and the value of the catalyst is comparatively low.	Consume as little catalyst as possible (run the reaction as slowly as possible)	Maximize process efficiency	Profit margin will decrease. You will sacrifice revenue that you could have made by not making enough product to meet market demand.
Market demand of chemical product is low and price is low.	Consume as much catalyst as possible (run the reaction as quickly as possible)	Maximize process production	Profit margin will decrease. You will make more product than you can sell and will have spent more resources than needed to create the product you can sell on the market.

Don't Prioritize Goals; Balance Them Instead

Programming optimization routines and other algorithms also encourages programmers to rank or prioritize goals. But when designing brains that will learn to trade off competing goals and strategies, prioritization is not the right approach.

For example, I have had many subject matter experts tell me that "throughput is their highest priority" and that "efficiency is a subordinate lower priority." That is like saying that my first musical priority as a composer is release and my second priority is tension. If I apply this prioritization technique to the chemical process above, we will maximize throughput as a first priority incorrectly for the scenario where the market demand of the chemical product is low and the price is low.

Instead of prioritizing goals and objectives, focus on defining the cost benefit of the trade-off. Your job as a brain designer isn't telling the system what to do in every situation, it's to set up the trade-off and let the intelligent system learn how to navigate the trade-off in a nuanced way.

Watch Out for Expert Rules Disguised as Goals

I have one more word of advice for you about how to set goals for your AI before I discuss types of goals. Watch out for expert rules masquerading as goals. Often process experts identify expert rules that lead to success under a common (but not every) scenario, then communicate them to the less experienced as goals. The risk of this practice is that if the expert rule is pursued as a priority goal, it will fail when it is used in the wrong scenario. Remember, expert rules are like portable, dehydrated strategies. They only work when matched to the right scenario and goal.

I worked with a railroad company to design a brain to manage loading train cars on trains. Trucks deliver train cars and park them in large parking lots (called rail yards). Rail yards can be miles across and contain thousands of spaces to park containers. Specialized trucks called hostlers tow the containers to the train tracks, where cranes load them onto trains. The task is to assign hostler trucks to containers in a way that loads the train as quickly as possible. We want the brain to make sequential assignments for each hostler in the yard until the train is loaded.

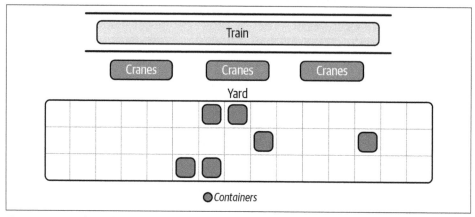

Figure 6-2. Rail yard with containers that need to be delivered to cranes, which will place them onto a train

We can already see that one of the goals of the task is to move all of the train containers from their disparate locations in the yard to the cranes to be loaded as quickly as possible. That's the throughput of the system. The opposing goal is how much fuel and labor it takes to load those containers onto the train. This is the efficiency goal of the system. This is where it gets interesting. There was much debate about whether it is a goal to minimize the amount of time that hostler trucks travel around without a container. This is related to efficiency but it's really an expert rule that provides guidance for how to keep the operation efficient. If hostlers drive across the yard without a load to pick up a container, they are potentially wasting gas and time. But this expert rule (which is really the seed of a strategy) isn't the best thing to do in all scenarios. That's how I know it's not an overarching goal for the process. Instead, it points to another trade-off:

- Wait for a hostler truck to become available near the container.
- Send an available hostler truck to pick up the container now, even if it is not close by.

I discovered this trade-off by asking if there was an alternative action to this "goal." Watch out for guidance masquerading as goals.

Ideal Versus Available

The railroad example also illustrates another common trade-off pattern: ideal versus available. In the first trade-off pattern above, making and moving more goods is balanced against the cost required to make them. The more that you make, the less efficiently you will make it. The more efficiently you make things, the more care required and the less you will make. There's no simple right or wrong answer. It's a trade-off. In the ideal versus available trade-off, you balance doing the best thing possible, which isn't available right now, later, against doing something less ideal right now. Do you see the ideal versus available trade-off in the rail yard example?

I see this trade-off a lot in production scheduling for manufacturing. Imagine that you have multiple machines for making products on a manufacturing line. Some machines have greater capacity than others. If I'm making chemicals, a larger tank might represent greater capacity. So let's say that I'm creating a schedule that determines the sequence for the product that I want to make. If my schedule has a list of all the same products, then higher-capacity machines are ideal. If my schedule contains a list of products that are all very different, lower-capacity machines are better.

As I'm building my schedule, I need to make the ideal versus available trade-off. Should I wait until the highest-capacity machine is available, or should I claim a low-capacity machine now?

Setting Goals

The first step to setting goals for your AI is to identify scenarios. Those scenarios often have separate goals (remember how each phase of the walking gait in Chapter 4 had completely different goals?). Then, goals map to strategies. The next chapter discusses teaching strategies, but the third step below is where you start.

Step 1: Identify Scenarios

Scenarios help us make sense of how complex systems interact over time. They partition large decision-making environments into sections. Certain strategies work well in certain scenarios or market regimes, while others don't. Scenarios are sections that help decision-makers organize vast environments.

Decision-makers call these sections different things for different activities. Let me take you through examples from chess and manufacturing. There are three commonly discussed stages or phases of a chess match: the opening, the mid-game, and the endgame. A chess match typically lasts somewhere between 20 and 40 moves. There are a tremendous number of potential board positions in chess. Humans and AI can organize this ocean of information by identifying and treating the game stages differently.

The goal during the mid-game is to gain material advantage (win strategic pieces) and spatial advantage (set yourself up to attack or defend well). In contrast, the goal of the endgame is very different: checkmating, or pinning your opponent's king so that they cannot move.

Manufacturing lines have operating regimes similar to phases of a chess game. The startup regime is typically the hardest to control. The conditions during startup vary tremendously, and the process requires significant adjustment to make the end product pass quality control inspection. Many manufacturing lines use human operators for the startup even if the other phases are automated because it is so difficult. The goal for the startup regime is typically to reach a state where the majority of products can pass quality inspection as quickly as possible. This is the definition of *steady-state*.

The goal of the steady-state regime is to trade-off throughput and efficiency effectively. The goal of the shutdown regime is to fix issues that are preventing effective startup or steady-state operation. For example, during shutdown, you might replace a pump that is near the end of its life and is making it difficult to control the process well. Table 6-4 shows some examples of scenarios that help organize goals and strategies over time for complex processes:

Table 6-4. Examples of scenarios that categorize conditions in complex systems

Activity	Scenario	Examples
Trading stocks	Market regimes	Bull market, bear market
Manufacturing process	Operating regimes	Startup, steady-state, shutdown
Chess	Game stages	Opening, mid-game, endgame
Equipment maintenance	Wear states	New mid-life, end of life

So you see that because different goals have different scenarios, it's impossible to set the goals correctly without acknowledging the scenarios that categorize the process. First identify the scenarios, then set the goals for each scenario.

Step 2: Match Goals to Scenarios

For each scenario, set one or more goals that define success. Many scenarios will take a single goal, but some will take multiple goals. Goals work together in a scenario when they either complement each other (e.g., maximize the products you manufacture, but avoid making product that you need to throw away because they don't meet quality specs) or when they compete with each other. You will need a comprehensive understanding of the process and access to a subject matter expert to do this effectively. Table 6-5 lists the three regimes that we expect to see in a typical manufacturing process:

Table 6-5. Goals for the operating regimes in a manufacturing process

Regime	Goal
Startup	Minimize time to steady-state
Steady-state	Trade off throughput and efficiency based on customer demand
Shutdown	Fix issues that prevent startup or effective steady-state operation

Step 3: Teach Strategies for Each Scenario

By this time, the scenarios and the goals that you've learned from the process experts have already suggested some promising strategies. In the next chapter, I'll show you how to flesh out and finalize the strategies that you want to teach your AI brain. Each strategy will map to specific scenarios. First, let's discuss the goal objectives that you will use in your AI.

Goal Objectives

There are six basic goal objectives that you will commonly use to teach your AI brains skills and strategies. For each learning brain module, identify which goal objectives the concept needs to satisfy. The goal of each concept is the composite of all its goal objectives. The most basic goal objectives are to maximize and minimize key parameters.

What About Multiple Goal Objectives?

It is fine for each skill to have multiple goal objectives, but well defined skills tend to carry simpler, cleaner sets of goal objectives.

Maximize

The maximize goal objective controls a process to increase a parameter as much as possible. For example, you might want to maximize throughput, the amount of miles a vehicle can travel on a single charge, or the lifetime of a part.

Minimize

The minimize goal objective decreases a parameter as much as possible. For example, you might want to minimize heat generated by a process, emissions generated by a factory, or the frequency of part failure.

Reach, like the Finish Line for a Race

Sometimes the objective for a process is to reach a particular state. If you reach the goal state, you satisfy the goal. For reach goals, usually the scenario ends when the goal objective is satisfied. See Table 6-6 for a list of examples of reach goals.

Table 6-6. Examples of reach goal objectives

Activity	Goal state	Result
Chess	Put the opponent in checkmate	Win game
Drone landing	Bring the drone to zero vertical position without crashing	Mission complete
Autonomous racing	Complete specified laps before other drivers	Win race
Machine calibration	Bring the equipment within tolerance	Machine ready for operation

Drive, like the Temperature for a Thermostat

Sometimes you want the system to reach a state and stay there. Thermostats work like this. When I get home on a hot day, I set the thermostat to 72 degrees Fahrenheit (22.2 degrees Celsius). The thermostat turns on the air conditioning system and drives the temperature from the current 78 degrees Fahrenheit (25.6 degrees Celsius) to 72 degrees and keeps it within 1 degree Fahrenheit of that set point. See Table 6-7 for a list of examples of drive goals.

Many parameters of industrial processes must stay within a certain range as part of the definition of success. Drive goal objectives keep these parameters in bounds.

Table 6-7. Examples of drive goals

Activity	Target
HVAC	Keep temperature within range of setpoint
Chemical processing	Keep viscosity within range of setpoint
Oil refining	Keep flash point of resulting gasoline within range of setpoint
Discrete manufacturing	Keep dimensions within tolerance across products that are coming off the manufacturing line
Logistics	Keep delivery time within range of scheduled delivery

Avoid, like Dangerous Conditions

Some situations define specific states to avoid which represent bad things that you don't want to happen. See Table 6-8 for a list of examples of avoid goal objectives.

Table 6-8. Examples of avoid goal objectives

Activity	State to avoid
Drone landing	Crashing (hitting the ground with enough force to damage the craft)
Machine component control/maintenance	Breaking
Oil drilling	Collapsing bore hole
Baggage handling	Missing connecting flight for bag

Standardize, like the Heat in an Oven

Consistency and uniformity is often a goal. For example, one of the goals of world-wide service restaurant chains like McDonald's or Starbucks is to ensure that the menu selections and the taste and quality of each item are consistent from store to store. I want to make sure that when I'm craving a Big Mac, what I order looks and tastes like the Big Macs I remember.

The same is true for heat in an oven. If the oven heat is not uniform when baking bread with yeast, the bread may not rise. I once designed a brain for a company that makes computer chips. The wafers that will eventually become computer chips are baked in an oven-like reactor using a process called epitaxy. These ovens use multiple heat lamps arranged in 3D space and fans to make sure that the temperature not only reaches the set point but also is uniform throughout the reactor. The wafers could be ruined if the temperature is not uniform, so heat uniformity is a goal of the process. Saturation, the extent to which something is dissolved or absorbed, is a form of uniformity. Last, coatings and films must reach a target thickness but also have a goal of uniform thickness.

The *standardize* goal objective keeps multiple state variables within certain proximity to each other. For example the standardize goal objective might keep multiple temperature sensor readings in a reactor within 2 degrees of each other or multiple thickness sensor readings along a film within 3 mm of each other.

It is possible to express this goal objective using other goal objectives like this first code sample for a hard constraint and this second code sample for a soft constraint:

```
avoid (difference between sensors) > 2 (hard constraint)

drive (difference between sensors) < 2 (soft constraint)
```

See Table 6-9 for a list of examples of uniformity goal objectives.

Table 6-9. Examples of uniformity goals

Activity	Uniformity
Wafer epitaxy	Uniform temperature in reactor
Paint formulation	Uniform pigment particle (color) distribution
Steel galvanization	Uniform zinc coating thickness
Plastic extrusion	Uniform film thickness

Smooth, like a Line

Sometimes good control of a system must satisfy goal objectives like maximize or minimize, but it must also do so without bouncing the control actions all over the place. For example, many systems wear more on startup than at other times, so constantly starting up and shutting down will wear the system more. The *smooth* goal type keeps the actions from being volatile (moving around a lot).

Expanding Task Algebra to Include Goal Objectives

Using the goals I describe above, we can expand the task algebra for a brain to include the goal objectives that describe the concept. Each concept (skill) can be substituted with the goals that compose that skill. Using the goals I describe above, we can expand the task algebra for a brain to include the goal objectives that describe the concept. Each concept (skill) can be substituted with the goals that compose that skill.

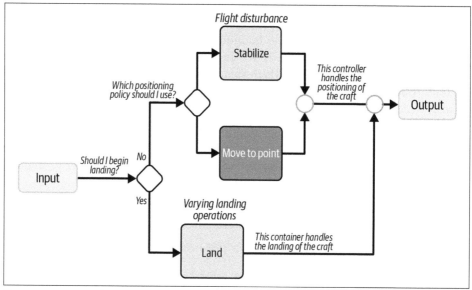

Figure 6-3. Brain design for teaching an autonomous AI brain to fly a drone

Landing involves descending to the ground without crashing, which is a very different skill from controlling the drone during flight. When flying the drone, moving from point to point is a very different skill from avoiding obstacles and stabilizing the craft. We teach each of these skills separately. Each of these skills have different goals, as shown in Table 6-10.

Table 6-10. Skills and goals for flying a drone

Skill	Goal
Move to point	*Reach* landing zone X and Y position
Stabilize	*Avoid* obstacles and *maintain* stability
Select flight strategy	*Minimize* fuel consumption
Land	*Reach* landing zone Z position and *avoid* crashing

Do you see how each skill has different goals related to its purpose in the brain?

The task algebra that I introduced in "Brains Are Organized by Functions and Strategies" on page 99 describes the brain skills using a mathematical expression. Let's expand this expression to include the goals for our drone control AI:

```
Minimize Fuel Consumption[Drive Stability, Reach Landing Zone X and
Y Position] → (Reach Landing Zone Z Position and Avoid Crashing)
```

We replace each skill in the task algebra with the goals that comprise the skill. See Table 6-11 for other examples.

Table 6-11. Mathematical description of example brain designs expanded to include their goals

Activity	Task algebra	Task algebra (with goals added for each skill)
Drone control	Fly to target[stabilize, move to point] → land	*Minimize* fuel consumption[*drive* stability, *reach* landing zone X and Y position] → (*reach* landing zone Z position and *avoid* crashing)
HVAC control	Control HVAC[recycle air, freshen air]	Control HVAC[*drive* comfort and *minimize* energy consumption and *avoid* unlawful CO$_2$]
HVAC control	Control HVAC[day control, night control]	Control HVAC[*drive* comfort and *minimize* energy consumption, *drive* comfort and *minimize* energy consumption]

Setting Goals for a Smart Thermostat

Now that I've described how to set goals for autonomous AI, we can set goals for our smart thermostat.

There are two goal objectives for our smart thermostat: *maintain* comfort and *minimize* energy consumption. I'm choosing the maintain goal objective for comfort instead of the maximize type goal because when the temperature and humidity are in the comfortable range, I do not want the AI to waste energy (and money) trying to maximize comfort. Note that these two goals oppose each other. You have to spend more money to be more comfortable (heat cold air and cool hot air).

In Chapter 5, we determined which actions we wanted our AI to take. In this chapter, we learned how to set goals for our AI. Next, I will show you how to teach your AI skills and strategies.

CHAPTER 7

Teaching Skills to Your AI Brain

By the time that you finish setting goals for your AI brain, you should have a good idea about which skills you need your AI to practice to succeed at the task you are designing it to perform. By the end of this chapter, you will be able to translate this list of key skills into a brain design that serves as a mental map to guide and focus the AI as it practices and explores. In "How Humans Make Decisions and Acquire Skills" on page 29, I presented a framework for skill acquisition for specific tasks to AI. The performance of your AI will depend most, though, on your level of teaching sophistication. Figure 7-1 shows the levels of teaching sophistication you can achieve. The further you progress up this ladder as a teacher, the more expert your AI can become.

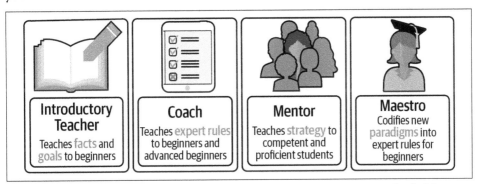

Figure 7-1. Levels of teaching sophistication. The farther you progress up this ladder as a teacher, the more expert your AI can become.

Teaching Focuses and Guides Practice (Exploration)

Batting in baseball demonstrates this well. Unlike in basketball, football, and soccer, where many skill motions are used to launch the ball and score (e.g., jump shot, hook shot, or layup in basketball; pass or punt in football; throw in, instep kick, back-heel kick, header, and bicycle kick for soccer), baseball has only one method to propel the ball from home plate: batting.

Figure 7-2. Stages of batting

This observation, combined with the amount of money that is spent on succeeding in baseball and the age of the sport, suggests that batting is the most sensible way for humans with two arms and two legs to use a bat to propel the baseball a long distance. So if a human or AI is practicing using a bat to propel a baseball a long distance, and we limit the practice to the batting skill, we are focusing the exploration on the skill that we know will succeed. This prevents exploration in areas that we already know are not promising, like the stance shown in Figure 7-3.

Figure 7-3. Just one of the infinite ways to try to propel a baseball from the batter's box, after it is pitched at you. This picture is actually a demonstration for how to grip the bat before you enter the baseball swing, but a naive AI will indeed try this and many other things instead of the baseball swing.

 Teaching focuses and guides exploration and practice on the most promising areas likely for success.

Autonomous AI, with its built-in tendency to *explore* (try new and different ways to succeed) and *exploit* (use known methods of success to meet objectives), will try infinite ways to hit the ball that are not batting, unless you confine the practice to a specific skill. That's what *machine teaching* is all about (see Figure 7-4).

Figure 7-4. Teaching focuses exploration on skills that the teacher already knows will lead to success at the task. The student develops and customizes the skill by practicing under a variety of conditions and pursuing success at the task. I credit my friend Mark Hammond for this graphic and analogy.

Don't worry, there's plenty for the learner to practice within the boundaries of the skill. Table 7-1 and Figure 7-5 outline the many different ways to execute the baseball swing. Competent and proficient batters adapt their swing to hit varying pitches well. Expert batters cement a batting style, which adapts to various pitches but also works well with their anatomy and helps keep them from managing too many different variations of the baseball swing.

Table 7-1. Scenarios, goals and strategies for chemical production with a catalyst

Dimension	Variation
Height	High swings
Height	Low swings
Extension	Close swings
Extension	Extended swings
Grip	Choked (high) grip
Grip	Low grip
Speed	Fast swings
Speed	Slow swings

After a lot of practice and experimentation with different ways to perform the baseball swing skill, as the player moves from the proficient to the expert stage of skill development, they settle into a style, a tendency, a gravitational center which anchors their adaptation to pitches and their future exploration. Figure 7-5 shows batting adapted beyond mere variations: they are tendencies that expert batters adopt to suit their batting style and anatomy. They adapt their batting swing (perform the skill) from the starting point of these tendencies. (Analysis courtesy of Jeffrey Beckman's 2011 article "MLB Power Rankings: 23 Quirkiest Batting Stances in Baseball" (*https://oreil.ly/uYErL*).)

Figure 7-5. Baseball swing styles (from left to right, Magglio Ordóñez, Carlos Quentin, Prince Fielder, Orlando Cabrera). Image credits: Ezra Shaw/Getty Images, Norm Hall/Getty Images, Andy Lyons/Getty Images.

Skills Can Evolve and Transform

As you explore how to perform a skill to succeed under specific conditions, the skill can flex and transform to the point that it becomes something different. Remember how I said that there is only one sensible, well-proven skill for propelling a baseball from the batter's box? Well, some baseball coaches teach bunting as a separate skill. A sacrifice bunt is a specific strategy that uses the bunting skill to place the ball far enough from fielders to help a runner (who is often on third base) to score. The batter is making a sacrifice because they will be thrown out (they will not make it to first base), but the run will be scored anyway. In order to execute this strategy, the batter must place the ball precisely on the field in a way that gives the runner enough time to score. The grip used to perform the bunting skill is very high (choked grip) with the bat held close to the body. The batter intentionally meets the ball with bat and taps slowly.

The bunt differs from the baseball swing in its grip and in the fact that it's not really a swing but a tap. This specialized batting skill evolved from the desire to accurately place the baseball in a particular zone on the field. The related skills of batting and bunting can be presented in relation to two defining variables: grip and extension, as shown in Figure 7-6. In the presence of a specific goal, when there's leeway for exploration with grip and extensions, the batting skill transforms and the bunting skill emerges.

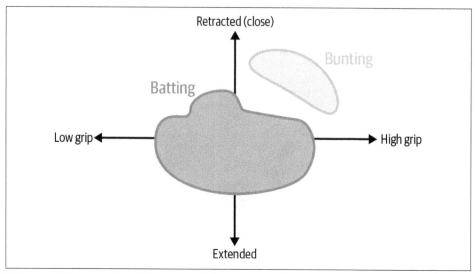

Figure 7-6. Relationship of batting and bunting as skills

Skills Adapt to the Scenario

In the same way that skills can evolve and transform, skills adapt to scenarios to succeed. In baseball, batters must adapt their swing to match the positions of defensive players on the field and the position of the offensive players on the bases to successfully score. The same is true for skills that you will design into your autonomous AI.

Levels of Teaching Sophistication

Teachers are crucial to the development of skills in humans and AI. Learners cannot and will not predictably and efficiently ascend the ladder of skill acquisition without teaching. More sophisticated teaching methods increase the likelihood of learners achieving higher levels of skill acquisition. You will use the following levels of teaching sophistication to improve your own machine teaching and guide your architecture choices for the AI brains that you design.

- Introductory teacher
- Coach
- Mentor
- Maestro

The Introductory Teacher Conveys the Facts and Goals

The *introductory teacher* expresses facts and goals to the AI. This is a crucial aspect of teaching, but the information is rudimentary and the skill level of the learner is low. The analogy is preschool teaching for children. Much of the preschool curriculum teaches children the facts about the world around them, for example, "this is a banana," "this is the letter A," "this is a cat," and goal definitions for basic skills such as "good job raising your hand when you wanted to speak," "that is not the right way to wait in line," "keep your hands to yourself," and it offers rewards for meeting goals. If you stop here in your teaching, you are expecting your AI to learn a whole lot on its own. Imagine if we only taught our preschoolers how to identify objects and goals for behavior, then let them discover everything else by trial and error.

The Coach Sequences Skills to Practice

By the time we finish defining goals, we are starting to see expert rules for students to practice. The next level of teaching sophistication is a coach who provides expert rules for both new beginners and advanced beginners to practice. Each of these rules is like a dehydrated strategy that the AI (or human) will hydrate into a customized, specialized skill for the task. Eventually, it is built into the learner's intuition and memory. I introduce this idea in "So, what is a skill?" on page 65, but now is a good time to discuss this principle in more detail.

Imagine if someone tried to teach you a skill by describing all of the nuances to you from the beginning. There's just too many rules to digest. Instead, teachers dehydrate a juicy, nuanced concept that they've learned from a lot of previous practice into bite-sized expert rules that are simple to communicate, don't overwhelm the student with details, and allow plenty of space for the learner to practice and customize the skill as they build it out. This is what I mean by "Expert rules inflate into skills" and "Teach expert rules, let the learner inflate the skills by practicing" in Chapter 4.

You might still be wondering what there is to practice about an expert rule, so I'll give you an example. One of the most fundamental skills for a football running back is "finding the hole" to run through toward the goal line (to ultimately score). The learner here is the running back, the teacher is the coach who gives the running back plays and expert guidance for finding the hole. Figure 7-7 provides a diagram of football running lanes that a back might run through during a play.

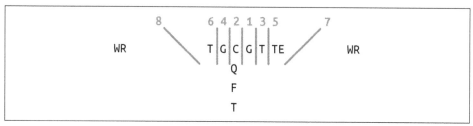

Figure 7-7. Football running lanes

The running back moves forward toward scoring a goal between players marked by letters (guard, center, tight end and so on). As the defense evolves during a football play, these lanes will expand and contract. Finding the hole means choosing a running lane where you perceive that the hole will emerge and then running through that hole. Each offensive running play is a strategy that opens up a running lane for the running back. So, the skill of finding the hole requires testing different running lanes against the other team's defense to see which works best.

The *coach* is a master at feeding the right expert rule for each student (usually the player of a game like football or basketball) to practice at just the right stage of their development. In the same way, great brain designers get really good at identifying expert rules that encapsulate fuzzy skills: that is, pare the skill down to a format that a beginner can easily understand and practice. As they practice, they can begin to identify exceptions to that rule (see "Expert Rules Inflate into Skills" on page 87 for more details). For a brain designer, this means compiling expert rules from process experts and architecting them into your brain design as skills that the AI will learn. As illustrated in Figure 7-8, remember that skills are concepts that take action toward goals. As the learner identifies exceptions to each rule, the concept fleshes out. As a brain designer, you will provide rules for autonomous AI to practice.

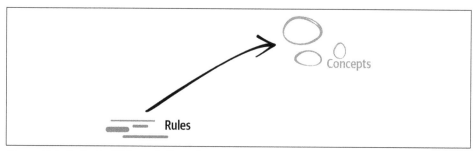

Figure 7-8. Rules build into skills with practice.

The Mentor Teaches Strategy

The *mentor* teaches strategy: how to implement each strategy and which strategy to use under various conditions. Strategy is the main vehicle that humans use to exchange skills for accomplishing complex tasks. The mentor often shadows the learner as they practice tasks and provides feedback in real time about strategy options. Imagine a football coach blowing their whistle during practice, asking their players to read the defense, then talking their offensive players (particularly the running back for a running play or the quarterback for a passing play) through the options of which strategy to deploy. This is common for chess coaches as well. They stop their students between moves and discuss strategy options with them. Sometimes this discussion includes guidance; sometimes it just helps the students think through the options for themselves and debate the pros and cons of each strategy.

The Maestro Democratizes New Paradigms

The *maestro* has a very special role. Maestros help students cement the hundreds of skills and strategies that they've learned into a unique style, as well as codifying new skill paradigms, then packaging them for beginners, advanced beginners, and competent learners to practice (see Figure 7-9).

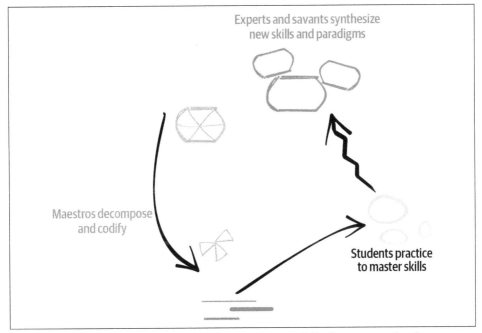

Experts and savants synthesize
new skills and paradigms

Maestros decompose
and codify

Students practice
to master skills

Figure 7-9. Maestros study experts and codify the new skills that experts develop into rules that less-expert students can practice.

Let me give you an example of how maestros codify new paradigms for less proficient students. I play the alto saxophone and I've studied jazz music ever since the seventh grade. Without question, the most influential alto saxophone player in jazz history is Charlie Parker. Along with trumpet player Dizzy Gillespie, Parker invented the jazz paradigm of bebop (*https://en.wikipedia.org/wiki/Bebop*). Jazz music is an improvisational art form that relies heavily on practiced skills where a common musical structure supports collaborative creation. Each player weaves together and adapts known improvisational skills to spontaneously create melodies that match both the chord structure and the way the other musicians play.

Like many art forms, jazz is an evolution of styles where revolutions periodically introduce new paradigms. Bebop was a new paradigm in the 1940s following the swing era. In the swing era, jazz was the popular music of the day in America. Bebop introduced more complex, dissonant melodies with wider swings between tension and release. It allowed more creative expression but was harder to understand and master.

So, as shown in Table 7-2, a small group of expert, savant jazz musicians evolved a new paradigm by combining and modifying skills from the previous jazz paradigms of ragtime, Dixieland, and swing.

Table 7-2. Skills from previous jazz paradigms that bebop pioneers transformed.

Skill	Expert rule to practice	How bebop transformed skill
Outline the chord tones for each chord (in the melodies you create).	Play the root (first note), third, fifth, and seventh.	Include the 9th (second note), 11th (4th note), and 13th (6th note).
Play the notes of the scale that matches the chords in the underlying structure (in the melodies you create).	Play the scale ascending or descending and try to land on chord tones, particularly the third and seventh.	Play the notes of scales that match other chords related to the chords in the underlying structure.

When bebop first emerged, it was exclusive to a small group of genius jazz practitioners (Bud Powell and Thelonious Monk on piano, Charles Mingus on bass, Dexter Gordon and Sonny Rollins on tenor saxophone and Max Roach on drums). Very few others knew how to play it. In a lot of ways, the current state of autonomous AI (in 2022) is similar to the state of bebop jazz playing in the 1940s. A small group (though not as small as the group of bebop practitioners) of savant AI practitioners produce the lion's share of the autonomous AI in the world.

Enter the maestro of bebop: Sonny Stitt. Sonny Stitt was an expert bebop player as well as a maestro, much the same way that Phil Jackson and Steve Kerr won NBA basketball championships as both players and coaches. But I want to focus on Stitt's role as a maestro. Stitt's way of playing and teaching codified, distilled, and made more clear what specific skills and devices the bebop pioneers were using. This allowed exponentially more players (even novice players) to practice these skills and weave them into their playing. It is difficult for nonexpert practitioners to hear a new paradigm, understand what is happening, digest how this paradigm evolved from previous paradigms, and imitate it. That's the role of the maestro: digest and codify new paradigms into bite-sized skills that all learners can practice as expert rules.

The maestro has an important role in democratizing AI, and you will practice the competency of a maestro as you (1) interview experts about their control paradigms, (2) digest and codify these paradigms into modular skills that your AI will practice, and (3) design an AI from these modular skills that can succeed at the task in real life.

Max Petrie, an executive at PepsiCo in R&D, recently told me that their most valuable asset is their operators' experience in running their manufacturing lines. PepsiCo is a company that makes $67B in annual revenue making snack foods like Cheetos, Doritos, Annie's Pretzels, and Quaker Oats, in addition to beverages. Let that sink in for a minute. If this company's most valuable asset (more valuable than the manufacturing equipment, the factories, or even the executive leadership) is the *skills that the operators develop and pass on*, then teaching is of paramount importance.

The primary competence that I've developed as a designer of intelligent systems is the ability to quickly (sometimes extremely quickly under various constraints and demands) understand a high-value process, absorb the control paradigm that the process experts use to manage that process, and decompose the control paradigm into skills that I can codify in an AI brain that will practice and learn how to control this high-value process. I strive to be a maestro. If I succeed, I will have identified and built high-value skills into autonomous AI that in turn will enable many more operators to succeed in the future. In that way, I'm democratizing valuable control paradigms. As you build the sophistication of your machine teaching, you will further this democratization as well.

The end goal is to enable a diverse and ambitious population of machine teachers that power a skills-based industrial and social justice economy.

Machine teachers respect and value experts, codify their high-value skills, store them, and transfer them to autonomous AI and humans to practice and master.

How Maestros Democratize Technology

In the early 1990s there was turmoil in the software community over whether software should be designed and built as a single monolith or whether software should be modularized into composable objects. The result of this debate was the software development practice we now know as object oriented programming (OOP).

Most technology that reaches material scale experiences a similarly tumultuous transition from applied research technology where it is developed, usually at a very low level by a small number of innovators, to mass market technology where it is consumed by a wider audience. Programming itself experienced this transition from assembly language code, which is very similar to the code that the machines input directly, to higher-level languages that more closely resemble human language and make it easier for more programmers to write. In this case, the maestros who democratized software programming were the pioneers of higher level software languages and later the "Gang of Four," who wrote patterns for object-oriented software development.

This happened again when database platforms and the SQL programming language enabled users to ask a database questions about their data in a form that resembles human language instead of programming machine level code and writing algorithms that compress, store, and retrieve data. Sometimes, as with OOP, the transition includes both an abstraction and a modularization of the technology to make it easier to manipulate. For the database, one maestro that codified this new paradigm and democratized it for the masses was Donald Chamberlain, the inventor of Structured Query Language (SQL). SQL provides a predictable way to ask a database questions without needing to interface with specialized data management algorithms.

The originators of higher level software languages and Donald Chamberlain both democratized new technologies by understanding the new paradigm well enough to codify it for the less experienced to practice. You will perform the same function for process experts when you codify their control paradigms into brain designs.

As machine teachers increase their level of teaching sophistication, they also increase their ability to shepherd learners, whether AI or human, through the stages of skill acquisition. As a brain designer, you will need to leverage more and more sophisticated brain design architectures to increase the skill acquisition potential of learning systems. Each of the brain design architectures in the next section represents a level in the skill acquisition model.

Levels of Autonomous AI Architecture

Greater levels of teaching sophistication advance learners through the levels of skill acquisition. Humans increase their potential for skill acquisition as they move through the stages. Teachers *accelerate* the skill acquisition as they scaffold the levels of teaching sophistication. Good machine teachers use the levels of teaching sophistication as templates for their brain designs. Remember, the intelligence of your autonomous AI is captured in the design. As modular brain structures progress in sophistication, the learning AI that they produce has the capability for greater and greater skill competence, as you can see in Figure 7-10.

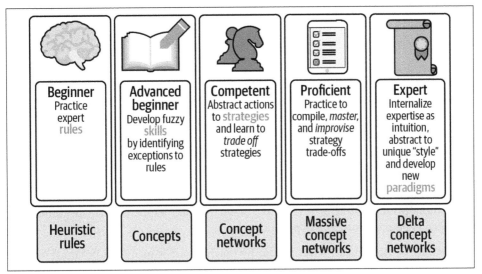

Figure 7-10. Your brain designs will progress in capability to learn and acquire skills as you move farther up the skill acquisition ladder. Each level of teaching sophistication leverages more sophisticated brain architectures.

In this section, I will map a series of brain design templates to levels of increasing teaching sophistication. The later templates open autonomous AI to move toward greater expertise because they mirror the teaching sophistication that teachers practice with humans.

Machine Learning Adds Perception

Machine learning models that perceive but do not act are the most rudimentary form of autonomous AI (see Figure 7-11). After all, they are not actually making the decisions. Even though they build extremely powerful correlations and prove very useful for decision-making, they must be paired with brain components that can actually make decisions. One famous example of a complex machine learning perception model is GPT-3 (*https://oreil.ly/nG771*) from OpenAI (*https://openai.com/*). There are plenty of nuances and limitations to this model, but this largest AI network in the world (as of this writing) has significant capability. As *Forbes* describes it, "GPT-3 can create anything that has a language structure—which means it can answer questions, write essays, summarize long texts, translate languages, take memos, and even create computer code." In fact, one online demo (*https://oreil.ly/qobGn*) shows GPT-3 using a plugin for the app-design tool Figma to create an app similar to Instagram.

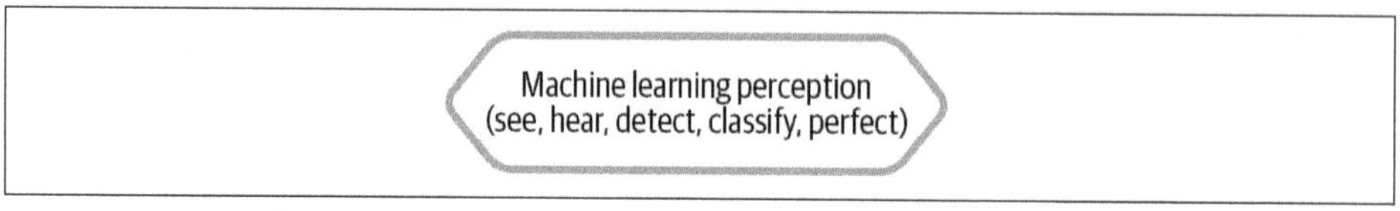

Machine learning perception
(see, hear, detect, classify, perfect)

Figure 7-11. Machine learning perception needs to be paired with decision-making capability to function as autonomous AI, but it can learn and is an important building block of autonomous AI.

Monolithic Brains Are Advanced Beginners

Now let's add decision-making. A monolithic brain comprises a single deep reinforcement learning module which practices a task and pursues reward based on feedback. This monolithic treatment of tasks is similar to what happens when beginners and advanced beginners practice expert rules.

For example, most chess players begin by playing games using the point system (see Figure 2-4 for details). In the point system a pawn is worth one point, so losing or gaining a pawn results in an exchange of a single point. A queen, on the other hand, is worth nine points. The high point value for the queen incentivizes using her with caution and intention because you don't want to send this powerful piece careening around the board at risk of losing her. The beginner is using math to make decisions in a simple but reasonably effective way. This is fine for the beginner, because the same mathematical calculations point to principles that will evolve into strategies later on. The beginner is treating the recipe like the law. She follows expert rules verbatim as prescribed to each situation. The beginner will not go beyond the rules.

The advanced beginner starts to identify exceptions to the rules and breaks the rules when it leads to success. There are some situations where it is strategically advantageous to sacrifice the queen, even though she is worth the maximum nine points in the point system. Likewise, there are other situations when particular pawns in strategic positions are worth far more than one point, like when they form edifices that block opponents or protect other pieces. The advanced beginner has integrated the rule system (manuals) into a deeper, more nuanced intuition of chess as a single monolithic skill.

Monolithic AI is an advanced beginner who is flexible and understands nuance, but treats the entire task as one huge monolith. This would be like training an AI brain to play chess using the point system as guidance (rewarding it with points based on the system) but also holding it accountable for wins and losses. With a lot of practice, the AI will pick up some of the same nuances that human advanced beginners gain as they discover exceptions to the implied rules of the point system. Until the autonomous AI or human learns different skills that apply to different situations, it will remain an advanced beginner. Table 7-3 provides examples of expert rules that beginners practice and build into skills.

Table 7-3. Expert rules that beginners practice in chess and Go

Skill	Expert rule to practice	Examples of rule exceptions
Skill	Point system	Sacrifice queen for line or position
Skill	Capture as many stones as possible	Capture fewer stones for position advantage

The Fantasy of Monolithic Black Box AI

In the US comic strip *Calvin and Hobbes,* Calvin creates a magic machine that can turn him and his friends into whatever they want. It's really a cardboard box, but hey, imagination is a truly wonderful thing. Unfortunately, some schools of thought about AI are just like this transmogrifier. Machine learning models are often nicknamed "black boxes" because it's difficult or impossible to see inside. You can't tell very much about how or why the model made each decision. This may be fine for research applications, but it's not acceptable for real applications where people's safety, valuable equipment, and products are on the line.

David Pugh, principal data scientist from Anglo American mining, said it well: "While I understand that a monolithic concept might come up with really novel strategies, the people and process concerns require decomposition."

Just as monolithic buildings and software have their place, monolithic AI has a purpose. Just understand the limitations well before using in your Autonomous AI designs. See Figure 7-12 for a diagram of monolithic AI.

Monolithic AI

Or

Figure 7-12. Monolithic AI learns all of its skills or all of its directive skills together. This approach gives a wide but unpredictable range of possible skill levels for the resulting AI (anything from beginner to competent). It also lacks explainability.

As scientifically interesting as it is to contemplate black-box AI that becomes a savant with no human intervention or expertise, not a single AI that I reference in this entire book is a monolithic agent. Not Tesla AI, not AlphaGo or AlphaChess, and certainly not many of the AI that I've designed. This is because most high-value tasks are complex enough that the most efficient way to learn them well is to learn and practice multiple skills.

Concept Networks Are Competent Learners

Most complex tasks require multiple skills and strategies to succeed. Remember *Pac-Man* and *Montezuma's Revenge* from Chapter 2? Monolithic AI struggled to learn those games by self-guided practice alone because they both require deploying different strategies for different situations. So, in order for your AI brains to make the leap from advanced beginner to competent learner, they must learn multiple skills and strategies.

> The concept network is a matrix of brain modules that each perform a unique skill and combine to the full decision-making power of the brain.

The term *concept network* is just another term for an AI brain with multiple modules. Each modular skill in the brain is a node in the concept network. The idea of a concept network was introduced in the Bonsai AI blog post "Deep Reinforcement Learning for Dexterous Manipulation with Concept Networks" (*https://oreil.ly/ Bdoi3*). The concept network is inspired by hierarchical deep reinforcement learning (*https://oreil.ly/SbLrO*) and later federated learning (*https://oreil.ly/UH5Zg*), but it doesn't have to use DRL for each of its skills and doesn't necessarily arrange its skills in a hierarchy. Concept networks learn perceptive, directive, and selective skills separately. Figure 7-13 shows an example of a concept network, though not a concept network designed for learning a particular task.

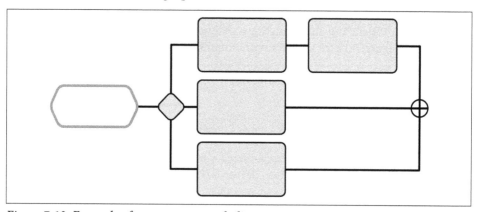

Figure 7-13. Example of a concept network diagram

Skills in a concept network can perceive or take action and they can be arranged in a hierarchy, sequenced, or executed in parallel. See "Brains Are Organized by Functions and Strategies" on page 99 for details. A concept network can include any number of nodes (skills), each of which can be performed by any decision-making technology.

A concept network represents the competent learner. The competent learner shifts away from one monolithic skill, like the point system in chess, and toward multiple strategies like chess openings. Chess openings exist because most players need a manual to help them navigate the treacherous conditions of the first few moves. There are many ways to make game-ending mistakes in the first few moves, so opening sequences provide a step-by-step guide to secure footholds to get you safely to your objective.

To achieve AI brains that are consistently, predictably competent, we must shift from a monolithic architecture to an architecture that leverages multiple skills. Each node that you design into the concept network is a unique skill that you teach explicitly. The AI will practice each skill and how to use the skills together. Concept networks push the capability of autonomous AI solidly into the competent and possibly even proficient levels of skill acquisition because they learn, practice, and use skills separately.

Massive Concept Networks Are Proficient Learners

As learners transition from the competent level of skill acquisition, where they first understand and use a strategy to perform a task, and the proficient level, where they acquire many more strategies, the *learner practices a huge number of skills*. So, in order to transition from generally competent concept networks to generally proficient concept networks, the number of skills in the network must significantly increase.

There is no known definition for how large a concept network needs to be before it moves into the realm of potential proficiency for a task. Instead of using the number of nodes as a criterion, compare the ratio of the number of nodes in the network to the number of known skills for a task. The number of known skills (for a well-explored task landscape) is a proxy for the overall complexity of the task; therefore, the percentage of those known skills that the AI has acquired is a good indicator of how likely that AI is to become proficient at the task.

As discussed earlier, there are 12 typical opening sequences in chess. A concept network with nodes that teach 3 out of those 12 strategies learns 25% percent of the known strategies, but a chess AI that learns 9 learns 75% of the known strategies. In contrast, there are many more known strategies for the chess endgame (around 80), so a concept network of similar size (10 nodes) is now only learning an eighth of the known strategies. What matters is not how many nodes are in the concept network, but what percentage of the known strategies the concept network is teaching.

There is, of course, an argument that the skill acquisition percentage is not complete because there are still parts of the chess space that are unexplored. Acquire the known skills explicitly and explore the rest. Figure 7-14 provides a hypothetical example of a massive concept network that learns many skills.

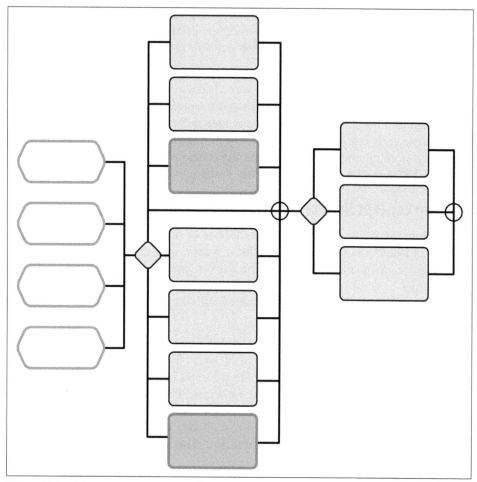

Figure 7-14. Massive concept networks imitate proficient learners by amassing large numbers of skills and learning how to navigate between them effectively while performing tasks. This diagram is just an example of a concept network, not a concept network designed for learning a particular task.

Pursuing Expert Skill Acquisition in Autonomous AI

The human brain contains three major sections divided into nine major regions. Each of these regions have distinct functions and capabilities. I don't claim expertise on human neurology, but based on my research on machine teaching and autonomous AI (much of which I have presented in this book), it stands to reason that expert skill acquisition will require modular AI where each module performs a unique and purposeful function.

In the next sections, I present four advanced machine teaching techniques and architectures you can use to pursue expert skill acquisition in your autonomous AI:

- Brains that come with hardwired skills
- Brains that define skills as they learn
- Brains that assemble themselves
- Brains with skills that coordinate

Brains That Come with Hardwired Skills

What if we build a library of hardwired skills as a base of skill acquisition for specific tasks? Animals are born with instincts and humans seem to display hardwired skills and tendencies (*https://oreil.ly/2abAu*). Hardwired skills are like instincts to an AI brain. Think of this like the firmware installed directly on computer chips before the operating system is installed.

Some skills are reusable across many tasks, so this may help us generalize intelligent behavior across tasks. Imagine the skill of selecting which strategy to apply. I've given many examples of strategy selection in games and real-life industrial problems. Can we build a selector that learns how to select strategies in multiple games?

If we can describe scenarios in terms of characteristics that they share, then we can learn and prescribe similar strategies for similar scenarios, even across tasks. Remember, scenarios break up problem spaces into regions where they operate well. The first step is to provide some useful metadescriptions of problem space regions.

So, what is a metadescription of a problem space region? Metadescriptions cut across individuals to comprise a category or cluster of similar things. For example, drones are small aircraft with more than two rotors. They are not planes because their spinning rotors produce lift, not wings. They are not helicopters either because they are smaller and have more than two rotors.

Problem space regions are the mathematical shapes that describe scenarios. Remember the three phases of a chess game (opening, mid-game, and end-game)? Well, underneath those scenarios lie math that describes what it's like to make decisions in those phases. The pictures of landmasses that I drew in Chapter 4 are visual representations of problem space regions. Metadescriptions of problem space regions describe clusters of similar problem spaces.

For example, some problem space regions are easy to explore. Others have easily recognizable terrain that maps to known mathematical relationships, like the ideal gas law that we discussed in Chapter 1. Some problem space regions are unexplored. Others are treacherous (like chess openings), unpredictable, and hard to navigate. A selector that learns to select strategies across different task environments needs to know something about the properties of the problem space regions where the strategies will be applied. Table 7-4 shows some example problem space regions and their metadescriptions.

Table 7-4. Metadescriptions of problem space regions

Metadescription	Problem space characteristics	Example problem space
Explorable	Problem spaces within a task where trial and error is relatively low risk and unconstrained exploration leads to good results.	*HVAC control*: Exploration for how to control heaters and air conditioners is relatively cheap and risk-free. What's the worst that could happen?
Calculated	Problem spaces where there is a known mathematical model that leads to good decision-making in the space.	*Robot joint control and drone rotor control*: Mathematics describes the relationship between servo actions on the joints and robot positions for robots well. The same is true for the relationship between drone rotor control and drone position.
Treacherous	Problem spaces where trial and error is risky because there are many ways to lose. This may also include situations where exploration is unsafe.	*Chess opening*: Trial and error is risky because there are many ways to lose a chess game early. This is why chess opening sequences are so prescriptive.
Unknown	Problem spaces where we don't know the terrain because they are unexplored.	*Controlling a nuclear fusion reactor*: No one knows how to control a fusion reactor yet. The problem space is unknown.

These metadescriptions not only provide clues for which strategy to select but also give us a great idea of which decision-making technique to use to make decisions in that space.

Once we have these metadescriptions, we can train a selector to select strategies across very different tasks based on the metadescriptions of the subdivisions where the skills will operate. So a selector might learn how to select strategies for chess, Go, baggage handling, and chemical manufacturing. This works because each of those tasks have scenarios that can be described with the same metadescription.

As concept networks become larger and larger to pursue further potential expertise, this may be the only reasonable way to continue along the path.

Brains That Define Skills as They Learn

A concept network provides multiple skills for the selector to choose from to make the next decision. But what if the defined set of strategies does not provide all the skills the AI needs to succeed? Back to the game of chess. We know that AlphaGo discovered the 12 most common opening sequences in chess, which shows us that those 12 opening sequences cover much of the decision-making territory of the chess opening. But that doesn't mean that there are no more chess strategies to discover.

Imagine a concept network with a selector that chooses which strategy to assign control. What if the selector doesn't find any of the strategies in the concept network to be good matches for the scenario? That's where brains that define skills as they learn come into play. If we give decision-making power to the supervisor selective skill, it can (1) assign decision-making control to lower-level skills, (2) decide if none of the existing skills will execute the next decision well, and (3) learn what to do if none of the existing skills will work.

This special selective skill *defines and practices a new catch-all skill as it learns*. Let's give it a special brain design diagram symbol, the chevron. You can think of this skill as a hands-on supervisor (see Figure 7-15). This is like a supervisor who assigns work but also jumps in to help make lower-level decisions when the workers need a little help.

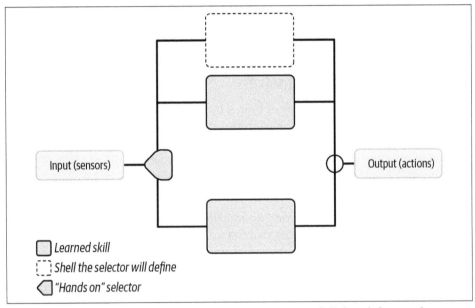

Figure 7-15. Concept network with a hands-on supervisor skill that defines and practices a new skill as it learns.

Here's how to use this architecture pattern in a brain:

1. Create a concept network with one directive skill for each known strategy that you will teach.

2. Create one extra directive skill to hold an undefined strategy that the brain will discover as it learns. This skill has a dotted outline in Figure 7-17.

3. Create a learned selector to supervise the directive skills as part of a hierarchy.

4. The selector will control the decision about which strategy to assign control; if it doesn't find any of the defined strategies a good match for a scenario, it will choose an option that represents the alternate strategy and also select the lower-level actions itself.

This brain architecture uses the selective skill to learn which strategy to leverage from the strategies you already know about *and* to define a new strategy as it learns. The more strategies you teach, the more specific and effective this catch-all skill will be. For example, I worked with trading experts to design a brain that makes financial trades for a commodity. I used this architecture pattern in that brain design. There were hundreds of known strategies. If you teach the concept network all known strategies, the hands-on selector will learn a very specific strategy that covers the decision-making space that you don't know how to navigate. But, if you teach the concept network only 10 of the known strategies, the hands-on selector will have to learn a bunch of strategies that you already know *and* figure out which parts of the decision making space you don't know how to navigate. If you combine the idea of pretrained skills with brains that define skills as they learn, we can imagine brains that assemble themselves.

Brains That Assemble Themselves

Now I'd like to take this concept of brains that define skills as they learn one step further. It is possible that once the concept network becomes large enough, the best way to manage hundreds or even thousands of skills is to select which skills should be loaded from the skills library and leverage different *sets of skills* at different times. This might be analogous to how the brain assembles groups of neurons between thought processes.

Well, why can't skills in our AI brain do something similar? We can envision another skill type called the *assembler* that determines which skills should be in play for a particular decision. At various points in the decision-making process, the assembler picks the skills that will be used to make a decision, much like the human brain assembles the neurons to activate before it enters each thought process. I discussed this in the intro to Part II.

To represent the assembler, we pick an upward pointing triangle that usually represents extraction or storage of raw materials in workflow diagramming, as shown in Figure 7-16.

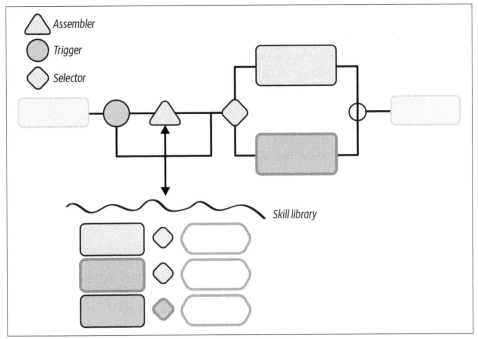

Figure 7-16. A concept network with an assembler that decides which skills to extract from a library; a trigger programs the conditions that call the assembler to extract new skills; once the assembler extracts skills, those skills are used for decision-making in the brain until the assembler extracts the next set of skills.

Brains with Skills That Coordinate

Sometimes, skills need to coordinate with each other to make decisions well. Think about a soccer team. It's possible to envision an AI brain taught to play soccer that divides the playing field into regions and asks each skill to cover a region. We could also architect a brain that divides playing soccer into skills like passing, shooting, and dribbling but oversees all of the skills. But at the end of the day, soccer is a game played by 11 players with a mind of their own that need to work together.

That's where specialized reinforcement learning algorithms come into play to enable *multi-agent reinforcement learning*. Multi-agent reinforcement learning (*https:// oreil.ly/r7Mwy*) is the study of numerous artificial intelligence agents cohabitating in an environment, often collaborating toward some end goal. When focusing on collaboration, it derives inspiration from other social structures in the animal kingdom. It also draws heavily on game theory.

I have seen multi-agent architectures suggested for lots of tasks that don't actually require coordination between skills that each have a mind of their own. Most industrial applications require oversight from one well-designed brain. A good question to ask when considering multi-agent architectures is: *do the skills in this brain really require a mind of their own?*

Now that I have explained the levels of teaching sophistication and matched those levels to modular brain architectures, I will give you a framework for architecting autonomous AI: first identify the skills that you want to teach, orchestrate how the skills work together, and then choose a decision-making technique to perform each skill.

Steps to Architect an AI Brain

Architecting an AI brain is like snapping together Lego blocks. Rarely will you invent a new decision-making technique, but if you snap existing techniques together as skills in a brain, you will likely devise a novel and effective AI. You might even invent a new AI paradigm by combining techniques in interesting ways.

Step 1: Identify the Skills That You Want to Teach

The first step to architect an AI brain is to identify the skills that you want to teach. Whether the skills perform *perception* like vision or classification, *action, supervision* (such as with a selector), *hands-on selection* or even *assembly*, I always name and label each module in my AI brain as a skill.

If you think in terms of diagramming an AI brain design on a whiteboard, this first step is about figuring out which skills to put on the board. We're not worried about how the skills relate to each other or which technology to use to perform the skills yet.

Remember, *the more skills required to complete the task that you explicitly teach your AI brain, the faster your brain will learn to succeed* (sometimes exponentially faster). You explicitly teach skills by including them as modules in your AI brain design.

To ensure that you have a complete inventory of skills, complete an interview with a subject matter expert. That's the best way to understand what we already know about performing the task. Remember, *the fewer skills required for the task that you include in your AI brain, the exponentially longer it will take your brain to learn to succeed.*

I like to interview people who get paid to perform this task for a living. Fill out this heuristics table to list and organize all of the known skills for performing the task. Table 7-5 provides an example of a skill arranged in the three column table format. The first column is for the scenario. It describes conditions where the skill should be used. The second column explains the meaning of the scenario. The third column contains the expert rule, abbreviated as an action. This is the skill to consider adding to your brain design.

Table 7-5. Heuristics table to fill out with skills from your subject matter interview

When the environment looks like this	It means that this is happening	Do this
Commonly used perishable goods arrive in the warehouse.	These goods will likely be required by many trucks arriving to pick up orders.	Distribute these goods throughout the warehouse so that order pickers can retrieve them quickly from many locations in the warehouse.

You will likely end up with more heuristics in this table than strategies you will want to teach your brain. That is OK. Here's a quick procedure and checklist for narrowing down the number of skills that you want to design into your brain as separate modules:

1. Look for duplicate strategies or strategies that you can merge together.

2. Eliminate strategies that apply to scenarios outside the purview of the brain.

3. Eliminate functional skills that take actions that the system cannot accept from the brain.

Some skills that you surface in the heuristics table cover scenarios that are outside the purview of the brain. AI brains that you design will not be all-seeing and omnipotent. Save that thought for your love of science fiction movies. Each brain will have a defined scope of influence that you and the subject matter experts you work with decide will provide the best return on investment (ROI) for building the AI.

Sometimes skills that you identify for your brain take actions that the real system can't accept. Other times systems don't provide the information that skills need to succeed. One of my colleagues designed a brain for a mining process. The human operators performed one of the skills by manually turning a valve, and the valve didn't report back how much liquid was flowing through it. If we can't tell the brain the information it needs to take an action, it can't learn. So, my colleague removed this skill from the brain. See Chapter 8 for details on giving your AI brain the information it needs to make good decisions.

After you whittle down the skills that you want to teach, you should have a core set of skills that you will design into your brain. If the skill is a perceptive skill, include a perception concept module in your brain design to perform this skill. If the skill takes action, include a directive concept module in your brain design to perform the skill.

Step 2: Orchestrate How the Skills Work Together

After you identify the skills and strategies that you want to teach, you need to wire them together. Determine how the skills relate to each other and document that relationship in the brain design.

I call this phase of brain design "drawing the lines on the page" because from the perspective of drawing a brain design diagram using our visual language, it's the lines that describe how the skills work together. For a refresher on how to organize skills using functional skills and strategies, see Chapter 4. Here are a few questions to guide your thinking:

- Are there any skills that should be performed in a sequence?
- For skills that should be used in sequence, is the sequence fixed or variable?
- Are there any skills that can or should be performed in parallel?
- Are there strategies that should be arranged in a hierarchy?

Step 3: Select Which Technology Should Perform Each Skill

Now it's finally time to determine which technology to use to perform each skill. This is the phase of machine teaching where we map the skills in our brain to the best decision-making technology to make that decision. In this phase, we use our understanding of the strengths and weaknesses of math, menus, manuals, machine learning, and any other decision-making technology. See Chapter 1 for a refresher on the difference between math, menus, manuals, machine learning, and DRL.

In your diagram, use color to map each skill in your AI brain to a suitable decision-making technology.

Now I want to point out some pitfalls to avoid while teaching skills and describe what happens if you jump the gun and lead with technology selection before identifying and orchestrating the skills for your AI brain.

Pitfalls to Avoid When Teaching Skills

Some of us, me included, love thinking about technology. So, it's tempting to jump straight into discussion about which technology is best to use in our AI brain. This tendency is so strong that sometimes people associate whole classes of problems with a particular decision-making technology. You may hear "Logistics problems are optimization problems" or "Robotics is an inverse kinematics problem." Machine teaching freely mixes math, menus, manuals, and ML in modular AI that controls and optimizes better than any of them on their own. For the best autonomous AI, avoid these pitfalls as you teach skills.

Pitfall 1: Confusing the solution for the problem

The first pitfall is coupling the two so tightly that you forget there may be other ways to solve the same problem. Attributing solutions for problem types to a specific technology may result in missing key opportunities to design a superior solution with a brain.

This is what is happening when people say that logistics problems are optimization problems. While it's true that logistics problems are large spaces, optimization algorithms are great at exploring. These landscapes also require separate strategies that optimization algorithms don't recognize. Machine teaching to the rescue! It doesn't mind mixing optimization, DRL for strategies, and ML for perception.

Avoid this pitfall by starting with the engineering process instead of the decision-making technology. Let the problem and the process guide your technology decision. You can design a superior brain by designing with the right modular components.

Pitfall 2: Losing the forest for the trees

If you focus too much on one component, you can lose your big-picture view. I've entered many brain design endeavors to find stakeholders laser focused on one part of the problem to the neglect of the whole task.

Often skills and trade-offs don't reveal themselves until you see the whole end-to-end process. To avoid this pitfall, it is critical to examine the whole process before decomposing subcomponent modules and selecting decision-making technologies.

Example of Teaching Skills to an AI Brain: Rubber Factory

One of the students in my brain design class, Andrii Antilikatorov, designed the brain shown in Figure 7-17 as his final assignment. It's a great example of using the machine teaching framework to design a brain.

He designed this AI brain for a project that he worked on at a rubber factory. The task was to decide what to do when alarms sound in the factory. These alarms are split into three categories. The first is the safety-critical category, meaning it's important for the safety of everyone in the plant to do the exact right thing in response. This category can be built using simple mathematical calculations and statistics. The second category is not safety critical but still easy to calculate. Math describes what to do quite well. The third is also not safety critical but more nuanced and difficult to calculate.

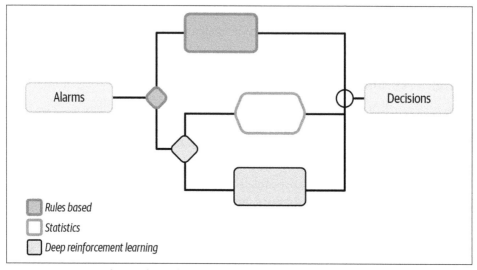

Figure 7-17. Brain design that takes action on alarms in a rubber manufacturing plant

In his brain design, he decided to place a selector (a rules-based selector first) to separate the safety-critical alarms from the rest. This was a great choice—no need for advanced machine learning to decide which alarms are safety critical when we already have a quantitative list of what conditions are unsafe. The rule-based selector routes safety-critical alarms to expert rules. Manuals are a perfect choice. Expert rules can codify exactly what to do in each safety critical situation. For the alerts that are not safety critical, he used a learned selector to determine which alerts can be handled with statistics and which require more humanlike decision-making. This is a good brain design choice as well because it's hard to determine which alerts belong in the second category and which alerts belong in the third category. The boundary between them is fuzzy. He uses a statistics or machine learning module to make decisions for the second category and deep reinforcement learning to make decisions for the third category.

Machine learning is not deterministic, which means it might not give you the same answer every time. This is the exact opposite of what we want for safety-critical situations. We also don't want the brain exploring and trying different things when it's trying to handle safety-critical alarms. The opposite is true for the third category of alarms. We don't have experience that tells us how to handle each of these alarms that require nuanced decision-making, and even if we did, we'd have to program many many rules into an expert system to make it happen. It's possible to use optimization to search for what might work best for this third category of alarms, but if perception is required then this might not work well either.

Brain Design for Our Smart Thermostat

Now let's put everything we've learned about the machine teaching framework together into a brain design for our smart thermostat. First, I'll list the skills that I want the brain to perform (Table 7-6), then I'll draw a diagram that describes options for how to arrange the skills in the brain (Figure 7-18).

Table 7-6. *List of skills for smart thermostat*

Skill type	Skill description	Description
Perceptive	*Predict* outdoor air temperature based on hour of day, month of year, cloud cover and wind conditions.	This skill predicts the temperature.
Perceptive	*Perceive* the number of unique people in the home.	This skill uses computer vision to determine how many people are in the house. If 0, no HVAC is needed (unless the brain decides to anticipate arrivals), if greater than 0, the more people, the more cooling required.
Perceptive	*Predict* the arrival time of additional occupants.	This skill controls the system based on what's happening right now.
Directive	*Anticipate* demand.	This skill anticipates periods of high HVAC demand and high energy cost and precools or preheats the house in response.
Directive	*Control* the system.	This skill controls the system based on what's happening right now.
Selective	*Select* a cooling strategy.	This skills decides whether to anticipate or to control current conditions.

This is just one of many possible brain designs that I could have created. Can you think of any modifications that you might make to this brain design?

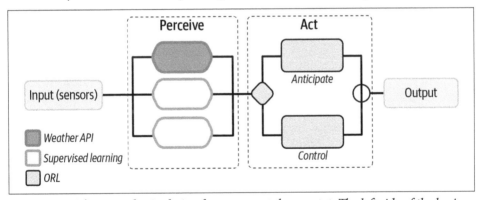

Figure 7-18. *This is my brain design for our smart thermostat. The left side of the brain perceives what is happening in the house and with the weather, the right side of the brain controls the system.*

Let me explain my logic and assumptions. It's really important to be able to clearly articulate the design choices that you've made for your autonomous AI. Brain designs often change during reviews with process experts and always change during brain implementation. Don't be afraid to create multiple designs for your clients to discuss and choose from.

First I decided which skills I wanted to use in my brain. I've designed quite a few brains for HVAC systems and interviewed a lot of experts. That helps. I know that the volume of HVAC heating or cooling output is determined far more by the outside air temperature and sunlight shining in the windows than by the price of energy and the number of people in the building.

It's important to know how many people are in the house at any given time. I'll need some machine learning for this. The brain could perceive this from a camera, or perhaps predict occupancy from historical patterns. Predicting outdoor air temperature is also important. There are many weather services that my AI can call to get this information.

When the price of energy is high, one common strategy is called peak shifting or peak shaving. Nobody wants to pay full price for energy when it's most expensive. I'd rather heat or cool when the price of energy is less expensive. That's how I formulated the anticipate strategy. When I don't need to anticipate, I can control for what's happening right now.

I designed in a learned selector that uses DRL to decide whether to anticipate or not. It's fuzzy, and this concept will need to consider the weather and occupancy predictions to select well. This selector determines which directive concept will control the system at any given time.

In case you were wondering, this is an original brain design even among other autonomous AI that I've designed to control HVAC systems.

CHAPTER 8

Giving Your AI Brain the Information It Needs to Learn and Decide

Reality is complex and nuanced.

Most of the systems and processes for which you will design autonomous AI are like complex three-dimensional objects. Imagine you're trying to explore the surface of a Picasso sculpture (*https://oreil.ly/4ZsCw*). The surface is asymmetrical and irregular, so to truly understand it, you're going to have to look at it from different angles.

The same is true for decision-making. Humans and autonomous AI need to look at each process they optimize or system they control from a variety of perspectives. They try different scenarios and consider different variables during their practice. When designing autonomous AI, consider what information the AI will need to make decisions well under lots of different conditions. I like to start by considering what information I would need to make the same decision. If I don't know, I ask experts.

Most AI that you design will learn by practicing in a virtual environment. This allows the AI to learn without experiencing the financial and safety consequences of trial and error on the real system. Virtual environments also usually significantly accelerate (sometimes by orders of magnitude) the training by allowing much more practice in the same amount of time.

Simulations are the virtual environments that provide the training gym where your AI will practice. They are the digital version of sensors that measure what's happening in the real system. As a machine teacher, you will need to consider which scenarios to simulate and which information from the simulation to show the AI during training.

Sensors: The Five Senses for Your AI Brain

Sensors take measurements of the world around us. They serve as senses for your AI brain, providing the feedback from which it learns and reports the results of its actions, step by step. Sensors report data to AI brains using variables and trends.

Variables

Variables are individual streams of data from the sensors. Each variable represents one piece of information that your AI brain needs to learn and make decisions. Table 8-1 shows some examples of variables from the AI brains that I have presented so far.

Table 8-1. Examples of sensor variables from AI brains

Autonomous AI	Sensor	Purpose
Robotic arm control	Position of each joint	The position of each joint combines to form the pose of the robot.
Robotic arm control	Velocity of each joint	You need to know how fast each joint is moving to know when it might reach a destination.
Robotic arm control	Acceleration of each joint	This is important for force and inertia calculations.
Chess	Position of each piece on the board	The state of the game is based on the position of each piece on the board.
Drone control	Pitch of the drone	This tells us how much the drone is tilted side to side.
Drone control	Yaw of the drone	This tells us how much the drone is tilted up and down.
Drone control	Roll of the drone	This tells us how much the drone is tilted front to back.
Rock crusher	Speed of the conveyor	This determines how much rock is entering the crusher.
Rock crusher	Position of the mantle	This determines part of the crusher behavior.
Rock crusher	Thickness of the lining	This changes over time and determines how the rocks respond in the crusher.
Baggage handling	Destination gate for each bag	This tells you where each bag needs to go.
Baggage handling	Departure time for each bag	This tells you when each bag needs to be at its gate.
Baggage handling	Number of bags in the conveyor system	This tells you how full this transportation method is.
Baggage handling	Number of bags in the cart system	This tells you how full this transportation method is.

For each skill that you design into your brain, you will need to determine which variables you need to report to that skill so that it can learn. There are two basic types of variables: discrete variables and continuous variables. I also want to discuss derivatives as a special kind of variable.

Discrete variables

Discrete variables are like integers or categories. They have specific values that represent specific things, and they don't blend into each other.

Continuous variables

Continuous variables cover an entire range. There are no gaps between continuous variables. They're like a gradient.

Derivatives

Derivatives are special variables that tell you the direction that other variables are headed. Derivatives measure trends and track inflection points and the trajectory of variables. For example, velocity is a derivative of position. It tells you how much the position of an object is changing. Acceleration is a derivative of velocity. It tells you how much you're speeding up or slowing down. Make sure to pass derivatives to your skills when they need to understand the trends of other variables in order to control the system well.

Proxy Variables

Sometimes you can't measure important variables, but you can measure other variables that give you clues because they're related. These related variables are called soft sensors or proxy variables. Let me give you an example.

I worked on a brain design to help control a Formula 1 racing engine. An internal combustion engine has about 10,000 parts. The racing team that I was working with figured out that there are about 20 crucial parts that determined whether they would win a race or not. If you could minimize the failure of those 20 parts, you're much more likely to win the race. The goal of the AI was to control 8 other parts that minimize the failure of these 20 important parts.

Part failure is a tricky thing. Whether you're talking about Formula 1 engine parts, machine components on an assembly line, or parts of a robot, failure doesn't happen often, so it's hard to learn about it enough to prevent it. There's a whole branch of applied machine learning called predictive maintenance which tries to use data from the past to predict failure. The problem is failure happens so infrequently that there's hardly enough data to use to predict it.

So we turned to proxy variables to help. Stress and strain are proxies for failure. Stress measures the internal forces of the material and strain measures the deformation or bending of a material under stress. Sensors can measure stress and strain in real time, while it's impossible to measure failure in real time. It just happens all of a sudden. So we included stress and strain as sensor measurements to pass to the skills in this AI brain to help it learn how to prevent failure.

Trends

Trends are important for designing autonomous AI too. Derivatives describe trends. Ask the experts what trends they monitor to make decisions and make sure to include those trends as information you pass to the skills in your brain.

Simulators: A Gym for Your Autonomous AI to Practice In

When I was in college, I spent hours in practice rooms playing my saxophone. These are small cement rooms with metal doors. Saxophone players like to stand in the corner so that they can hear the sound reflected back to them as they play. Musicians repeat exercises over and over again until they can get it right, both sound and technique, at various speeds.

Simulators are like the practice rooms for autonomous AI or gyms where they can work out. In fact, there's a famous software interface built by OpenAI called OpenAI Gym, which is exactly what it sounds like: virtual environments for autonomous AI to practice specific tasks.

Figure 8-1. Microsoft Flight Simulator.

Every autonomous AI needs a place to practice (and get feedback).

Practicing in virtual environments like simulations has some critical benefits. The first is that it makes practice safe. Trial and error can be really dangerous and expensive for some tasks. Imagine learning how to control a steel mill by trial and error. Simulation also speeds up practice significantly. One reason for this is that simulations can literally speed up time in their virtual environments. So an hour of real time can be just a fraction of that amount of time in simulation. Powerful computers and cloud computing allow practicing on multiple environments at the same time. This is very similar to what happens when chess players play multiple opponents at the same time. In the same way, autonomous AI can practice controlling many simulations simultaneously on the cloud.

One of the issues that I'm really interested in tackling with autonomous AI is the issue of climate change. I truly believe that autonomous AI can help make decisions that will mitigate the influence of climate change and prompt better climate policy. As I was looking into this area, I realized that I needed a simulator to model the effects of climate change actions. I came across Climate Interactive's climate action simulations (*https://oreil.ly/sM6Zl*), and the En-ROADS simulation in particular (*https://oreil.ly/kXM4K*) caught my eye. Simulation models the effect of climate change policy decisions on the temperature of the Earth. Using a simulation like this, it would be possible to design an autonomous AI that could recommend climate change policy decisions.

This simulation was designed to run what-if scenarios, which brings me to an important point about simulation. Many simulations were not created for AI to practice making decisions. One major exception is simulations that were created for humans to practice on. These tend to be great environments for AI to practice in with very few changes. Most simulations were not created for humans to practice on. They were created to model systems during the design process, or they were created for running what if scenarios. Here's a list of important criteria to make sure that you can use a simulation to train autonomous AI:

Can computers connect to the simulation?
> For AI to practice on the simulation, it needs to be able to connect to it programmatically to exchange information. Usually this means a simulation needs to have an API for exchanging messages.

Can an AI tell the simulation what it wants to do?
> Simulations run entire scenarios with preprogrammed actions. For autonomous AI to learn, it needs to be able to tell the simulation what action it wants to take and then receive a response back from the simulation about what will happen as a consequence of its actions. So, your simulation needs to be able to accept actions and pass back sensor variables at every time step or decision.

Can the simulation tell you what will happen in a reasonable amount of time?

After you give it an action that you want to take, some simulations can respond with the consequences of that action, the sensor variables, in a fraction of a second. Some simulations are actually slower than real time. For example, compressible fluid dynamics (CFD) simulations might take an hour or even a day to simulate a second of real time. It takes millions of practice decisions for autonomous AI to learn a skill. Consider the amount of time that it will take your simulation to respond to millions of decisions in practice. Ideally, this should be able to happen in a few hours. This means that if it takes much more than a minute to respond to an individual action with the state of the system, training with this simulation is probably not feasible.

Can you run multiple copies of the simulation on a computer?

More practice can occur, and more experience can be gained, if your AI can practice in parallel. It's possible for autonomous AI to gain years or even decades of experience in hours or days with the right simulation on the right amount of simulations in parallel. For example, I helped one client run 5,000 copies of their simulation in parallel on the cloud during training. To run simulations in parallel, you need to be able to run multiple simulations on the same computer. This could happen in the cloud or on a local machine. One convenient way to do this is in containers.

Does the simulation accurately represent reality?

This is a nuanced and controversial topic. Autonomous AI doesn't need perfect accuracy to learn. In fact, if the accuracy of a simulation is perfect, the autonomous AI might memorize how to control that specific system and miss the opportunity to acquire the skill. What you actually want is directional accuracy. If you make a decision, do the sensor variables move in the correct direction? Is the value of each of the sensor variables reasonable? Remember when an autonomous AI practices to learn a task, especially at the beginning, it doesn't know anything about what it's doing. Only after significant practice, as it gains competence at the skill, does significant accuracy matter. There's a rule of thumb that I like to follow: if the simulation is good enough to model and validate actions from a control system in the real environment, then it's good enough for AI to practice on.

Now I want to talk about the ways that simulation can be used to model reality. There are three basic ways to simulate reality so that Autonomous AI can get feedback as it practices. The first is physics and chemistry, the second is statistics and events, and the third is machine learning. I also want to discuss simulating reality using expert rules. Just like automated decision-making capabilities, each method of simulation has its strengths and weaknesses.

Simulating Reality Using Physics and Chemistry

The most accurate way to simulate reality during your AI practice is science. Usually this boils down to physics and chemistry that describe how the system will react to control actions. While this method is very accurate, it is also time consuming to create the simulations and to run the simulations. This also assumes that you have a good mathematical model for how the system will respond to decisions. Use physics and chemistry when you have a good mathematical model and when you need very accurate responses.

Simulating Reality Using Statistics and Events

Some systems are best modeled with statistics and events. Logistics is a good example. Logistics is about moving goods from one place to another—generally, from the people who make them to the people who buy them. Understanding and managing logistics involves computing the statistical likelihood that events will take place. What are the chances that a truck will arrive on time? What are the chances that a traffic accident will extend the transportation time on a route? What are the chances that a ship will arrive in port at the scheduled time? These kinds of simulations are called *discrete event simulations*. Use discrete event simulations when you need to model events and the statistical likelihood that events will take place.

Simulating Reality Using Machine Learning

Machine learning can be used to simulate reality too. Machine learning is really good at building correlations between variables. Machine learning simulation is attractive when you have a lot of data from the past and when it's difficult to model the system based on science. You might not understand the mathematical relationships well or simulation using physics and chemistry might just be too slow. I've worked with many clients who started with a physics- or chemistry-based simulation but realized that it was too slow for training autonomous AI or that they didn't have all they science they needed to build that kind of simulation.

The problem with simulating reality using machine learning is that in your historical data you only have information about the states that result from the actions that you always take. If you want your AI brain to explore and come up with new solutions and new ways to control the system, you need to understand how the system will respond to actions you don't have any data for. There are two ways to address this, and both involve getting data for actions that you don't normally take.

One method is to do a design of experiments, or a state space sweep. This means turning on the system and taking random actions on real equipment to see what will happen. Use this method in situations where it's safe and not too costly to take these random actions. If it is too expensive or not safe to perform a design of experiments, then you should pair up a subject matter expert with a data scientist to create synthetic data. Together they will make educated guesses about what will happen in different areas of the problem space and add synthetic data that describes these educated guesses. The subject matter expert uses their experience to predict with some degree of accuracy what will happen in the system, and the data scientist adds the synthetic data.

It is also possible to take a hybrid approach between simulating reality, using physics and chemistry, and machine learning. If you have an accurate but slow simulation, you can extract the data from that simulation and use it to build a multivariate machine learning model. In this case, you get the best of both worlds: the accuracy of a physics-based simulation with the speed of a machine learning simulation.

Simulating Reality Using Expert Rules

There is one last way that I have seen people simulate their systems for autonomous AI to practice on. Sometimes the subject matter experts have so much experience with the system that they can use expert rules to describe how the system will respond. These expert rules can be combined into a simulation. They also can be combined with machine learning and with physics and chemistry to create a good model of reality.

This is not meant to be a complete primer on simulation. There are lots of places that you can go to learn about simulation, simulation platforms, simulation vendors, and how to build simulations. My intention here is to teach you what you need to know to evaluate simulations so that you can determine whether you have what you need to train the autonomous AI that you are designing.

Sensor Variables for Smart Thermostat

Let's list the sensor variables that our smart thermostat will use to make decisions:

- Temperature setpoint (determined by users)
- Current outdoor air temperature
- Outdoor air temperature forecast (this is an output of the predict skill)
- Energy price
- Future energy price
- Home occupancy (this is an output of the perceive skill)

Teaching machines requires solid understanding of the learning process and a framework to apply learning constructs to technology. Our machine teaching framework has provided just that. First, determine what actions your autonomous AI will take. Next, set goals and objectives for your AI. Teach skills explicitly to your AI by defining skills, orchestrating how the skills relate to each other, and selecting which techniques will perform each skill. Finally, provide the AI the information that it needs to make its decisions.

Now that we've discussed machine teaching in detail, let me provide you with some tools to help you.

PART IV

Tools for the Machine Teacher

Every trade has its own set of tools for getting the job done, and I want to provide you with some tools that have been helpful for me as I've designed autonomous AI. I created an AI specification document that I've used to document hundreds of AI brains that I've designed and that I teach machine teachers to use as they design their autonomous AI.

I created this document to better organize and communicate all the information that I was getting from the subject matter experts and pass it on to the people who were going to build the AI that I designed.

The second tool that I want to give you is a platform for building the autonomous AI that you design. There are so few AI experts in the world that can build autonomous AI from scratch that it's important to have a platform that subject matter experts, and engineers like myself, can use to build the autonomous AI that you design. Platform is also really important for combining the various decision-making technologies that you'll use in most of your brain designs. But first, I want to discuss how designing and building autonomous AI are fundamentally different activities.

- Chapter 9, "Designing AI Brains That Someone Can Actually Build"

Designing AI Brains That Someone Can Actually Build

My first two summer internships in college, I worked for Ford Motor Company. The first summer, I worked as a manufacturing engineer with two MIT graduate students to figure out how to manufacture a newly invented air-conditioning compressor. We reduced the time to create a prototype compressor housing from 6 weeks for a sand-cast part to 45 minutes to send the manufacturing instructions over the phone line directly to the CNC machine which would cut it.

The second summer, I worked on the same product from the design side. I worked with University of Michigan acoustics professors to suggest design changes to reduce the noise vibration harshness of the compressor. While at Ford, I witnessed firsthand the natural and healthy tension between designers and builders.

Designers and Builders Working Together in Harmony (Mostly)

Both summers at Ford I attended many meetings where designers and builders interacted. Design engineers designed the parts and manufacturing engineers were responsible for making the parts. Design engineers were typically younger college graduates in mechanical engineering. The manufacturing engineers varied. They tended to be more experienced and some of them got their engineering education with that experience in the manufacturing plants.

In most meetings there was a conversation that sounded a lot like this. The design engineer makes a presentation and says, "This is what I want to build." The manufacturing engineer responds by saying, "No way, we're not building that," and then the manufacturing engineer lists the reasons why the design is too difficult or costly to build. There's a healthy tension here. The design engineer is pushing for the best-performing design, but the manufacturing engineer needs to worry about how much it costs to build that design and how long the part will last.

This same thing happens with autonomous AI.

Some machine teachers focus on brain design. Other machine teachers focus on teaching AI how to perform its skills, which is equivalent to building autonomous AI. Designers and builders have different concerns. Like the designers I met at Ford, brain designers are focused on designing high-performing autonomous AI. The machine teachers who build brains have a different concern. They want to make sure that the brain designs can actually be built within the time and budget allotted to the project.

Just like there's always a tradeoff between brain goals and objectives, there's always a tradeoff between brain design and brain implementation. Sometimes the brain design is more of the focus for a project. This would be like a famous architect designing a fancy, important building. The implementation is important, but what's more important for this building is the award-winning design. In other projects, implementation is more important. Here you can imagine a community of tract homes: sure, there's a quality design, but what's important here is building each home to specification and within budget. Learn how to navigate this tradeoff for the AI brains you design and build.

My wife and I bought a house in 2020. It was an older house and we decided to remove walls and make significant changes. We hired a designer to sketch out the design changes and we hired a contractor to build the design. The contractor and the designer were different people with very different skill sets. The same thing is true for AI brain designs. Those who design brains and the people who build AI brains are often different people and that's OK. Machine teachers who design AI brains just need to remember that someone is going to have to build what they design.

The unifying factor that held our home project together was the plans for the construction project. These blueprints provided the interface between the designers and the builders. Whenever there was a question about what needed to be built, all parties would consult the blueprints. I recommend the same for your autonomous AI. The AI design specification document later in this chapter (see "Specification for Documenting AI Brain Designs" on page 188) serves the exact same purpose for the autonomous AI that you will design and that someone else might build. Each section of the AI design document outlines key aspects of the AI brain that we've discussed in this book.

The challenge that prevents this process from working smoothly is that neither the design nor the implementation of autonomous AI is linear as in Figure 9-1.

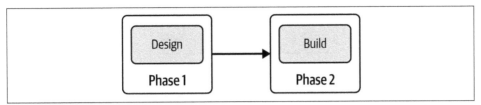

Figure 9-1. Idealized autonomous AI design and implementation. The idealized process assumes that the design phase ends, then the build phase proceeds exactly as planned. (It never works this way.)

The Autonomous AI Design Fallacy Designs but Won't Iterate

Almost every brain that I've ever designed was built by someone else. I designed the brains, wrote the brain design document, and handed over the spec for another team to implement. This is where I made my biggest mistake. I assumed that because I understood the problem well and spent lots of time with experts on how the process worked, that my brain design should be final. Sometimes I even resented the fact that others would come and change my brain designs later while building the brain. This is the autonomous AI design fallacy. It assumes that autonomous AI should be designed like a bridge or a steel mill. You can't design a bridge on the fly. You need to complete the design, verify the design with engineering calculations, and then once the design is complete, build it exactly to spec. It's the only way to ensure the bridge is safe and reliable.

Designing an AI brain is more like building software, though. It's iterative. Because brain design is about teaching skills to a learning system, you never exactly know what that system is going to learn until you let it try. When you see what it learns, you might reformulate your teaching strategy. This happens with people too. Many teachers develop lesson plans, then update them later after they see how well their students learn.

Take a look at Figure 9-2. Follow this scheme to avoid the autonomous AI design fallacy. Agile software design and development originated to exploit the opportunity that software affords to build and test smaller pieces of the software instead of implementing the entire design at once. Software affords the luxury of starting with a small piece of the system, building, testing, and letting that information influence the design as you build out from there. You can learn more about agile software development in James Shore and Shane Warden's book *The Art of Agile Development* (*https://oreil.ly/4EVhw*) (O'Reilly) and in Eric Reis's classic treatise on continuous innovation, *The Lean Startup* (Currency).

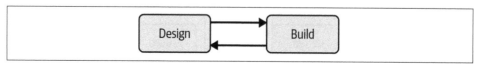

Figure 9-2. Realistic design and implementation of autonomous AI recognizes that, like lesson plans that teachers create, brain designs are iterative and change based on how the students learn.

The Autonomous AI Implementation Fallacy Skips Design Altogether

You can take this approach too far though, and that's where the autonomous AI implementation fallacy comes in. Yes, it's important to iterate. There's no way to come up with the perfect design the first time. But most of the systems that I've designed autonomous AI to control are much more like steel mills than they are like pieces of software. Bulldozers, robots, cars, warehouses, oil drills, chemical plants, CNC machines, and the automated systems that control them are designed for specific functionality and reliability, then built to spec. Updates are made very slowly over time—so slowly that you could consider them entirely new designs.

The autonomous AI implementation fallacy wants to ignore all this and treat autonomous AI just like other software applications. The intent here is to keep from being locked into misguided brain designs by only including design elements that are validated by experimentation. This means you build a prototype and design as you go. Wait a minute—this goes against our understanding of how teaching works. There are lots of things we already know about how to complete tasks. That's what we learned in our subject matter expert interviews! The subject matter experts help us, the machine teacher, learn the landscape of the problem, and they tell us about skills that have helped them navigate that landscape.

This means that we can't take a completely agile approach. We do need to design. But we're going to revise that design as we get feedback during implementation. This quote attributed to the famous architect Frank Lloyd Wright says it very well: "You can use an eraser on the drafting table or a sledgehammer on the construction site."[1]

Specification for Documenting AI Brain Designs

This brain design document (*https://oreil.ly/brain-design*) contains an end-to-end specification of what the AI is designed to do. Let's review each section of the brain design document. The template is filled out with an example AI design. Feel free to modify this document to match specific requirements for your organization.

---

1 Quoted in Edgar Tafel, *Years with Frank Lloyd Wright: Apprentice to Genius* (New York: Dover, 1979).

Project Description

The project description section gives the basic background of the project for the AI that you want to build. The project description should be written in plain language so that any stakeholder who picks it up could understand what the project is about and what the AI is supposed to do. Start with a bit about the process. Describe how the decisions are currently being made, then describe the pain point. Last, explain how the autonomous AI in this document will alleviate the pain point by making decisions better than the current method. See the example document for details.

Value

The value section should define the value of solving this problem with autonomous AI. As I discussed earlier in the book, value is not always monetary, but the value statement should be crisp. Here's an example of a great value statement: A 1% increase in the product yield for the manufacturing process is worth $5 million USD per year at the Sageville plant.

Optimization Goals

The optimization goal section describes each of the goals and how they trade off against each other. It gives specific metrics with units that describe how each goal is measured. See the example document for a solid goal statement.

Current Method

The current method for optimizing the system or process is either human labor, one of the automated decision-making methods, or a combination of humans and automation. Select the checkbox in the document for each decision-making method that matches the current decision-making methods.

Limitations of Current Method

In Chapter 2, I taught you about math, menus, and manuals, the prevailing methods for making automated decisions. Each of those methods has limitations. I also taught you how to determine when autonomous AI will likely outperform those methods. The limitations of current method section describes the pain points that this autonomous AI will address.

Control Actions

The control actions section describes the decisions that this autonomous AI will make to improve the process.

Configuration Scenarios

I've talked a lot about scenarios in Chapter 6. The configuration scenarios section describes the scenarios that the autonomous AI in this specification needs to operate in.

Concepts and Skills

This section of the specification describes each of the skills that you're building into your autonomous AI. These are the skills that you explicitly teach by incorporating them in your design. You should include a brain design diagram in the visual language format that we described in Chapter 4. You should also include the heuristics table from your subject matter expert interview in this section.

Environment States

This section of the document describes the sensor variables that your brain requires to learn.

Perception Models

The perception models section contains a detailed description of each of the perception skills that will need to be built as a machine learning model into your AI brain.

Simulation Environment

The simulation environment section of the specification describes lots of details about the simulation that you will use to train your autonomous AI. In all of the brains that I have designed, providing the virtual environment for the AI to train has proven the most consistent challenge. That is why this is an important section and why it includes so many details about the simulation and who will build it.

Platform for Machine Teaching

It is important for every machine teacher to understand both the design and building concerns of autonomous AI. So I want to discuss one more important consideration. I've built autonomous AI with many open source and commercial platforms. I want to point out two pieces of functionality that I have learned are important for building autonomous AI. The first is the ability to wire together brain modules as skills in a brain. Second is the ability to mix math menus, manuals, machine learning, and DRL into autonomous AI.

Platform for Wiring Multiple Skills Together as Modules

There are many sophisticated open source toolkits and commercial platforms for building DRL agents. Almost all of these are designed to train single monolithic AI. Wiring together multiple skills, especially when more than one of them is a DRL agent, can be challenging. A platform that abstracts some of the complexity away from and performs some of the tasks that train RL agents and arrange skills in sequences and hierarchies will provide the leverage you need to efficiently build the Autonomous AI that you design.

Platform for mixing math, menus, and manuals with AI

As you've seen from our smart thermostat design and the many other examples presented in this book, the most effective brain designs almost always mix math, menus, and manuals with AI. Our machine teaching framework allows us to design these components into autonomous AI. You will also need a platform that allows you to do the same when you're building these AI brains. Otherwise, you will need to develop a significant amount of software to weave the pieces together.

What Difference Will You Make with Machine Teaching?

I've covered a whole lot of ground in this book. We started by talking about what autonomous AI is and why you might need autonomous AI. Then we talked about situations when automation doesn't work and the humanlike decision-making that autonomous AI can deliver. I introduced machine teaching, the set of principles and a framework for teaching autonomous AI skills and strategies.

Machine teaching draws a lot from what we know about teaching humans. This is appropriate because with technologies like machine learning and DRL, AI algorithms can now learn. Anything with the capacity to learn is going to learn most effectively when taught. This is true even if learning involves significant self exploration, improvisation, and discovery. We spent a lot of time talking about how to teach machines: teaching autonomous AI the actions that it should take, setting goals for the AI, decomposing tasks into skills and strategies that we want to teach the AI, and giving the AI the sensor information that it needs to understand the world and learn to complete tasks. I also provided some tools to help you with your machine teaching efforts. Thank you for reading! With practice, you should be able to design sophisticated autonomous AI that outperforms existing methods.

Last question I have for you is, what difference will you make with machine teaching? We have a tremendous opportunity in front of us. Autonomous AI can do things that no other technology previously could do. So, what will we do with it? I hear a lot of talk about all the evil things that people could do with autonomous AI, but what about the good things that we could do with it? Any technology can be used for evil. And the only way to ensure, to truly make sure, that autonomous AI gets used for good is to do something good with it. I hope that I've given you the tools to start on that journey.

Glossary

artificial intelligence
> Computer systems that can perform tasks that normally require human intelligence.

automation
> Intelligence applied to industrial tasks, usually using mathematical calculations, optimization, and rule systems.

autonomous AI
> AI-powered automation that optimizes equipment and processes by sensing its environment and responding in real time to maximize the chance of achieving its goals.

machine teaching
> A framework for using human teaching methods to help machines learn concepts and acquire skills.

expert rule
> Direction for acting based on previous experience.

concept
> A notion or idea that comprises a composable unit of knowledge.

skill
> A unit of competence for a specific task that provides guidance for practicing, exploring, and successfully completing that task.

scenario
> A segment of an environment that helps decision-makers organize a vast decision-making space.

strategy
> A labeled course of action for completing a task.

heuristic strategy
> A strategy acquired by previous experience.

goal
> A high-level specification of what you want the AI to learn; the goal represents success at the task.

objective
> One of the components of a goal.

simulation
> A virtual environment where an autonomous AI can practice; the AI accepts an action and responds by predicting what state of the environment will result from the action.

Index

A

abstracting to strategy for complex tasks, 31

action masking, 103

actions

    defining actions and action frequency for smart thermostat, 127

    delayed consequences for AI brain actions, handling, 125

    determining for AI brain, 122-124

    directive concepts that act, 96

    distinction between programmed and learned concepts, 99

    perception versus in autonomous AI, 42

    separation from perception, 96

    separation into groups by functions, 102

    triggering in your AI brain, 124

advanced beginner stage (Dreyfus model of skill acquisition), 33

    monolithic brains, 156

AI

    automated decisions by machines, 3-25

        how machines make decisions, 5

        solutions as points on a map, 11

        solving the game of checkers, 15-17

        uncertainty, 19-21

        using control theory and math, 5

        using expert systems, 21-25

        using optimization algorithms, 9

        using reconnaissance, 17-19

    autonomous AI brain for CNC manufacturing, 27

    deep reinforcement learning (DRL), 36-40

    demonstrating using games, 48

    teaching allowing us to trust AI, 58-60

AI brains, 41, 74

    (see also brain design)

    building blocks for autonomous decision-making, 73

    giving information for learning and deciding, 173-181

        sensor variables for smart thermostat, 180

        sensors, 174-176

        simulators, 176-180

    learning multiple skills simultaneously, 53

    setting goals for, 129-141

        expanding task algebra to include goal objectives, 140

        goal objectives, 137-140

        identifying scenarios, 135

        matching goals to scenarios, 136

        setting goals for smart thermostat, 141

        teaching strategies for each scenario, 137

        trade-offs, 129-135

    teaching skills to, 143-172

        brain design for smart thermostat, 171

        coach sequencing skills for practice, 149

        focusing practice through teaching, 144-147

        how maestros democratize technology, 153

        introductory teacher, 149

        levels of autonomous AI architecture, 154-160

        maestro democratizing new paradigms, 151

        mentor teaching strategies, 150

        pitfalls to avoid, 168

About the Author

Kence Anderson is director of autonomous AI adoption for autonomous systems at Microsoft. Kence has pioneered uses for autonomous AI in industry and designed over 150 autonomous decision-making AI systems for large enterprises including Pepsi, Bell Flight, Delta Airlines, and Bayer. He now teaches autonomous AI design and consults enterprises on how to transform their organizations and practices with autonomous AI.

Colophon

The animal on the cover of *Designing Autonomous AI* is a white-necked raven (*Corvus albicollis*), named for the large patch of white feathers on its neck. It has a heavy bill with a white tip and is known for its distinctive call, which sounds like a hoarse croak. The white-necked raven is native to eastern and southern Africa and is sometimes confused with the smaller African pied crow, which has an overlapping range, and with the larger thick-billed raven, whose range is further north. White-necked ravens can be taught to imitate human speech, though they only show this behavior in captivity.

They are opportunistic foragers, eating fruit, grain, insects, small animals, and carrion. They are generally found in rocky or mountainous territory, but they can also be seen scavenging in cities. The white-necked raven is a species of least concern. Many of the animals on O'Reilly covers are endangered; all of them are important to the world.

The cover illustration is by Karen Montgomery, based on an antique line engraving from *Wood's Animate Creation*. The cover fonts are Gilroy Semibold and Guardian Sans. The text font is Adobe Minion Pro; the heading font is Adobe Myriad Condensed; and the code font is Dalton Maag's Ubuntu Mono.

O'REILLY®

Learn from experts.
Become one yourself.

Books | Live online courses
Instant Answers | Virtual events
Videos | Interactive learning

Get started at oreilly.com.

Milton Keynes UK
Ingram Content Group UK Ltd.
UKHW052300050724
445127UK00002B/2